Not White Enough

Not White Enough

The Long, Shameful Road to Japanese American Internment

Lawrence Goldstone

University Press of Kansas

Published by the University Press of Kansas (Lawrence, Kansas 66045), which was organized by the Kansas Board of Regents and is operated and funded by Emporia State University, Fort Hays State University, Kansas State University, Pittsburg State University, the University of Kansas, and Wichita State University.

Library of Congress Cataloging-in-Publication Data

Names: Goldstone, Lawrence, 1947– author.
Title: Not white enough : the long, shameful road to Japanese American Internment / Lawrence Goldstone.
Description: Lawrence, Kansas : University Press of Kansas, 2023. | Includes bibliographical references and index.
Identifiers: LCCN 2022029963 (print) | LCCN 2022029964 (ebook) ISBN 9780700634255 (cloth)
ISBN 9780700634262 (ebook)
Subjects: LCSH: Japanese Americans—Legal status, laws, etc.—History. | Japanese Americans—Forced removal and internment, 1942–1945.
Classification: LCC KF4757.5.A75 G65 2023 (print) | LCC KF4757.5.A75 (ebook) | DDC 342.7308/73—dc23/eng/20230105
LC record available at https://lccn.loc.gov/2022029963.
LC ebook record available at https://lccn.loc.gov/2022029964.

British Library Cataloguing-in-Publication Data is available.

Printed in the United States of America

10 9 8 7 6 5 4 3 2 1

The paper used in this publication is acid free and meets the minimum requirements of the American National Standard for Permanence of Paper for Printed Library Materials Z39.48-1992.

For Nancy, always

Contents

Prologue
Bigotry Triumphant

On December 8, 1941, one day after the Japanese navy launched an attack on United States air and naval bases at Pearl Harbor in Oahu, Hawaii, President Franklin D. Roosevelt addressed a joint session of Congress. He told lawmakers that December 7, 1941, was "a date which will live in infamy," and asked that a state of war be declared between the United States and Japan. While his denunciation of an unprovoked attack when the two nations were in theory actively negotiating to resolve their differences was certainly justified, three years later, on December 18, 1944, there was another date that has lived in infamy, one about which Roosevelt remained silent. The reason for his lack of outrage on this occasion was perhaps because he had been directly responsible for what would later be widely seen as an indelible stain on the country's honor.

On that day, with the defeat of fascism glimmering into sight, the Supreme Court, by a 6–3 vote, ruled that the forced displacement of more than 100,000 Americans, two-thirds of whom were United States citizens, to what government officials themselves called "concentration camps," was fully justified under the Constitution. Not one of these Americans had been accused of a crime, nor had they been shown to be disloyal to the United States. They had been torn from their homes, jobs, schools, and communities, and deposited in tawdry, makeshift housing behind barbed wire solely because of their race.

Roosevelt had authorized this action on February 19, 1942, with Executive Order 9066, which said effectively that anyone of Japanese heritage, citizen or not, was an "alien," a potential saboteur or enemy agent, and could thus have any rights guaranteed under the Constitution annulled in the name of national security. And so, the United States joined Fascist Italy and Nazi Germany as nations that forcibly displaced citizens without trial simply because of the circumstances of their birth.

The case in which the Supreme Court upheld the same practice for which the United States had condemned its enemies, *Korematsu v. United States*, is now one of the few decisions in Supreme Court history

Poster ordering Japanese Americans to leave their homes and businesses and report for internment. Courtesy of National Archives and Records Administration.

that both liberals and conservatives list among the worst ever. In a blog on the legal website FindLaw, *Korematsu* was listed third, behind only *Dred Scott v. Sandford* and *Buck v. Bell* (in which Carrie Buck, a Virginia teenager, was sterilized against her will because she had been judged, incorrectly as it turned out, to be "feeble minded"),[1] but ahead of such other travesties as *Plessy v. Ferguson* and *Citizens United v. Federal Election Commission.*[2] To make the decision even more damning, the Court's two great champions of civil liberties, Hugo Black and William O. Douglas, voted with the majority. Black was the author of the opinion.

But as damning as *Korematsu* might have been, to tell the story of the stigmatizing and imprisonment of these thousands of innocent Americans as an isolated incident, an aberration, a temporary loss of national purpose would be to miss the point entirely. In fact, both the Court's decision and the events that preceded the case were simply the natural extensions of decades of blatant and unapologetic discrimination against men, women, and children whose only offense was to have Asian or otherwise nonwhite forebears. And the discrimination against these people was not initiated because of acts of terrorism or a rejection of the American ethos, but rather because they demonstrated a willingness to toil tirelessly for paltry recompense, absorb insult and abuse without complaint, and give up even the most meager luxury for the benefit of their children—all values that Americans claim to respect.

Nor were the justices unaware of the nature of the case before them. White supremacists in the American West were as open in their intent to discriminate against Asian Americans as were white supremacists in the South willing to announce their intention to discriminate against African Americans. Law after law was passed to strangle immigration, and to prevent those immigrants from Japan and China who were successful in the entering the United States from becoming citizens. Further legislation then prevented Asian noncitizens from owning land, entering into real estate or commercial contracts, or enjoying constitutional protections afforded to most who lived within the nation's borders. Children of first-generation immigrants born in the United States, granted automatic citizenship by section 1 of the Fourteenth Amendment, were subject to other forms of discrimination designed to keep them separate from American whites, measures that the Supreme Court had deemed constitutional in *Plessy v. Ferguson* in 1896.

Although all but a few thousand Japanese immigrants and citizens lived on the West Coast, the tensions between them and the white population had exploded into a national issue decades before the attack on Pearl Harbor. In January 1921, for example, a prestigious academic journal, *The Annals of the American Academy of Political and Social Science*, published in Philadelphia, devoted an entire issue to "Present-Day Immigration with Special Reference to the Japanese." There were twenty-three articles from such diverse contributors as the openly and proudly racist former U.S. senator and mayor of San Francisco, James D. Phelan, to Baron Shimpei Gotō (now Gotō Shinpei), who had been the Japanese minister for foreign affairs. The arguments on both sides were almost identical to those that would appear twenty years later.

Baron Gotō asserted that the Japanese in California "live very plainly and work very industrially and fulfill a useful and, I should say, almost unreplaceable function in the economic life of the state. Their honesty is unimpeachable, so much so that I have often heard it said that banks will advance them money on the conditions which (if proposed by Americans), will be refused. They are, of course, entirely peaceful."[3]

Senator Phelan, on the other hand, in an article titled "Why California Objects to the Japanese Invasion," called for Congress to act immediately on the "Japanese problem," and said that "we admire their industry and cleverness, but for that very reason, being a masterful people, they are more dangerous." Phelan went on: "The people of Asia have a destiny of their own. We shall aid them by instruction and example, but we cannot suffer them to overwhelm the civilization which has been established by pioneers and patriots and which we are dutifully bound to preserve." Then in words similar to those of many of today's politicians regarding other races, Phelan said, "We are willing to receive diplomats, scholars and travelers from Japan on terms of equality, but we do not want her laborers."[4]

Another critic, John S. Chambers, the California State controller, insisted, "Assimilation is impossible," and compared the Japanese to rodents: "Watch the gopher at work. He starts to bore into a levee, and as he progresses, he is joined by more of his kind; then, in due time, the other side of the embankment is reached, and a little stream of water passes through. As the dirt crumbles, a flow increases and unless promptly checked, the bore soon becomes a wide gap with the water rushing through and overflowing the land. That is the flood that means loss, and perhaps eventual disaster. That is exactly what is happening in the state of California today through the Japanese policy of peaceful penetration."[5]

During the next two decades, however, many Japanese not only assimilated, but also showed every sign of becoming a vital and indispensable part of the economies of western states, which infuriated the anti-Japanese faction all the more. As one scholar observed, "An official report noted that by 1910, the Japanese produced about half of the entire amount of [Californian] agricultural products marketed. Their position was substantially the same as that of the Chinese except that the sector of agriculture which they occupied had grown to be very much more important than it had been at the time of the Chinese."[6]

In the aftermath of Pearl Harbor, white supremacists had their opportunity. They were able to claim foresight for insisting the Japanese were a treacherous race, but were also able to finally persuade the government in Washington to take the sort of action they had urging for decades. And so, more than 100,000 people were deported, their homes and businesses either seized or vandalized, and in many cases their lives ruined forever.

It would be sad enough if Japanese internment and the closed-door racism that propelled it could be dismissed as unfortunate anachronisms. But like the perpetuation of the Jim Crow era through a two-tiered system of criminal justice, the feelings and reasoning that resulted in the injustices of the past are all too present in the United States today. On December 7, 2015, the seventy-fourth anniversary of the Japanese attack on Pearl Harbor, the *Washington Post* reported, "Donald Trump called Monday for a 'total and complete shutdown' of the entry of Muslims to the United States 'until our country's representatives can figure out what is going on.'"[7] After his election, President Trump attempted to institute just such a ban. For a time, federal district and circuit courts, the lower two rungs on the federal judiciary ladder, ruled against the Trump administration, calling the proposal racially motivated. Eventually, however, after the initiative was transparently sanitized by restricting the order to citizens of specific countries that Trump claimed, without evidence, were hotbeds of terrorism, the Supreme Court in *Trump v. Hawaii* upheld the ban, as in *Korematsu,* on the grounds of national security.

Ironically, Chief Justice John Roberts, in his majority opinion in *Trump v. Hawaii,* made a point of stating, "*Korematsu* has nothing to do with this case," because, he claimed, *Korematsu* was openly racist, whereas his opinion was based on national security grounds.[8] But the chief justice was either unaware of the precedent he had disavowed or simply disingenuous. As one legal scholar noted, "In a manner very much akin to Roberts's opinion in *Trump v. Hawaii,* Justice Hugo Black's opinion for the Court in *Korematsu* danced around and downplayed the openly racist context from which the government's exclusion order emerged."[9]

But banning visitors on the basis of religion is not the only parallel with the imprisonment of Japanese Americans. The Trump administration also launched what can only be called a war against immigrants and asylum-seekers from parts of the world that are home to nonwhites. "The country is full," he declared in April 2019 on Fox News. Those that do make it across the border were often shoved into camps built on the same principles as those that housed the Japanese. And, of course, Trump made building a wall on the U.S.-Mexico border one of the cornerstones of his presidency. Here again, the same five justices who allowed for the restriction of Muslims into the United States chose to ignore racist intent and allow the Trump administration to divert funds allocated for military projects, including improved housing for soldiers in uniform, to be used to build the wall.

Although Trump is no longer in office, the support his policies garnered have outlasted him. And so, the American government's treatment of the Japanese is also a story of today's United States, and the lessons of that terrible period in our history are the lessons the nation cannot be allowed to forget. To combat bigotry and discrimination is, at least in theory, the job of every American, but the Supreme Court, as it has been so often in the past, will almost surely again be the venue where racism is either accepted or rejected in American law.

1 | Free and White

The U.S. Constitution makes no mention of the qualifications for citizenship. Excluding slaves and "Indians not paying taxes," who were assumed to be under the jurisdiction of their various tribes, anyone living in the United States when the Constitution was ratified seemed to qualify as a citizen. Citizenship was made even murkier in Article I, which required anyone elected to the House of Representatives be a U.S. citizen for seven years and to the Senate for nine, this in a nation that in 1787 was not yet officially seven years old.[1] To be elected president, a person needed to be either born on American soil or be "a Citizen of the United States at the time of the Adoption of this Constitution," and have been a "resident" for fourteen years, but the difference between "citizen" and "resident" remained undefined. Citizenship requirements for immigrants were also not stated, but Congress was empowered to "establish a uniform rule of naturalization" for those arriving in the country after ratification.

In addition, national citizenship, however defined, did not create a uniform standard for voting rights: rules for suffrage were left to the states. In every state, in order to qualify to vote, a person—almost always a man—needed to be twenty-one years old and either own property or pay taxes. (In New Jersey, where a technicality allowed women with property to vote, an amendment to the state constitution soon closed the loophole.) In fact, the language of both the Constitution and its first ten amendments did not explain what would later be termed "privileges and immunities" of citizenship at all, but Article IV did state, vaguely, "The Citizens of each State shall be entitled to all Privileges and Immunities of Citizens in the several States." Specific rights that were enumerated were in terms of "people," and made no distinction between citizens and noncitizens.

The First Congress did not further elaborate on "original" citizenship, but it did take up how those who did not live in the United States at the founding could become naturalized citizens. Immigration was to be enthusiastically encouraged. The new nation would need a significant influx of new arrivals for both the nation's economic growth and self-defense. As John Lawrence of New York observed in the debates over naturalization in February 1790, "The reason of admitting foreigners to the rights of citizenship among us is the encouragement of emigration, as we have a large tract of country to people."[2]

Still, there was also general agreement that the country did not want just anybody. When discussing a residency requirement, James Madison warned, "When we are considering the advantages that may result from an easy mode of naturalization, we ought also to consider the cautions necessary to guard against abuses; it is no doubt very desirable, that we should hold out as many inducements as possible, for the worthy part of mankind to come and settle amongst us, and throw their fortunes into a common lot with ours," but, "those who acquire the rights of citizenship without adding to the strength or wealth of the community are not people we are in want of." Madison concluded, "I should be exceeding sorry, sir, that our rule of naturalization excluded a single person of good fame, that really meant to incorporate himself into our society; on the other hand, I do not wish that any man should acquire the privilege, but who, in fact, is a real addition to the wealth or strength of the United States."[3]

In the end, Madison's hesitation worked itself into the final bill. On March 26, 1790, President George Washington signed "An Act to establish a uniform Rule of Naturalization" into law. It stipulated: "That any alien, being a free white person, who shall have resided within the limits and under the jurisdiction of the United States for the term of two years, may be admitted to become a citizen thereof . . . in any one of the states wherein he shall have resided for the term of one year at least . . . that he is a person of good character, and taking the oath or affirmation prescribed by law, to support the constitution of the United States."[4]

In addition to limiting naturalization to free whites, even though just what would determine race was left unspecified, the use of "he" was not an accident. In practice, few women could become naturalized citizens, except by application with her husband, or sometimes her son. As with most matters, naturalization was left to the states to decide who qualified for U.S. citizenship under the law.

Although almost every member of Congress, and President Washington, favored the limitation of "whites of good character," there were dissenting voices. Senator William Maclay of Pennsylvania, who served only one two-year term and left a lacerating often hilarious account of the experience, wrote, "The truth of the matter is that it is a Vile bill, illiberal. Void of philanthropy and needed mending much. We Pennsylvanians act as if we believed that God made of one blood all families of the Earth."[5]

Maclay left Congress in disgust with no mending of the 1790 law to be had. In the end, the only part of the legislation that caused widespread controversy was the residency requirement, which was directly related to the understanding that over time it would become easier (for men) to vote, with the property-holding prerequisite likely to eventually disappear. Residency was raised from two years to five in 1795, and then in 1798, with Thomas Jefferson's populists threatening to displace John Adams's more stodgy Federalists, to fourteen years. (It would not help Adams, who would lose to Jefferson in 1800, not because landless whites were counted for electoral votes, but because three-fifths of the slaves were.) In 1802, with Jefferson in the President's House—it wasn't officially called the White House until 1901—the requirement was again put at five years, where it has remained since.

Citizenship did not become a matter for the courts until the 1850s, and then only as an aside. The case began in 1836, when a U.S. Army major, Lawrence Taliaferro, performed a wedding ceremony. The groom was about forty and the bride about ten years younger. Both were simply dressed. What made this ceremony unusual, however, was that the groom, Dred Scott, and the bride, Harriet Robinson, were both Black and, depending on whom one asked, were either former or current slaves.

There was no question that both had been slaves previously, but their owners had moved from slave states to free Wisconsin, which had left their status in question. In 1820, Congress had passed and President James Monroe had signed, "An Act to authorize the people of the Missouri territory to form a constitution and state government, and for the admission of such state into the Union on an equal footing with the original states, and to prohibit slavery in certain territories." Known as the "Missouri Compromise," the legislation admitted Missouri to the Union as a slave state—balancing the admission of free Maine—and prohibited slavery in all other sections of what had been the Louisiana Purchase north of 36°30′ latitude. Although the legislation affirmed fugitive slave provisions in the now-free area, it did not address the status of slaves who had been brought north by their owners.

Northerners insisted the omission was moot—the prohibition was absolute. The legislation read, "Slavery and involuntary servitude, otherwise than in the punishment of crimes, whereof the parties shall

Dred and Harriet Scott. Courtesy of Library of Congress Prints and Photographs Division.

have been duly convicted, shall be, and is hereby, forever prohibited." If southerners could own slaves in free states, the law had no meaning. Any slave, therefore, traveling from a slave state to a free state would automatically be freed.

Not surprisingly, southerners vociferously disagreed. To them, slaves were property, and it would be the same as saying if a northerner came south with cattle, the cattle would be freed. Of course, the law had not addressed property, only slavery, which had been specifically outlawed. Dred's and Harriet's owners must have agreed they were free. Marriages were only recognized between free people, and if they were still slaves, the ceremony would not have taken place.

The question of the Scotts' status gained importance when their new owner returned to Missouri and hired the Scotts out to work as slaves for a local farmer.[6] Scott tried to buy his family's freedom, but his offer was refused. Instead, backed by abolitionist lawyers, he sued for his freedom in state court. He lost, as he did later in federal court. After many twists, turns, and long delays, in 1856 the case of *Dred Scott v. Sandford* finally reached the Supreme Court and Chief Justice Roger Brooke Taney.

Taney was a former slaveholder from Maryland who had been appointed to the high bench by another former slaveholder, President

Photograph of Roger Brooke Taney by Matthew Brady. Courtesy of Library of Congress.

Andrew Jackson. Taney had been Jackson's attorney general and had replaced John Marshall, whom Jackson loathed, and was chosen to protect the rights of states from incursions by the federal government, which included states, perhaps especially, in which slavery was an institution.

The Supreme Court's decision was not handed down until March 1857, with Taney writing the opinion for a 7–2 majority. During deliberations, President James Buchanan had approached some of the justices, including Taney, insisting that they had a grave responsibility because a definitive judgment on the legality of slavery was needed to head off the threat of war.

Taney's opinion was as definitive as Buchanan could have hoped for. He ruled not only that slaves could not be U.S. citizens, but also that "a free negro of the African race, whose ancestors were brought to this country and sold as slaves, is not a 'citizen' within the meaning of the Constitution of the United States."[7] Since Black people—slave or free—could not be citizens, they had no standing to sue in federal court. In addition, since the Fifth Amendment guaranteed the property rights of slaveowners and slaves were property, Congress could not pass a law that forbade slaveownership anywhere in the nation. The Missouri Compromise legislation, therefore, was unconstitutional.

Although his personal views had no bearing on the case, Taney included them anyway. Black people, he wrote, "had for more than a century before been regarded as beings of an inferior order, and altogether unfit to associate with the white race . . . and so far inferior, that they had no rights which the white man was bound to respect."

For his decision in *Dred Scott*, Taney, who was otherwise a respected legal scholar, has been vilified, not unfairly, as epitomizing bigotry, ignorance, and intolerance. Newspapers, members of Congress, and even other jurists described the departed chief justice as a blight on American democracy. After his death in 1864, one editorial observed, "History will expose him to eternal scorn in the pillory she has set up for infamous judges."[8] A move to erect a bust of Taney mounted next to that of his predecessor, John Marshall, in the Supreme Court room in the Capitol was blocked by outraged members of Congress.

In perhaps the biggest irony of all, rather than prevent a war with his definitive judgment, Taney helped start one.

2 | White, Black . . . and Gold

On January 24, 1848, a carpenter named James Marshall was supervising the construction of a sawmill for John Sutter near the American Fork River in north-central California. He noticed some metal flakes near a stream. The flakes were gold.

Marshall, Sutter, and the other workers tried to keep their find a secret, but word inevitably leaked out. By the following year, the gold rush had begun and upward of 80,000 would-be millionaires descended on California. San Francisco's population grew from about 800 people in 1848 to 25,000 just two years later. Most came overland or by steamship from the east, but others came from across the Pacific, almost all from China. Most Chinese arrived intending to stay only long enough at "Gold Mountain" to allow them to return home rich. By the end of 1849, "there were 781 persons of Chinese origin in San Francisco and the goldfields. The following year (1850), this number had increased to 4,025 and, by the end of 1851, to approximately 12,000. By 1854, there were more than 40,000 Chinese in the state of California."[1]

At first, the hardworking Chinese were accepted by the other miners. But as gold became scarcer and Chinese became more plentiful, resentment developed. In 1850, California began taxing "foreign" miners. Most white immigrants avoided paying simply by saying they were American, but Chinese miners, and Mexicans, did not have the same option. Of those Chinese who did pay the tax, many became victims of violence by whites.

With the tax in place and violence against those who continued to work their claims becoming commonplace, Chinese miners reluctantly gave up the hunt for gold and entered more prosaic lines of work. Some hired themselves out as workers in mining camps, some became farm laborers, while still others settled in cities—mostly in booming San Francisco—and either worked for white business owners or opened their own. Among the less entrepreneurial Chinese, railroad construction siphoned off large numbers of laborers in the 1860s, but that opportunity eventually came to an end. Still, with the West growing quickly, there was a constant need for cheap labor, and the Chinese could be worked hard, paid little, and often physically abused. Much like with

Chinese Miners in California. Courtesy of Library of Congress Prints and Photographs Division.

today's South and Central American immigrants, the grim working conditions and the pittance they were paid were still better than they could expect in their home country.

In 1868, China and the United States signed the Burlingame Treaty, the first agreement between the Qing dynasty and a Western power that was considered "equal."[2] China was granted most-favored-nation trade status, immigration and economic cooperation were encouraged, and, significantly, subjects of each nation—which included American missionaries—were guaranteed full protection of the law while living or working in the other.

As the Chinese population expanded, many who had crossed the Pacific decided to remain permanently in the United States, some migrating as far east as New York. For the first time, their eligibility to apply for U.S. citizenship came under question, which in turn led to the question of just who was and was not "white" according to the 1790 law. Until that point, the rule of thumb for naturalization seemed to be that any immigrant who looked white and claimed to be white was allowed to apply for citizenship as white. In addition, since no federal immigration bureau existed, an entrant denied naturalization in one state might simply reenter the country where state inspectors were either more tolerant or more corrupt. In New York, Tweed's Tammany Hall was propped up by a slew of immigrants who were shepherded to jobs, housing, and registration as Democrats. Well-paid-off inspectors made scant attempts to determine whether the new entrants were of "good character."

Naturalization law became more complicated in 1870. In the wake of the Civil War, Congress debated whether naturalization should be altered in favor of those of "African descent." The aim was to allow naturalization of any former slave or descendant of slaves who had left the United States and then returned. For the first time, whether race should be included in naturalization law at all came under question. As such, the subject of citizenship for the Chinese was also hotly contested.

Extending naturalization rights to the Chinese had many supporters, almost all of them from the East or Midwest. Senator Charles Sumner of Massachusetts said, "I content myself for the present with saying that the word 'white' be struck from the statute book."[3] Pennsylvania senator Simon Cameron agreed: "I am in favor of the position of the Senator from Massachusetts because it invites into our country everybody: the negro, the Irishman, the German, the Frenchman, the Scotchman, the Englishman, and the Chinaman. I will welcome every man."[4] Senators Richard Yates and Lyman Trumbull, both of Illinois, supported multiracial citizenship, as did Indiana's Oliver Morton.

Not everyone was so open-minded. Opposition to Chinese citizenship was almost universal in the West, much of it expressed vehemently in openly racist terms. California representative James Johnson, who had earlier introduced a resolution stating that the Fifteenth Amendment "never intended that Chinese or Mongolians should become voters," told his colleagues, "I hope large majority of the good people of this country believe its future greatness can best be secured by preserving the Caucasian blood in its purity; that the white is superior to the Chinaman; that our country would be better off peopled entirely with our own kind than if mixed with an inferior and degraded race." He added later, "How can any lover of this country ask for free Chinese immigration, which is Chinese citizenship and Chinese suffrage? . . . If the Hottentot, the cannibal from the jungles of Africa, the West India negro, the wild Indian, and the Chinaman are to become a ruling element in this country, then call your ministers from abroad, bring your missionaries home, tear down your school houses, convert your churches into dens and brothels, wherein our young may receive fatal lessons to end in rotting bones, decaying and putrid flesh, poisoned blood, leprous bodies, and leprous souls."[5]

With western congressmen immovable in opposition, any effort to fully end racial criteria for naturalization was doomed. The Naturalization Act that emerged in 1870 had seven sections, the first six of which were lengthy dissertations on curtailing the rampant fraud in the naturalization process, much of which took place in the Port of New York. The seventh section was but a single sentence: "The naturalization laws are hereby extended to aliens of African nativity and to persons of African descent."[6] Whether this provision was inserted to gain the support of Charles Sumner and other equal rights advocates cannot be definitively determined, but it seems likely given the structure of the bill and the debate that preceded its passage. In addition, intended or not, the phrasing of section 7 opened the citizenship door to those who had never been slaves at all, and so, for the first time in American history, people who were not "white" were officially allowed to become citizens, but the legal definition of "white" remained as elusive as ever.

Chinese immigration had continued to increase, but the Chinese in the United States remained a minuscule percentage of the total population—35,000 out of 31,000,000 in 1860 and 63,000 out of 38,500,000 in 1870. Still as the numbers grew, western whites grew more and more determined to halt what they saw as pollution by an inferior race. Chinese laborers were key targets, since they were lowering wages for white workers. By the mid-1870s, early union leaders, such as Denis Kearney of the Workingmen's Party of California and Daniel Cronin of the Washington Territory's Knights of Labor, were demanding West Coast politicians stanch the flow of Chinese labor.

Kearney in particular played on race hatred in his personal rise to power. Born in County Cork, Ireland, in 1847, he had arrived in San Francisco in his early twenties as a hand on a clipper ship, married, and set up a hauling business. Although he built a successful operation, he turned his attention to local laborers, and demonstrated a flair for demagoguery. He at first spoke to small groups of mostly unemployed workers, stressing the need both to organize and to eliminate sources of cheap labor. In case anyone was unclear what he meant, he closed every speech with a ringing "The Chinese must go!" Eventually his followers grew into the thousands and formed the Workingmen's Party, a local offshoot of an organization that had been growing across the United States.

The more powerful the group became, the more Kearney consolidated his own power and harangued against Chinese immigration. By 1878, Kearney's autocratic rule had alienated the rank-and-file of the group he had founded. In May, they held a meeting in which the Executive Committee deposed him as president, and it added, "Henceforth, he is no more than a member of this Committee, and neither honored nor trusted even in that capacity."[7] Kearney left San Francisco in 1879, traveled east to attempt to resurrect his fame, but with little success.

Even after his career faded, Kearney never ceased boasting that he kindled Chinese immigration as political issue, and he may well have been correct. Race prejudice was a winning strategy, and California politicians were all too pleased to seize on the fervor Kearney had stoked.

The most prominent of these in the mid-1870s was an opportunistic transplant from western New York, Horace Page. Born in 1833, and "brought up with Puritanic rigor," but with little education, Page left the family farm and moved to Placerville, California, when he was twenty.[8] He started a successful sawmill business, then a livery stable, and then made a series of astute business investments, becoming a respected member of his community. He was vocal about curbing the power of the railroads and requiring them to pay higher fees and taxes, both state and local. Although he initially claimed no interest in politics, he decided to run for Congress in 1872 as a Republican, solicited the support of the working class, and won an upset victory in a campaign marked by a good deal of mudslinging on both sides.

During his first term, Page attacked the exorbitant prices charged by private firms that carried the U.S. mail and succeeded in the saving the government an estimated $3 million. But Page's targets were not only railroads and government price-gougers. "Ever mindful of the Asiatic curse resting upon California, at the first opportunity and within a few weeks after his arrival in Washington," Page introduced a resolution demanding that the United States "check or altogether prevent Chinese immigration to the United States."[9]

By his second term, he had become the most outspoken anti-Chinese member of Congress. When Page discovered that the naturalization laws had been transcribed into the *Revised Statutes*—the first official record of the laws of the United States printed by the government—with the requirement that an immigrant be "white" left out, he brought it to the attention of Congress, and "free white persons" was reaffirmed in February 1875.

Page thundered in Congress that only action by the federal government could stem Chinese immigration. He took aim on Chinese laborers, "coolies," and also Chinese women, who were assumed to be brought to the United States to be prostitutes, as many actually were.[10] In 1875, Page, a California Republican, sponsored a bill to "end the danger of cheap Chinese labor and immoral Chinese women."[11]

The law Page proposed would be the first in U.S. history that restricted the entry of specific "undesirable" elements. Rather than target the Chinese as a race—which would have run afoul of the treaty signed in 1868—Page proposed banning unskilled Chinese laborers and Chinese women entering the country with the intention of becoming prostitutes or "concubines." Since few Chinese marriage ceremonies were recognized as legal, this definition included just about every Chinese woman arriving at an American port.[12] As Page put it in his speech in Congress, he intended to "place a dividing line between vice and virtue," and "send the brazen harlot who openly flaunts her wickedness in the faces of our wives and daughters back to her native country." White Americans, he added, were "stout-hearted people," who "with their wives and children . . . staked everything" to come to California, but now face a "deadly blight."[13]

Page had a good deal of support from labor groups, churches, and other politicians who had come to view Chinese exclusion as a winning campaign issue. But he also had the backing from some unexpected sources, such as the American Medical Association, which announced that the Chinese, especially the women, were carriers of diseases that would resist cures if they infected whites.

In the end, Page's bill had little trouble in Congress, easily passing in both houses. It was signed into law by President Ulysses S. Grant on March 3, 1875, two days after the president had signed the Civil Rights Act of 1875, guaranteeing to Black Americans equal access to theaters, restaurants, public conveyances, and hotels. Eight years later, the Supreme Court would declare the later law unconstitutional. The Page Act, however, would stand.

The Page Act was only marginally successfully at keeping out men because western employers, not displeased with laborers they could work to exhaustion and pay almost nothing, often found ways to spirit them into the country. But Page had successfully eliminated the entry of virtually all Chinese women.

Concurrent with throttling Chinese immigration, state and local lawmakers in the West took aim at Chinese already in the country. Prompted again by organized labor, a series of faux public health measures was enacted, intended to deny Chinese immigrants employment or housing, "to create an environment so hostile as to 'persuade' Chinese immigrants to return to China."[14] As early as 1870, San Francisco passed the "Cubic Air Ordinance," which required 500 cubic feet of air for every occupant of a residence or lodging. The law was enforced only in Chinatown, where immigrants, most of whom were working for impossibly low wages, lived in horribly cramped conditions: "Owners of lodgings would also be held responsible under the order. Violating the order was considered a misdemeanor, punishable by a fine of between $10 and $500, 5 days to 3 months in prison, or both."[15] Many Chinese who could not or would not pay the fines were sent to local jails more overcrowded than the hovels from which they had been removed.

In 1876, with the jails bursting, to encourage Chinese men to leave the country rather than risk imprisonment, the San Francisco Board of Supervisors enacted what became known as the "Pigtail Ordinance." The law, which had passed three years earlier but was vetoed, required prisoners to have their hair cut within an inch of their scalp. For the Chinese, cutting off the queue, the waist-length braid at the back of their necks, would not only cause great suffering in the afterlife, but also showed disrespect to the Qing emperor and would mean torture or death if a man returned to China. That either alternative was an unlikely incentive for the Chinese to emigrate seemed lost on city fathers.[16]

What was not lost on city and state officials, however, was that the Chinese turned out not to be the witless fools that most whites assumed they would be. Through hard work, diligence, and excellent business practices, a number of Chinese in the West became extremely successful and a few attained substantial fortunes. Then, rather than abandon their less successful brethren or the enclaves in which most Chinese lived, they formed benevolent associations, called "huiguans," with membership based on the region of China from which they had been born. Eventually, these associations joined together to form what was called the "Six Companies," although the number of actual affiliates varied. Most of the leaders of the Six Companies had not bothered to learn English or become involved in local government, but they nonetheless became a formidable political force. In something of an irony, they used much the same recruitment techniques as had the Tweed ring in New York and other East Coast Democratic political machines.

Every ship that arrived at San Francisco with Chinese immigrants aboard was met by an agent of one of the member companies, who escorted the new arrivals into the company's offices and offered them food and lodging while they sought employment: "They also provided facilities for recreational activities, such as reading, card games, etc., as well as for receiving medical attention in case of need. The association also took on the responsibility for burying the dead or sending their remains back to China for burial there."[17] Although membership was voluntary, once employed, most Chinese were happy to contribute to the organization that saw to their welfare.

A cornerstone of the Six Companies' success was a sophisticated understanding of the American legal system. Each time California passed a discriminatory law, Chinese businessmen hired white lawyers, often the best in town, to bring suit in either state or federal court. To the consternation of the authorities, the lawsuits were often successful, in some cases precedent-setting.

In April 1878, for example, a laborer named Ho Ah Kow was imprisoned for five days under the Cubic Air Law for failure to pay a $10 fine, and in jail had his queue hacked off. Members of the Six Companies hired two white lawyers, B. S. Brooks and J. E. McElrath, to bring suit against San Francisco sheriff, Matthew Nunan, an Irish immigrant who had also made a good deal of money as the owner of the city's highly successful Hibernia Brewery. For ordering Ho's hair shorn, they asked for $10,000 in damages. In addition, Ho's lawyers argued not only that the Board of Supervisors had overstepped its authority in enacting the law, but that the Pigtail Ordinance was a violation of their client's Fourteenth Amendment rights, denying him "equal protection of the laws," a novel argument in that never before had the Fourteenth Amendment been used to void a state or federal statute.

When Ho—predictably—lost in state court, the decision was appealed to federal court, where Supreme Court Justice Stephen Field was sitting on circuit, along with district court judge Lorenzo Sawyer. Field, who had come to California during the gold rush to get rich as a lawyer rather than a prospector, was the ranking judge in the case and hardly a friend of the Chinese. In a run for the California state senate in 1851, he had sought to reassure white residents. "I have always regarded the immigration of the Chinese in large numbers into our state as a serious evil," he wrote, "and likely to cause great injury to the morals of our people as well as their industrial interests."[18] Those sentiments were not

Justice Stephen Field. Courtesy of Library of Congress Prints and Photographs Division.

just for public consumption. As he observed to a friend three decades later, "You know I belong to the class who repudiate the doctrine that this country was made for the people of all races. On the contrary, I think it is for our race—the Caucasian race."[19]

Field was famously cantankerous, suspicious, vengeful, stubborn, and convinced of his own rectitude. He sometimes carried a gun in his judicial robes, and most of his colleagues assumed he would be happy to use it. He was a fierce defender of property rights, but also believed in "substantive due process," whereby the reach of Constitution went to the "substance" of guaranteed rights, not merely those specifically enumerated in the text.

Whether because of his judicial philosophy or despite it, Field stunned onlookers when, on July 7, 1789, in *Ho Ah Kow v. Nunan,* he ruled for Ho and declared the California law unconstitutional. Field, in atypically humanist language, agreed that the Board of Supervisors had exceeded its authority in passing the law, likening the shearing practice to torture, but the second part of his opinion was far more significant. Calling the law "spiteful and hateful," Field wrote, "It is special legislation, on the part of the Supervisors, against a class of persons, who, under the constitution and laws of the United States, are entitled to the equal protection of the laws. The ordinance was intended only for the Chinese in San Francisco. This was avowed by the Supervisors on its passage, and was so understood by everyone." He found the law to be "special legislation imposing a degrading and cruel punishment upon a class of persons who are entitled, alike with all other persons within the jurisdiction of the United States, to the equal protection of the laws."[20]

Field then added to the jurisprudence a definition of Fourteenth Amendment guarantees that hewed closely to what those who drafted it had in mind, namely, that because the amendment specifically read "any person" and not "any citizen," its protections were not reserved for the native-born: "The equality of protection thus assured to every one whilst within the United States, from whatever country he may have come, or of whatever race or color he may be, implies not only that the courts of the country shall be open to him on the same terms as to all others for the security of his person or property, the prevention or redress of wrongs and the enforcement of contracts; but that no charges or burdens shall be laid upon him which are not equally borne by others, and that in the administration of criminal justice he shall suffer for his offenses no greater or different punishment."

Field's pronouncement promised to be incendiary to the white population, as indeed it was. In an editorial, the *San Francisco Examiner* denounced the decision using the same states' rights reasoning southerners in the antebellum South had employed to defend their right to hold slaves: "Most alarmingly true will be that the States have no powers for self-protection; no powers, in fact, which the Government at Washington need to respect. . . . It is the very thing the Radicals are conspiring to consummate, to strip from the states the rights reserved to them under the original compact of the Constitution, and to subordinate them entirely to the paramount and arbitrary authority of the Washington Government."[21]

But what have might been the most important passage in Field's opinion, one that if adopted by the justices of the Supreme Court would certainly have changed the course of American history and thwarted violations of the Constitutional rights of the weak and powerless, turned out to be mere verbiage: "When we take our seats on the bench we are not struck with blindness and forbidden to know as judges what we see as men; and where an ordinance, though general in its terms, only operates upon a special race, sect or class, it being universally understood that it is to be enforced only against that race, sect or class, we may justly conclude that it was the intention of the body adopting it that it should only have such operation, and treat it accordingly."[22]

The Six Companies were not always successful, however, and the year before their victory in *Ho Ah Kow* they lost a far more important case, one whose repercussions would haunt Asian Americans for almost a century.

The 1870 Naturalization Act had contained no specific mention of the Chinese, and the status of Chinese immigrants already in the United States with regard to the 1790 law had never been adjudicated. In the 1870s, the United States lacked a national bureau of immigration, nor were there federal officers assigned to screen foreign arrivals at U.S. entry ports. Despite the attempts of the drafters of the 1870 law to apply strict rules to the naturalization process and control rampant fraud, inspectors remained state employees, which meant they were likely as not to have been appointed by the local political boss. Disputes were aired in court—not even necessarily federal court—and left entirely to the discretion of individual judges, which included whether or not Chinese were to be considered "white" for purposes of naturalization.

Where anti-Chinese sentiment was largely quiescent, away from the West Coast, allowing the occasional Chinese to become a citizen did not arouse much controversy. In Chicago, for example, in 1878, "Judge Tissot naturalized three Chinamen who applied to him to have themselves made citizens of the United States, they having made five years before a formal renunciation of allegiance to the Emperor of China, as required by law."[23] Also in 1878, the *New York Herald* reported, "For the first time in the history of the city of New York a native born live Chinaman has been admitted to all the privileges of citizenship provided by the Constitution of the United States. . . . The question of the naturalization of Mongolians has been a mooted one for many years, and the constantly increasing emigration of that mysterious and thrifty race has intensified the popular interest in the settlement of this difficult problem." The new citizen, Wong Ah Yee, who was granted citizenship by New York State judge, was described as "of unusual intelligence and ability . . . married to an Irishwoman and doing a good cigar-making business in Baxter Street."[24]

In the West, however, "unusual intelligence and ability" was of little importance to anti-Asians. Even the relative trickle of new immigrants from China who could circumvent the Page Act was too much for what whites came to speak of as a "plague." Chinese community leaders realized that unless they could become citizens, and then vote, they could do nothing to fight discrimination. One Chinese leader noted, "The moment you appear at the ballot box, you are a man and a brother and are treated to cigars, whiskeys and beers."[25]

In early 1878, the Six Companies hired B. S. Brooks, who would also represent them in *Ho Ah Kow*, to bring a test case in which a Chinese immigrant named Ah Yup applied for naturalization because, Brooks asserted, "Mongolians," as all Asians were classified, should be seen as "white." The case was heard in federal circuit presided over by Judge Lorenzo Sawyer, who would sit with Stephen Field in *Ho Ah Kow.*

Unlike many Californians, Sawyer had not expressed adverse sentiments toward the Chinese, but he was a close associate of Leland Stanford, who had done so often. To say nothing of the fact that thousands of Chinese had died building the transcontinental railroad that made Stanford his fortune. But the Six Companies could not have asked for a better judge. Sawyer was a thorough and respected legal scholar, known for fair, well-crafted opinions. He had been appointed to the federal bench by Ulysses Grant after a stint as chief justice of the California courts.

Sawyer was the first judge to be asked to create a legal definition of "white," and he undertook a careful, meticulous analysis, considering not only the evidence presented by the opposing lawyers but also examining the prevailing scientific analyses of race.

By 1878, questions of both the origins of the various races and whether or not there was a hierarchy among them and, indeed, whether

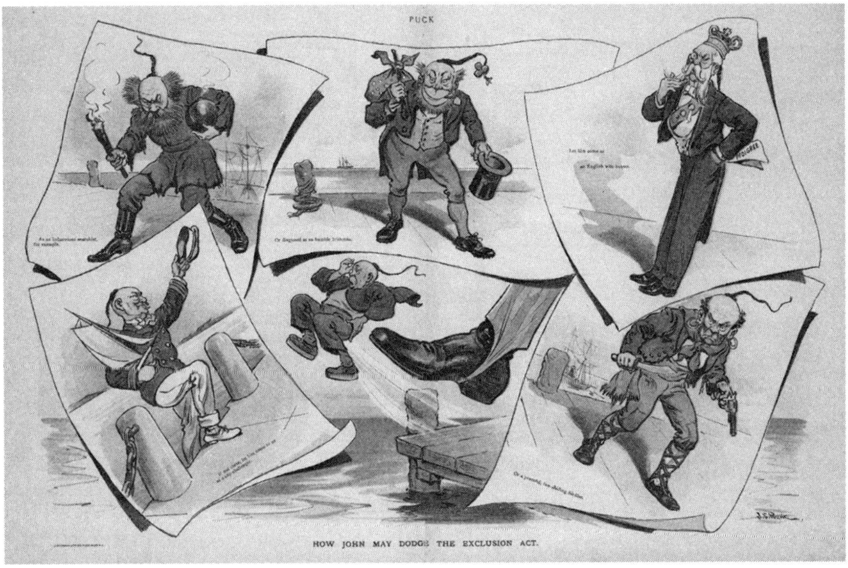

Later cartoon showing how the Chinese might try to sneak into the United States. Courtesy of Library of Congress Prints and Photographs Division.

they were from the same species, had become one of the pressing scientific questions of day. The process had begun a century earlier with Johan Frederich Blumenbach, a German anthropologist. Blumenbach had used skull size and shape to separate humans into five distinct racial groups: Caucasian, Ethiopian, American Indian, Mongolian, and Malay. Predictably, he found Caucasians—white Europeans—the most advanced and named them so because he believed they had descended from Adam and Eve and originated on the southern slopes of Mt. Caucasus in the country of Georgia. All the other races represented a "degeneration" from the Caucasian ideal. Racial stratification had been assumed for centuries, but Blumenbach was the first to put the case in scientific terms.

Although it did not question the existence of racial hierarchy, in the 1840s, a theory took hold that members of the various races had developed separately, from different antecedents. This model of human development, known as "polygenism," was developed by a Philadelphian, Samuel George Morton, a physician, geologist, and paleontologist. He had gained notoriety by analyzing the fossils collected by

Lewis and Clark. After studying hundreds of human skulls, Morton produced a catalogue that classified all the artifacts in his collection. He concluded there were five separate races, which he ranked by cranial capacity. These included, in descending order, Caucasian, Mongolian, Malay, Native American, and Negro. His treatise was published in 1849 and reprinted many times, making Morton "the most famous American anthropologist of his day."

The "Mongolian" type, which included the Chinese, placed relatively high on the scale; they were "tricky, clever and cowardly." Morton placed the "Ethiopian (Negro)" on the bottom rung of his comparative ladder, describing them as "joyous, flexible, and indolent; while the many nations which compose this race present a singular diversity of intellectual character, of which the far extreme is the lowest grade of humanity."[26] This characterization was, not surprisingly, seized on by American slaveholders, who pronounced Morton a visionary, and caused them to support Morton's description of Mongolians as well. Morton's rankings were much the same as Blumenbach's, but polygenism allowed white supremacists to deny that members of other races were even "human" in the same sense as whites.

Morton died in 1851, but the standard of polygenism was then hoisted by no less a champion than scientific titan Louis Agassiz, newly arrived at Harvard from across the Atlantic, and thought by many to be the greatest natural scientist in the world. Agassiz, born and educated in Europe, had been the first man to postulate that the Earth had undergone an ice age, and was equally expert in geology, paleontology, climatology, and ichthyology. He was brilliant at classifying subspecies by physical, environmental, and functional attributes, a skill, unfortunately, he would apply to the origins of the races.

Agassiz adopted both Morton's thesis and his methodology, and, like Morton, claimed simply to be following the data without prejudice, a statement difficult to square with his published conclusions.[27] But Agassiz and polygenism would be shattered less than a decade later when, in 1859, Charles Darwin published his ponderously titled treatise, *On the Origin of Species by Means of Natural Selection, or The Preservation of Favoured Races in the Struggle for Life*, which sold out in Britain the day it was published. When it was released in the United States the following year, the reaction was immediate and compelling. Agassiz, at the height of his fame, condemned it, as "a crude and insolent challenge to the eternal verities, objectionable as science and abominable for its religious blasphemies."[28]

Others saw things differently. The *New York Times,* for example, in a full-page review of more than 4,000 words, gushed, "It is clear that here is one of the most important contributions ever made to philosophic science. . . . Ten times the space given to this article would not suffice for any adequate treatment of this vast and complicated subject."[29] Whatever one's point of view, few denied that "natural selection" represented so massive an assumptive shift that the full repercussions were impossible to predict. Most theologians understood instantly that their lives had become more complicated. But how many other fields of science would be influenced—or infected—no one knew.

Some scholars tried to hold out against the tide. In 1861, for example, the American Academy of Arts and Sciences published a long dissertation by Agassiz's Harvard colleague Francis Bowen, a professor of "Natural Religion, Moral Philosophy, and Civil Polity." Bowen concluded that "development theory," as it was called, "fails entirely."[30] He asserted that "Mr. Darwin is too imaginative a thinker to be a safe guide in natural science; he has unconsciously left the proper ground of physics and inductive science and busied himself with questions of cosmogony and metaphysics."[31]

But Agassiz and his acolytes could not halt the inexorable tide of Darwinism. Agassiz died in 1873, and by the mid-1870s polygenism was in the dustbin. (Eight of Agassiz's most prominent students had converted to Darwinism, including Agassiz's own son.)[32] That monogenism had become axiomatic, however, did not mean that acceptance of racial equality would follow. If anything, natural selection, precisely because its underpinnings were so scientifically sound, would provide every bit as persuasive an argument for white supremacy as polygenism ever had.

To create that agreeable racial hierarchy, however, required a perversion of Darwin's construct. Natural selection as postulated was essentially a five-step process. It began with an individual variation, a mutation. The variation would be inherited and eventually work its way into the species as cumulative variation, in effect a new subspecies. The new and the old would compete for resources—by definition finite—in a "struggle for life." The struggle would culminate in the species more suited to its environment winning out over the lesser. Darwin made no value judgments. "More suited" did not mean "superior." In fact, "superior" and "inferior" were characterizations that had no place in Darwin's model. Evolution was a phenomenon of adaptability, not quality.

If, however, one began at the end of the five steps rather than the beginning, a different set of conclusions might be drawn. If, in civilized society (a definition that could be manipulated to suit) one race or ethnic grouping was doing "better" (another definition that could be manipulated to suit), did it not then follow that the more successful group was more suited to civilized society? And the less successful, less suited? How the superior group attained its success was unimportant—the success itself was the explanation.

The notion that prosperity, or even survival, is based not on chance, luck of the draw, or coincidental advantage but rather on measurable, scientifically verifiable evolutionary advantage held immense appeal.[33] Darwinism as social science could provide justification to society's winners—the rich, the well-placed, the powerful, and the white—and therefore had the potential to create a peculiar assortment of allies. In the United States, two groups that had been at odds for decades and had recently fought one another in the Civil War—southern planters and northern capitalists—each suddenly found themselves with a vested interest in Darwin's theory being proved applicable beyond biology. The same was true in the West, where the Chinese living in squalid conditions that seemed subhuman appeared to be proof that the Chinese existed lower on the evolutionary ladder than the white nativists who were denouncing them.

Equally appealing in legitimizing racial stratification was the ostensible Darwinist conclusion that tinkering with the social order, or allowing the races to live in close proximity, could have disastrous consequences. Doing so would encourage perpetuation of the less suitable group, thereby corrupting the evolutionary process and humankind in general. Prohibiting the Chinese to enter the United States would thus be a patriotic act rather a betrayal of democratic ideals.

But before the Darwinian creed could be functionally applied to questions of race, labor, or immigration, it needed to itself mutate, to wend its way out of natural science, out of biology, and find application in the smokier social sciences. Darwin himself would have had scant interest in such an endeavor; indeed, found it ludicrous. What was needed, then, was some reputable thinker to formulate a sound and logical extension of the theory.

An Englishman, Herbert Spencer, did just that.

Spencer was born in 1820. His father was a religious dissenter and admirer of empirical science. As a young man, Herbert, prodigiously bright, developed quickly into a free-thinking, free-market intellectual, with a deep antipathy to oligarchic authority, which he associated mainly with centralized government. For a time, he worked as a junior editor for *The Economist*, then, as now, a passionate and articulate advocate of free trade. Despite his predilections to human interaction uninhibited by law or custom, Spencer did not set out specifically to extend Darwinism to sociology. His goal was to create a framework that would explain human behavior using empiricist methodology. Spencer's work, therefore, although itself social science, is replete with analogies to natural science. Darwin was not so much his starting point—Spencer began formulating his theory almost a decade before *On the Origin of Species* was published—but rather a catalyst in producing his finished product.

Spencer began not with natural selection, but rather by importing the first law of thermodynamics, conservation of energy, an exciting subject for nineteenth-century physicists. In his social science application, the notion was termed "persistence of force."[34] Just as physical energy is never destroyed, but merely changes form, human "energy" never disappears, but evolves under pressure of the need for subsistence from lower to higher organisms.[35] To achieve this effect, Spencer employed the second law of thermodynamics, entropy, another concept new to the nineteenth century. Life, according to Spencer, had been traveling the path of increasing differentiation—"an advance from homogeneity of structure to heterogeneity of structure"—beginning with simple organisms, such as protozoa and amoebas, progressing toward increasing uniqueness, until, finally, the process had created "Man," the most unique organism of all.[36]

But even the appearance of *Homo sapiens* had not ended the progression. Man himself was evolving from lower to higher forms. "During the period in which the Earth has been peopled," Spencer wrote, "the human organism has become more heterogeneous among the civilized divisions of the species and that the species, as a whole, has been growing more heterogeneous in virtue of the multiplication of races and the differentiation of these races from each other."[37] Not only had "Man" evolved to a higher state than the animal life it supplanted, then, but Man himself, if unencumbered by false notions of do-goodism, would constantly tend toward higher and higher planes of existence.

Spencer left no doubt of those attributes that would move Man on his ethereal path: "A premium on skill, intelligence, self-control, and the power to adapt through technological innovation . . . had stimulated human advancement and selected the best of each generation for survival."[38] Spencer, not Darwin, initiated the phrase "survival of the fittest."

Spencer's theories were not specific to race—he would differentiate between poor and rich as readily as between Black and white. For Americans so disposed, however, a self-serving racial hierarchy could not have been simpler to extract: "Beginning with a barbarous tribe, almost if not quite homogeneous in the functions of its members, the progress has been, and still is, towards an economic aggregation of the whole human race, growing ever more heterogeneous in respect of the separate functions assumed by separate nations, the separate functions assumed by the local sections of each nation, the separate functions assumed by the many kinds of makers and traders in each town, and the separate functions assumed by the workers united in producing each commodity."[39] Those races or classes that seemed to thrive in modern society, even on a relative basis, could be seen as more suited to modernity than those that did not.

The wealthier, the more powerful one became, even at the expense of his fellows—perhaps *especially* at the expense of his fellows—the more he was contributing to the advancement of the human race. As a result, Spencer acquired a devoted following among the rich and successful and achieved greater popularity on the American side of the Atlantic than his own. He would eventually be feted by John D. Rockefeller and Andrew Carnegie, and among his followers would be famed Supreme Court Justice Oliver Wendell Holmes.

And so, when Lorenzo Sawyer sought to base his decision in *Ah Yup* on how to legally define "white" using prevailing science, even though there was no longer a question of whether the different races had sprung from a common antecedent, Spencer's social Darwinism and Blumenbach's racial stratification lurked in the shadows. Regardless of how evenhanded one attempted to be, stratification implied superiority for some and inferiority for others.

For this reason, Sawyer wrote, words should be taken in the commonly understood sense. "White" didn't refer merely to skin tone. Citing Blumenbach, Sawyer noted, "Those called white may be found in every shade from the lightest blonde to the most swarthy brunette," yet "as ordinarily used everywhere in the United States, one would scarcely fail to understand that the party employing the words 'white person' would intend a person of the Caucasian race."[40] Thus, as race theorists insisted, the Chinese, as Mongolians, were not "white."

Sawyer also relied on the congressional debates leading up to the 1870 naturalization law, in which those who opposed Charles Sumner's motion to remove the word "white" from the statute often did so specifically to ensure banning the Chinese. In conclusion, he wrote, "A Mongolian is not a 'white person' within the meaning of the term as used in the naturalization laws of the United States." As a result, no Chinese immigrant could apply for American citizenship regardless of how long he had lived in the country.

3 | Enter the Japanese

In July 1853, Commodore Matthew Perry led a flotilla of four warships into Edo Harbor (now Tokyo), with instructions to either persuade or compel the reclusive Japanese to open trade with the West. Japan, ruled for more than two centuries by the Tokugawa shogunate, a feudal, military dictatorship, had declared Japan closed to foreigners in 1640, although a Dutch trading station was allowed some limited activities in Nagasaki, under strict supervision. Those Japanese harboring "dangerous thoughts" were subject to arrest and even execution, but the Dutch provided a clandestine conduit for books and other printed material from Europe. The number of Japanese who could read Dutch was limited, but when books in Chinese on Western-style government appeared in the mid-nineteenth century—which many educated Japanese could read—interest in Western ideas began to percolate through the population.[1]

By the time Perry arrived, the shogunate was beset by a spate of economic and political problems. Tensions were sufficiently great to create the threat of civil war between reformers and traditionalists. The previous decades had also seen periods of famine and a number of flash uprisings by farmers unhappy about low prices and oppression by the ruling samurai class: "The samurai in the Tokugawa period was an unproductive class; they did not farm the land. They were fed by the farmers." Money had also replaced rice as currency, which "led to the development of urban districts and to the rise of the chonin (commercial) class to a position of influence."[2] Some of the merchants amassed immense fortunes, outstripping the wealth of the feudal lords under whom they theoretically served. Many samurai went into debt to the chonin, and others chose to join this new commercial class as their influence over farmers dwindled. Within the samurai itself, a good deal of tension existed between younger, lower-ranking members trying to make their way in a changing economic landscape and the older elites. The appearance of foreign ships in Edo Bay, therefore, was seen by feudal lords as precisely the sort of provocation they were desperate to avoid.

But avoidance would not be possible. Since previous overtures had been rebuffed, Perry arrived with permission to use force to gain compli-

The American Expedition, under Commodore Perry, Landing in Japan (July 14, 1853). Courtesy of Library of Congress Prints and Photographs Division.

ance. At first the local authorities refused to send anyone of significant rank to speak with the invader, but Perry's "black ships" were equipped with a formidable array of modern cannons, which he threatened to use to level the city, and so, hopelessly outgunned, the Japanese relented.

But Perry was prepared with the carrot and also the stick. He had filled the ships in his flotilla "with gifts and festive supplies. He and his crewmen held parades, technological expositions, and musical performances for their unwilling Japanese hosts, and these cultural activities constituted the core of expedition's approach to establishing diplomatic relations between the U.S. and Japan."[3]

One of Perry's primary objectives was to secure a coaling station for American vessels en route to China, but Japan and the Far East were also untapped markets for American goods as well as sources of other raw materials. The Americans also intended to convert the Japanese both spiritually and politically: "Commodore Perry and his crewmen believed they could elevate Japan to a higher state of civilization by exposing the Japanese to three civilizing forces: commerce, Christianity, and republican governance." The sentiment was unilateral—the Americans were not interested in whether or not the recipients were desirous of these gifts: "Japan's seclusion policy rejected the introduction of all three, yet Americans believed they were eminently exportable to Japan and the world at large."[4] Underpinning all their dealings was the conviction of racial superiority; Perry and his crew made little attempt to hide those views from the Japanese.

Unable to conclude arrangements in 1853, Perry left, but he returned the following year with nine ships. Tokugawa officials resisted allowing foreigners to any port but Nagasaki, but eventually, with European powers also pressing for access, agreed to deal with the Americans. The result was the Convention of Kanagawa, which gave Americans access to selected Japanese ports, initiated diplomatic relations, guaranteed humanitarian treatment of shipwrecked American seamen and provisioning of American ships, the beginnings of trade with appropriate currency exchange, and free movement of Americans within the port cities that were open to American commerce. Although in theory the terms were reciprocal, there was nothing in this agreement that Japan actually wanted, and the agreement precluded the Japanese from obtaining more favorable terms from other nations.

With the Tokugawa dynasty continuing to deteriorate, an even more unfavorable agreement, the Treaty of Amity and Commerce, was concluded four years later. Called the Harris Treaty after the U.S. trade representative who led the negotiation, the pact effectively destroyed what was left of Japan's efforts to insulate its culture from foreign influence. The Harris Treaty eventually served as a model for other agreements in which Tokugawa shogunate came to terms with France, Great Britain, the Netherlands, and Russia. And thus, key Japanese ports, including Yokohama, Kobe, and Nagasaki, would be accessible to foreigners, "who would be allowed to live and trade there with extraterritorial rights and according to low import duties specified by international standards. Accordingly, the once small town of Yokohama was soon filled with Tokugawa officials and foreigners, who soon displaced the local population."[5] Traditional Japanese society began to disappear: "The age of land economy, on which the feudal system was founded, was superseded by the age of currency economy, which was incompatible with the former, and then came the importation of foreign capitalism."[6] The new spate of commerce did not benefit all Japanese, however. "The opening of the ports caused a rise in prices and brought much suffering to the lower classes."[7] But the greatest loss was in sovereignty. "With a stroke of the pen, Japan lost its ability to control its own tariff rates and also punish outsiders who were economically breaking the law within its borders."[8]

Foreign influence initiated a series of reactions. One was a desire to expel the barbarians, and a number of the ruling clans rose up, always without success. The failure to dislodge Western powers, despite the individual bravery and skill of samurai warriors, emphasized to the Japanese, especially those who favored reform, how much isolation had resulted in technological backwardness. Eventually, the forces that had been resisting the shogunate banded together with a determination to end its rule. Although some of the ruling clans announced their intention to oust the leadership in Edo, the real threat came from groups that had been excluded from participation in government: "The wealthy farmers formed an alliance with the reformist lower class samurai—growing out of anti-feudal activity of the farming class and finally to the popular army, which was organized to fight against the Shogun regime and taking away the power of the feudal clans from the upper-class samurai."[9]

In November 1867, with support collapsing, the Tokugawa shogun resigned. Over the next months, the younger samurai and their merchant and farmer allies, bent on reform and modernization, established a new government, an odd hybrid of Western modernity mixed with traditional Japanese values of discipline, single-mindedness, and dedication to perfection. Although the nation was to be titularly led by fifteen-year-old Matsuhito, who was dubbed Emperor Meiji ("Enlightened"), the actual administration would be through a newly constituted national assembly and ministries, such as foreign affairs, finance, public works, education, and especially army and navy.

The new rulers immediately undertook to break down the old order, sweeping away the caste system, vestiges of the feudal economy, a medieval military, restrictive education, and, mostly, the unwillingness to interact with other nations. Ideas were readily borrowed from the West—railroad tracks were laid, factories built, plans for a modern army and navy initiated, and foreign trade encouraged.

Later in 1868, a few months after the installation of Emperor Meiji, the Japanese government concluded an agreement with King Kalakaua of Hawai'i for a group of contract laborers to work on the islands, most on Hawaiian sugar plantations.[10] The deal was brokered by an American merchant, Eugene Van Reed, who had been appointed to serve as the Kingdom of Hawaii's consul in Japan, and "the labor contractor who organized them was Tomisaburo Makino, a *ronin* (former samurai) who had joined the staff of a brothel in Yokohama, thus learning some English from sundry customers."[11] The workers' contracts would be for five years. Four hundred Japanese, mostly young and impoverished, applied to travel across the Pacific, to be paid $4 for twenty-six days of work per month, and also receive room, board, and medical care. One hundred fifty were chosen—143 men, 6 women, and 1 child. They were called "gannenmono," for "first year." Tomisaburo brought the group to Hawaii, then himself went on to San Francisco, to work there as a labor contractor.

The experiment soon seemed doomed to failure. Some of these new arrivals became domestic servants, but most were assigned to harvest sugarcane on plantations throughout the islands. Cutting sugarcane in stifling heat was far more torturous than the Japanese workers were accustomed to, and many began to regret their decision to emigrate. In addition, "The Portuguese labor managers, called luna, were mean and beat them with whips. There was at least one uprising after such a beating where the Japanese workers fought back and injured the labor manager. Three were taken to court and jailed for 300 days and with a $100 fine. Others were fined $25 each."[12]

Within two years, a third had returned home. Another third chose to sail in the other direction and settle in the United States, most in California. The rest remained in Hawaii, married local women and began families. Those fifty became the roots of what became a thriving Japanese community, a vibrant segment of Hawaiian society, which experienced little of the bigotry to which the Chinese were subject to on the mainland.

But for Japan, exporting a few laborers was only the beginning. As one scholar wrote, "Over the next twenty years [from 1868] Japan experienced a complete overhaul of its political and social structures and embraced Westernization, taking the world by surprise with the breakneck speed of its modernization."[13] As part of that overhaul, Japan exported what came to be seen by whites as an exotic and hypnotic culture, first to Europe and then to the United States. Japanese art and design became all the rage, with the French coining the term *japonais* to describe a school of art that borrowed liberally from painting, scrolls, pottery, and other artifacts that were sent to the West by the Meiji government. Artists such as James Abbott McNeill Whistler and Vincent Van Gogh were deeply influenced by Japanese craftsmen, and Gilbert

Porcelain from the Japanese exhibit at Philadelphia Centennial Exposition, 1876. Courtesy of New York Public Library Digital Collections.

and Sullivan's "Mikado" was an enormous success, first in Britain and then in the United States.

It was not until 1876, however, that Japanese culture exploded onto the American stage. At the grand Centennial International Exhibition of 1876 in Philadelphia, the United States' first world's fair, the Japanese exhibition proved to be one of the event's most popular attractions. And the competition was intense. Among the other marvels were the bicycle, the gasoline engine, a giant locomotive, the telephone, the typewriter, root beer, bananas, and Heinz ketchup.

The Japanese exhibit included a model home and a "bazaar, which presented and sold the types of Japanese wares that would soon become de rigueur in middle-class homes as displays of cultural refinement." The reaction from much of the press was fawning, the *Atlantic Monthly* noting that the "clean lines and simple elegance of Japanese design made everything else look 'commonplace and vulgar.' For the Japanese, 'the commonest object of pottery of cotton-stuff for daily use has a merit of design and color which it does not owe to oddity alone.'"[14]

Three years later, when former president Ulysses S. Grant stopped for an extended stay in Japan on his round-the-world tour, America's fascination increased. He wrote his visit to Japan had been "the most pleasant of all my travels." Grant was effusive in extolling Japan's virtues, where he was treated to a reception "the most extravagant I have ever known, or even read of." He added, "The country is beautifully cultivated, the scenery is grand, and the people, from the highest to the lowest, the most kindly and the most clean in the world."[15]

Grant was not, however, blinded to the forces that would soon make Japan a world power: "The progress they have made in the last 12 years is almost incredible. They have now Military and Naval Academies, Colleges, Engineering schools, schools of science and free schools, for male and female, as thoroughly organized and on as high a basis of instruction, as any country in the world."[16]

But modernity had not been achieved without dissension. The new Japanese army, clad in Western uniforms and wielding Western weapons, had been forced to put down an insurrection led by one of Japan's most respected samurai warriors, willing to die—as he did—to prevent the abandonment of the old ways.[17] The Harris Treaty and those like it with other nations were stifling Japan's growth, and Japan was embroiled in a dispute with China over ownership of the Ryuku Islands.

Grant's visit seemed opportune. The young emperor spent a good deal of time with the former president, who became something of a mentor and was said to have influenced Japanese government policy. Meiji often evoked Grant to buttress his arguments when discussing key questions of governance. "Grant spoke of the harm of foreign debts. His words are still fresh in my ears," he is reported to have said. During the composition of the Meiji Constitution, the emperor leaned on Grant's advice heavily. "On this question Grant said . . . on that question Grant taught me . . . "[18]

Still, despite the establishment of democratic institutions and the emperor's embrace of a United States president, Japan remained a class-stratified society, with samurai values predominant and the laboring class still little better off than the feudal peasantry.

By the time Grant left Japan in August 1879, the publicity his visit had generated in the United States was already translating into commerce. Americans had become sufficiently enamored with Japan to create "a booming export market, especially for art and artifacts from Japan's feudal past, of which the new Western-focused government was eager to rid itself." Japanese philosophy attracted a goodly number of adherents, and Americans saw the Japanese discards as height of style and fashion: "kimonos, paper parasols, and folding fans became fashionable among ladies of all social ranks."[19]

Although this exalted view of Japanese culture was largely confined to the eastern United States, a sprinkling of well-educated students or entrepreneurs began to migrate to West Coast cities, all of which led to a tentative belief that the Japanese were somehow "superior" to the Chinese, both personally and culturally. But tens of thousands of Chinese were still doing the work that white Americans were unwilling to undertake under similar dehumanizing conditions.

Although many farmers and industrialists in the West were pleased that a stream of Chinese laborers had managed to evade the Page Act, Horace Page and his supporters were not. Even the relative trickle of new immigrants from China who could circumvent the new law was too much. Once more, among the most vocal advocates of ending Chinese immigration were the leaders of growing labor movement in the United States, who saw low-cost Chinese labor as fatal to their own efforts to improve the wages of union members. State and city officials responded by demanding that Washington take steps to prevent the West Coast, and eventually the whole country, from being overrun.

Page responded as he had since entering Congress. In a later tribute to him, a fawning admirer wrote, "There has hardly been a session of Congress since his election, that he has not introduced an anti-Chinese resolution or bill."[20] One of those bills was introduced in the House of Representatives on April 12, 1882, in which he proposed a measure that would effectively ban all Chinese from entering the United States. Although specifically aimed at laborers, the bill was drafted in such a way as to make it extraordinarily difficult for anyone Chinese to prove he was *not* a laborer. The bill also reaffirmed that those Chinese already in the country could not become citizens.

Page's bill sailed through both houses of Congress and was signed by President Chester A. Arthur on May 6, 1882.[21] It was the first immigration law passed in the United States that barred a specific national or ethnic group. Coupled with the Page Act, the Exclusion Act halted virtually all Chinese immigration for almost a century. As a result, many farmers, timber barons, and industrialists were forced to seek a replacement for a labor pool that could be pushed to superhuman limits for subhuman pay.

They soon found one.

The change was not immediate—Japanese laborers did not instantly pour into the American West. But they did come to Hawaii.

Although Hawaii was not even officially a territory, the American business interests that controlled the economy pressured the Hawaiian government to abide by the Chinese Exclusion Act, and in 1883 a law was passed that did just that. But unlike in the American West, where the supply of Chinese workers was sufficient in the short term, Hawaii's sugar industry was booming and needed a constant supply of new workers.

Two years before, in 1881, with Chinese exclusion a looming probability, King Kalakaua had visited Japan and met with Emperor Meiji to request Japanese laborers be allowed to emigrate. The harsh treatment of the *gannenmono* had been considered an insult in Japan, and further immigration had been prohibited, but the king assured the emperor that mistakes would not be repeated. Although no action was taken immediately, shipping workers across the Pacific was an attractive prospect to the Japanese rulers. Economic conditions among the peasantry remained poor and, with strict class stratification still in place, laborers had scant opportunity to improve their lot. Finally, in 1885, Japan and the Kingdom of Hawaii signed a joint agreement to allow Japanese contract workers to travel to Hawaii.

The agreement was a boon for both sides: "From 1885 to 1894, nearly 30,000 Japanese government-sponsored contract workers—mostly from poor tenant farm families—came to Hawaii, setting the foundation for Hawaii's Japanese population to flourish in the coming years. The Japanese laborers earned on average $15 a month, which was considerably higher than the $4 a month the *gannenmono* had earned."[22]

The contracts obligated the workers to remain with their employers for a fixed term, usually three to five years. And though most of those who signed on were treated a good deal better than their predecessors, toiling day after in the sweltering cane fields was murderous: "Most Japanese immigrants were put to work chopping and weeding sugar cane on vast plantations, many of which were far larger than any single village in Japan. The workday was long, the labor exhausting, and, both on the job and off, the workers' lives were strictly controlled by the plantation owners."[23] Rumors of better conditions and enhanced opportunity in the United States prompted a trickle of those who had fulfilled their contracts to move to the West Coast. By 1890, census figures indicate that Japanese in the United States had increased from 148 in 1880 to 2,039.[24]

The pace increased in 1894, when government-sponsored contract employment ended. Although private contractors often charged fees to potential immigrants, there were also inducements, such as higher pay or the promise of improved living conditions. In addition, that year the United States and Japan signed the first treaty between Japan and the West in which Japan was treated as an equal partner.[25] The agreement "accords complete tariff autonomy to Japan. This is greatly to Japan's advantage. Under existing treaties with foreign nations, including the United States, Japan is not permitted to impose import duties of more than 5 per cent. This forces Japan to impose heavy export duties, to the injury of its own interests. . . . It is the most complete recognition of the Japanese nation, its position as a power, and its right to rule to suit its own affairs and conditions that has yet been accorded by a foreign nation."[26]

Although the principal focus was commercial, there were travel and immigration features that seemed less newsworthy but that would have greater long-term effect. One would require Westerners who committed crimes in Japan be tried in Japanese rather than consular courts, thus further enhancing Japanese sovereignty. Another guaranteed Japanese nationals the right of immigration to the United States, where they were to be treated equally with U.S. citizens, with reciprocal application in Japan.

In California and Washington State, contractors, many of whom were Japanese immigrants, began to partner with farmers and businessmen to lure laborers to the United States. At first, these new workers were welcomed by employers who congratulated themselves on solving their labor problem with a people they saw as clean and morally upright. But organized labor held a quite different view.

Even when Japanese immigration was minuscule, West Coast labor unions began agitating for their exclusion. As early as May 1892, prompted by union leaders, the *San Francisco Morning Call* ran a series of "investigative" articles that were little more than racist screeds. Estimating the number of Japanese in California at 15,000, a tenfold exaggeration, the first article warned, "Every steamer from Yokohama brings a full cargo of the pleasant little people from the Mikado's realm," and they "displace thousands of white girls and boys as domestics or in factories." The Japanese, the *Call* found, "will take anything they can get in way of compensation . . . much less, in fact, than the Chinese."[27]

In an ensuing article, the *Call*, after congratulating itself on awakening the public to the new threat from the East, admitted that the Japanese were less objectionable than the Chinese. However, "The simple fact that they use more soap, cut their hair short, and tuck their shirts in cuts no figure in the question. The problem is, shall we let these pleasant and agreeable little people in here by the thousands to ruin our labor market?"[28]

The series ran for weeks, filled with distortions, innuendo, and outright falsehoods. That the effect was not terribly significant was a result of there being so few actual Japanese in the country. But the series sold newspapers and set the stage for the torrent of anti-Japanese propaganda that would burst forth when the Japanese population increased.

Which would not be long in coming. In 1898, Hawaii was annexed by the United States, and all existing contract labor agreements were annulled, freeing Japanese workers to travel east. They were enticed to do so by earlier Japanese arrivals who had become labor contractors in fast-growing West Coast cities, such as San Francisco, Los Angeles, Seattle, and Portland. The new immigrants were recruited largely to work in agriculture, "but also in logging, mining, and the other local industries in need of manual labor."[29] More Japanese came until, in 1900, more than 12,000 arrived in a single year. Still, there were fewer than 25,000 in the entire United States.

But that was enough for white supremacists. Picking up from the *Call*, they termed the Japanese "sneaky," "clannish," "out to undermine white society," with Japanese women denounced as prostitutes. The artifacts of Japanese culture that had so fascinated Americans ten and twenty years before became symbols of an alien race that could never blend into American society: "The United States Industrial Commission, for example, declared in 1901 that the Japanese 'are more servile than the Chinese, but less obedient and far less desirable. They have most of the vices of the Chinese, but none of the virtues. They underbid the Chinese in everything, and are as a class tricky, unreliable, and dishonest.'"[30]

Organized labor stepped up its accusations that Japanese workers were destroying the lives of American workers, many of whom were immigrants from Europe. In its official magazine, the American Federation of Labor declared, "White workers, including ignorant ones and the newcomers from southern and eastern Europe, possessed qualities enabling them to join and contribute to the labor movement. They could be taught the fundamentals of unionism and would stand shoulder to shoulder with faithful workers. . . . Unable to be 'assimilated,' the Japanese could not become 'union men.'"[31]

Many ordinary white citizens took that one step further and insisted the Japanese could never become Americans at all.

4 | Birthright

Although Chinese immigration had been effectively choked off and there was no longer a threat of the Chinese who had immigrated to the United States becoming citizens, one key open question remained: Were children born in the United States to Chinese immigrant parents American citizens? The answer would be determined by how the indistinct language of one of the country's most widely debated pieces of law was interpreted.

Section 1 of the Fourteenth Amendment, which would ultimately spawn reams of controversial jurisprudence, states, "All persons born or naturalized in the United States, and subject to the jurisdiction thereof, are citizens of the United States and of the state wherein they reside." The amendment had clearly been intended to guarantee citizenship to freed slaves, but there was nothing in it that limited its application, unless "subject to the jurisdiction thereof" could somehow be turned into a restriction.

There were two theories that could apply. The first was called *jus soli* or "law of the soil." It meant that citizenship was determined by where a person was born. The second was *jus sanguinis* or "law of the blood," which meant that citizenship was determined by the nationality or ethnicity of one's parents.[1] Although the United States had always been a *jus soli* nation, there was no law that said it had to remain that way.

When the Fourteenth Amendment was adopted in 1868, there were so few Chinese that questions of their birthright citizenship hardly came up.[2] Even by 1880, there were barely 1,000 U.S.-born Chinese children in the nation.

In 1871, that number had increased by one, when, in San Francisco, a merchant named Wong Si Ping and his wife, Wong Wee Lee, welcomed a son, whom they named Wong Kim Ark. The elder Wong and his wife had lived in California for more than a decade but could never apply for United States citizenship.[3] But what about their child? Was he a citizen? By virtue of the Fourteenth Amendment, had Wong Kim Ark achieved by accident of birth what his parents could never attain under any circumstances?

Throughout Wong's childhood, the question did not come up. He was more or less accepted as a citizen, but "unnoticed as a citizen" would have been a more accurate phrase.

Wong's parents returned to China the late 1880s. He visited them in 1890, after which he returned to the United States some months later without incident. It appears that while in China he got married, but his wife remained behind when he left. Four years later, he traveled to China once more, by which time he had a son, whom he saw for the first time. He again remained for some months, fathering a second child, before returning to the United States in August 1895.[4]

This time, Wong Kim Ark was denied entry by a customs inspector in San Francisco. Although he had all the necessary documents to prove that he had been born in the United States, the inspector claimed he was not a citizen. Wong was a cook, a laborer, rather than a merchant like his father, and thus, according to the inspector, under the aegis of the 1882 Chinese Exclusion Act.

Wong's being denied admittance was widely viewed as a contrivance by the federal government to challenge birthright citizenship. "The decision was in accordance with an arrangement made with [U.S.] attorney general [Judson Harmon] who is anxious to test the right of native born Chinese to land here," the Associated Press reported. The intention was to prompt a judicial interpretation of the Fourteenth Amendment. A favorable decision would effectively eliminate Chinese citizenry in the United States. "According to the contention of the government," the article went on, "a person born in the United States must not be at the time of his birth subject to any foreign power, thus making it indispensable to citizenship by birth that the parent then be an American citizen." But, as the government was aware, the Chinese would not be the only ones affected. "If the contention of the government is upheld, the standing of all people born in the United States of alien parentage will be greatly affected."[5] If the decision in federal district court came down in favor of birthright citizenship, the government intended to appeal to the Supreme Court, where a conservative majority made it confident of victory.

Wong was held offshore for five months in a series of ships anchored in San Francisco Bay. In November, he was approached by representatives of the Six Companies, expressly to be the plaintiff in the lawsuit challenging his exclusion.

Establishing birthright citizenship for the small minority born in the United States was vital. With it becoming more difficult for Chinese already in the country to function in civil society "as aliens ineligible for citizenship," birthright citizens, even as children, could have property registered in their names and enter into contracts through adult nominees, both of which state and local authorities had been trying to restrict for noncitizens with discriminatory legislation.

What whites feared most, as always, was that birthright citizens could not be denied the right to vote. "If this young Chinaman should be declared to be a citizen," one newspaper complained, "then there are several thousand Chinese citizens in this State, and of course they will be entitled to the ballot. . . . It is enough to make one shudder to contemplate."[6]

The Six Companies had continued effectively challenging anti-Chinese laws using the very best white lawyers and had scored an enormous victory in 1886. Hall McAllister, for whom a statue was later erected outside San Francisco City Hall, was the lead lawyer in the landmark 1886 civil rights case *Yick Wo v. Hopkins*, in which the Court ruled that discriminatory administration of a nondiscriminatory law was unconstitutional.

For Wong, the Six Companies hired prominent Democrat Thomas Riordan. He filed a habeas corpus motion on Wong's behalf, and the case, *In re Wong Kim Ark*, was heard in federal district court in San Francisco in January 1896.

U.S. attorney Henry B. Foote "claimed that a Chinese could not become a citizen of this country, even though born here, under the Fourteenth Amendment to the Constitution."[7] Since Wong was born to parents who were subjects of China, Foote went on, he was also a subject of China and was therefore not, in the words of the Fourteenth Amendment, "subject to the jurisdiction" of the United States. Foote further pointed out that China, like Japan, granted citizenship based on bloodline. Children born to Chinese nationals regardless of location can claim citizenship in China if the birth is properly registered in China, which Wong Kim Ark's birth was. Therefore, Foote concluded, Wong's Chinese citizenship took precedence over any claim to U.S. citizenship he might file.

Riordan simply said that no matter how much the government tried to dodge the issue, the United States was a *jus soli* nation, had always been so, and the Fourteenth Amendment had been enacted under that rule. Like it or not, Wong Kim Ark was a citizen of the United States, entitled to all the privileges and immunities that citizenship afforded. And the case went beyond the Chinese. If Wong's birthright were denied, anyone born in the United States whose parents were immigrants would also lose their citizenship.

There was also precedent in Wong's favor. In 1884, Look Tin Sing, another native-born Chinese American who was refused reentry, had brought suit in federal court, and the government attorneys had made the same argument Henry Foote would make in *Wong*. But the circuit court dismissed the claim of dual allegiance. The Fourteenth Amendment had granted birthright citizenship to Look, the court wrote, and the phrase "subject to the jurisdiction thereof" was inserted specifically and exclusively to restrict children of foreign diplomats born in this country. The government had been widely expected to appeal the ruling to the Supreme Court, but for reasons never made public, it did not. With Wong Kim Ark, however, there was no question that the government would make every attempt to have birthright citizenship for Chinese Americans annulled.

Weeks before Wong's petition was filed, the federal district judge who would rule on the case, William W. Morrow, had ruled in another immigration case, this one of a Chinese immigrant, Gee Hop, who had become a naturalized citizen in Camden, New Jersey, in 1890, and had even been issued a U.S. passport.

Gee had traveled to China and then returned in September 1895, just after Wong Kim Ark, and, despite a valid passport, had been denied entry by the same customs official who had arrested Wong. Gee filed a petition of habeas corpus, to which government officials replied by recommending his deportation.

The U.S. attorney told the court that Gee's grant of citizenship had been an error by the New Jersey court, since it violated the dictates of current naturalization law. Morrow agreed. "Persons of the Mongolian race under American law," he wrote, "could at no time become naturalized. This was the view held by Judge Sawyer in the case of Ah Yup. Congress intended to exclude Mongolians." And so, "the judgment of the Court of Common Pleas of New Jersey naturalizing Gee Hop was absolutely null and void for want of jurisdiction, and that, therefore, Gee Hop was not and is not a citizen of the United States, as claimed by him, and cannot be permitted to land in this country." The passport had therefore also been issued in error, and the deportation order was sustained.[8]

In an editorial on the Gee Hop case called "A Wise Decision," the *San Francisco Call* exclaimed, "The laws governing the decisions regarding naturalization of this race were founded in an understanding that the race was incurably alien and wholly 'unadapted to citizenship,'" and expressed fear that, as citizens, Chinese would be "permitted to vote." It was also specifically noted that the decision would apply to the Japanese as well. "'All Mongolians' is the language of the opinion."[9]

Before *Wong*, in the last days of December 1895, Judge Morrow handed down a decision in another immigration case, this one involving a native-born Chinese American, Ching Too, who faced deportation after his release from prison for a felony conviction. Although the Geary Act, an 1892 law that greatly stiffened the Exclusion Act, mandated deportation of all Chinese felons, Morrow ruled that it could not apply to those born in the United States. California newspapers were not pleased either with the decision or the portent as regards the Wong Kim Ark case.[10]

On January 3, 1896, Judge Morrow rendered his decision for *In re Wong Kim Ark*, and the foreboding among anti-Asians proved justified. The *Call* reported, "That Chinese born in this country of parents not in the Chinese diplomatic service are citizens of the United States, and may exercise the elective franchise, and may go and come whenever and wherever they please, is the effect of United States District Judge Morrow's decision of the test case of Wong Kim Ark."[11] The Chinese were exultant: "There was great rejoicing in Chinatown over Judge Morrow's decision."[12] It was only after the decision that Wong was finally released on bail.

The reaction was different in the white community, with the vision of native-born Chinese as eligible voters particularly unpleasant: "At the headquarters of the United Parlor, Native Sons of the Golden West, it was learned that the Chinese estimate that there are at least 1000 native-born Chinese in that City, and a big vote might be polled among those of voting age."[13]

Judge Morrow had scarcely pounded his gavel ending the proceedings when the government announced its intention to appeal to the Supreme Court and ask for an expedited hearing for a very specific purpose: "Attorney-General Harmon had hoped to have the case advanced and placed on the spring calendar, so that a decision could be reached in time to prevent the voting of the 500 Chinese in San Francisco who claim to be native sons of California."[14] But the Court was in no hurry. The calendar was said to be too crowded to hear the case until the fall 1896 term, but it is far more likely that justices wanted to delay deciding on such an incendiary issue. In fact, they would not hear oral arguments until March 1897.

In the meantime, with the full blessing of the U.S. attorney general, officials in California announced that every effort would be made to prevent native-born Chinese Americans from voting. As reported in the *San Francisco Chronicle*: "Notwithstanding that the Supreme Court of the United States will not be likely to afford relief from the 500 Chinese of this City who threaten to cast their ballots in the fall, there is quite a strong feeling in this City over the question, and efforts will be made to put a quietus on the ambition of these young Chino-Americans. They will be, at least and by all means, examined most severely on the educational qualification, and to this end the 'native sons' are now learning the constitution by heart."[15]

There is no record of how many Chinese voted in San Francisco or elsewhere, but those who would deny them access to the ballot would wait until March 29, 1898, to learn that, at least on the basis of citizenship, they could not. In a 6–2 decision, the Court ruled for Wong.

Justice Horace Gray wrote the opinion and stated the issue to be decided narrowly.

> The question presented by the record is whether a child born in the United States, of parents of Chinese descent, who, at the time of his birth, are subjects of the Emperor of China, but have a permanent domicile and residence in the United States, and are there carrying on business, and are not employed in any diplomatic or official capacity under the Emperor of China, becomes at the time of his birth a citizen of the United States by virtue of the first clause of the Fourteenth Amendment of the Constitution.[16]

But the Fourteenth Amendment made no mention of "permanent domicile," so Gray had already limited the reach of the decision to certain category of immigrant.

From there Gray went on at great length to cite examples in English common law and from other cases in American jurisprudence, all to demonstrate that "there is, therefore, little ground for the theory that, at the time of the adoption of the Fourteenth Amendment of the Constitution of the United States, there was any settled and definite rule of international law, generally recognized by civilized nations, inconsistent with the ancient rule of citizenship by birth within the dominion. . . . The opening sentence of the Fourteenth Amendment is throughout affirmative and declaratory, intended to allay doubts and to settle controversies which had arisen, and not to impose any new restrictions upon citizenship."

Wong Kim Ark's American citizenship was therefore affirmed.

Gray's dissertation was prolix and circuitous, even for a legal opinion, and the excesses might have been unnecessary if Gray were not defending a decision at which many if not most Americans would be outraged. There was also the contrast of *Plessy v. Ferguson*, decided two years earlier, in which the same roster of justices ignored Fourteenth Amendment guarantees and upheld a blatantly racist Louisiana law forcing Black United States citizens to ride in smoky, dirty, substandard railroad cars on the grounds that separate facilities were constitutionally acceptable as long as they were "equal."

But perhaps the real reason for the Court's seeming pivot away from the shameless racism of *Plessy* can be found buried in the middle of Justice Gray's opinion: "To hold that the Fourteenth Amendment of the Constitution excludes from citizenship the children, born in the United States, of citizens or subjects of other countries would be to deny citizenship to thousands of persons of English, Scotch, Irish, German, or other European parentage who have always been considered and treated as citizens of the United States."

The scenario drawn by western whites of the Chinese arriving by the thousands to overrun white civilization had not persuaded the justices, almost all of whom were from the East. There were so few native-born Americans of Chinese descent that they were less concerned with them than with the much larger number of native-born children from "desirable" northern European countries.

Protecting the native-born children of "desirable" northern European immigrants, however, was of little interest to westerners, who saw themselves as manning cultural barricades, protecting the white Christian nation they loved from destruction at the hands of an invasion by an inferior race. Nazi Germany would use much the same reasoning thirty years later when trying to persuade Western Europe to support them in suppressing the Slavic hordes. As an editorial in a California newspaper read:

> From the point of view of public policy, the present decision of the supreme court seems to be a distinct retrogression. In this age of rapid transit and of large migratory populations, citizenship should have a more substantial basis than the ancient feudal doctrine of birth within the allegiance. Napo-

> leon, with the progressive spirit which characterized him in the formation of his Code, discarded the jus soli in favor of the jus sanguinis as the determining principle in citizenship. Great Britain has abandoned the doctrine of indelible allegiance. Almost all nations now accord to their citizens the privilege of expatriation. In view of these considerations, the wisdom of the supreme court in giving to a doubtful clause a construction which is contrary to the manifest tendency of rations may well be questioned; and if the matter is again brought before the court, it will not be surprising if the present decision is reversed.[17]

It has not been. Although *United States v. Wong Kim Ark* has remained precedent for more than a century, many American conservatives, led by former president Donald Trump, have suggested that the question of birthright citizenship be revisited, especially in the case of children born in the United States to immigrants who are in violation of current naturalization law.[18] Millions of adults and children who have always considered themselves citizens might then be left without citizenship, not only in the United States, but also in the country their parents had left.

5 | Yellow Peril

The decision in *Wong Kim Ark* protected a tiny minority of Chinese in the United States, but it did nothing to ameliorate the labor shortage caused by Chinese exclusion. That role was being filled by the Japanese. With a growing labor movement eager to demonize any group that worked for low wages, and with the Japanese subject to a stream of propaganda disseminated among the remainder of West Coast citizenry, politicians of both parties had found a ready-made campaign issue. Each would attempt to outdo the other in anti-Japanese vitriol. For the next three decades, one of the most successful race-baiters in the nation was also one of the most cultured men in San Francisco.

James Duval Phelan, classically educated, heir to a banking and real estate fortune, then a banker himself, was a fixture in San Francisco society. He gave elegant dinners at the Bohemian Club and was described as "an Edwardian gentleman with exquisite taste." A memoir written after his death in 1930 by the wife of San Francisco newspaper editor Fremont Older noted that Phelan "financed California playwrights, artists, and sculptors and their creations, together with European art and sculpture, filled his house and gardens. He would have preferred being a great poet rather than a millionaire, and in the redwood forest on the mountainside back of the dwelling he created a naturalistic shrine, placing in the circle of redwoods bronze busts of Joaquin Miller, Edwin Markham, and John Muir, using redwood stumps as pedestals. In the outdoor theater, back of the patio and swimming pool, his most enjoyable afternoons were experienced when poets read aloud their original verse. He, himself, contributed excellent sonnets."[1]

In 1896, having recently given up his post as president of the San Francisco Art Association, Phelan was persuaded to run for mayor by Fremont Older "to rid the city of the domination of bosses."[2] Although Phelan was initially incredulous and claimed no talent for politics, he ran as a Democrat and soundly defeated his Republican opponent, an impressive achievement since in San Francisco in the same election, Republican presidential candidate William McKinley handily outpolled Democrat William Jennings Bryan. Phelan came to office promising to improve the city's water supply, to work to pass a revised city charter, to

James D. Phelan. Courtesy of Library of Congress Prints and Photographs Division.

cut "the waste and extravagance which is the cause of high taxation," and to ensure that "municipal offices are conducted without extravagance, favoritism, waste or corruption."[3]

Phelan soon added another promise to the people of San Francisco—Chinese and Japanese exclusion. When he first took office in January 1897, before the Supreme Court ruled in *Wong Kim Ark*, Phelan seemed no more anti-Asian than most members of the city's gentility. He soon learned, however, that there were significant political advantages in public denunciations of the Japanese as an alien race and claimed that "the Pacific Slope [could be] overrun by hordes of Japanese," an odd accusation against a group that was only a microscopic percentage of the city's population.[4] In 1900, however, unprecedented numbers of Japanese landed on U.S. mainland shores—more than 12,000 would come that year—and Phelan's warning seemed prophetic. As his mayoral term wore on, Phelan became the most reliable spokesman for white supremacy, and thereby gained the enthusiastic support of San Francisco's labor unions, along with anti-Japanese business leaders, such as newspaper magnates William Randolph Hearst and V. S. McClatchy.[5]

In February 1900, dead rats were found on the streets of Chinatown. No one took much notice, but on March 6, "the body of Wong Chut King, a Chinese laborer, was removed from the basement of the old Globe Hotel to rooms of a Chinese undertaker." When a police surgeon was called in to issue a death certificate, he noticed enlarged glands and other signs that caused him to report the death to the Board of Health.[6]

City medical officials informed the police commissioner and the mayor's office that the likely cause was bubonic plague. Through increased awareness and proper sanitation, the disease would no longer spread unabated and kill thousands, but just the presence of what had been called the Black Death might easily spread panic across the city. Initial "bacteriological and microscopic examinations," however, found no evidence that the diagnosis was correct. Nonetheless, Mayor Phelan, who by then missed no opportunity to call the Chinese and the Japanese filthy races and menaces to public health, ordered Chinatown and the two tiny Japantowns to be roped off and quarantined. He likely expected to be cheered on all sides, especially since no other neighborhood in the city received similar treatment.

But Phelan had miscalculated. The prospect of plague in the West's largest city could strangle shipping and commerce and cost enormous financial losses. California governor Henry Gage, fearing economic disaster, issued a string of denials, claiming the reports were politically motivated. Some San Francisco newspapers supported him. The *Call*, for example, often a Phelan cheerleader, ran an article the day after the quarantine, "Fake Plague Part of Plot to Plunder." It opened, "There is not bubonic plague in San Francisco," and went on to accuse those who

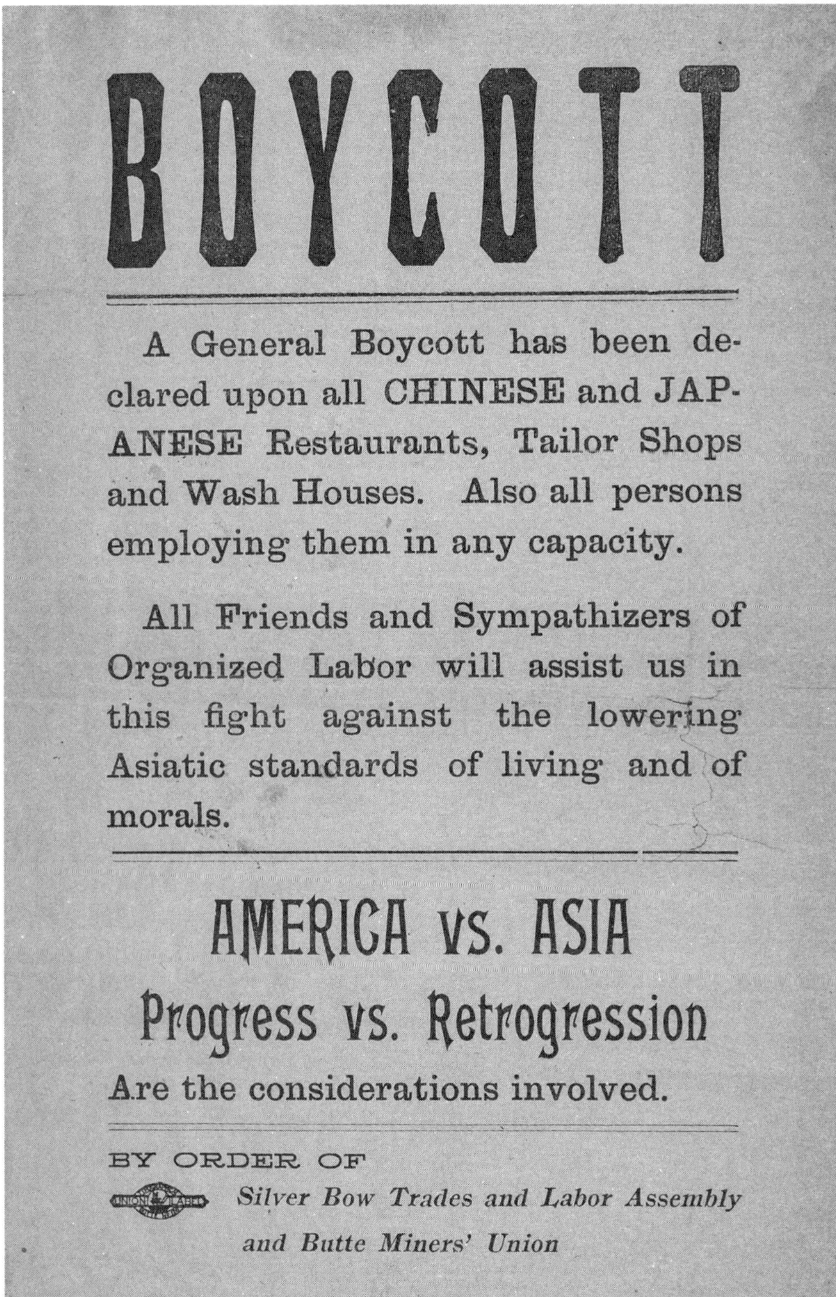

Union poster urging a boycott of Chinese and Japanese businesses. Exhibits from *Hum Fay et al. v. Frank Baldwin.* Courtesy of National Archives at Denver.

put forth such a ridiculous notion of making "a bold attempt to blackmail the city out of funds to feed a horde of hungry office-seekers who compose Mayor Phelan's only following."[7] Phelan must have been taken aback at being attacked for singling out Asians as carriers of a dread disease and a menace to the city.

Phelan may have misjudged the political reaction, but he was exactly right in the action he took. The day after the *Call* ran its article, a number of animals, including a monkey, inoculated with serum taken from the dead man, died. San Francisco would deal with the plague outbreak, indeed centered in Chinatown, for more than three years. Quarantine would turn out to have been exactly the proper course, and it helped limit deaths from the disease to slightly more than one hundred. Gage, by contrast, would be soundly defeated for reelection. Nonetheless, because most public officials and every newspaper initially described the situation as a hoax, Chinese and especially Japanese community leaders were convinced this was merely another attempt to cast them as scapegoats for the city's ills and provide an excuse to isolate them rather than the disease.

There was certainly no shortage of evidence to support their conclusions. On May 7, 1900, an "enthusiastic and largely attended mass meeting . . . under the direction of the united labor organizations of this city" met "to protest the violations of Chinese exclusion act and the alarming influx of Japanese laborers."[8]

The mayor was one of the featured speakers. He arrived late "to prolonged applause," and "after referring to the existing Exclusion Act and the fact that despite it the Chinese laboring class is constantly increasing," he said, "But it is not a local question, not a labor question, but a national question, an American question, a question that may affect the very existence of the Republic. . . . The framers of our naturalization laws considered only the Caucasian race when they said that America should be an asylum for the oppressed. . . . The Oriental races do not come here as an oppressed people seeking an asylum. . . . The decline of Rome dates from the time she brought her subjugated people to Italy as slaves and placed them on the farms and vineyards, driving the native-born population to the city. . . . If America permits the free and unrestricted immigration of the servile races, the history of Rome will be repeated."[9]

Perhaps the meeting's most important speaker, however, was Edward A. Ross, a Stanford sociology professor and noted eugenicist: "In a thoughtful and eloquent discussion of the economic phases of the problem, he declared that primarily the Chinese and Japanese are impossible among us because they cannot assimilate with us; they represent a different and an inferior civilization to our own and mean by their presence the degradation of American labor and American life." Ross demanded "protection for the American workmen as well as for American products . . . and should the worst come to the worst it would be better for us if we were to turn our guns upon every vessel bringing Japanese to our shores rather than to permit them to land."[10]

Along with cheap labor, the most serious complaint was that "native son" Chinese, such as Wong Kim Ark, were "stealing" the vote. The union leaders demanded their expulsion, ignoring the inconvenience of them being U.S. citizens. Mayor Phelan, to rousing applause, "sympathized thoroughly with the position taken by organized labor . . . from whatever point of view we look, Asiatic labor [is] unwelcome, unsolicited and unwholesome. More than that, the Chinese are springing upon us 'native sons,' full-grown men, votes and able-bodied voters. They are a menace . . . to our civilization, to everything we cherish."[11] The following day, citing gross fraud, San Francisco's district attorney announced that all Chinese arriving at the port of San Francisco claiming to be American citizens would not be allowed to disembark without a "thorough examination," regardless of any documentation they might possess.

The Labor Council drafted a number of resolutions that were forwarded to a variety of state and local politicians, including this:

> Resolved, By the citizens of San Francisco, in mass meeting assembled this seventh day of May, 1900, that we urge upon Congress to re-enact the Chinese exclusion act, with such additions as may be necessary to make it fully effective for the protection of American labor; and, be it further Resolved, That we also urge the adoption of an act of Congress or the adoption of such other measures as may be necessary for the total exclusion of all classes of Japanese other than members of the diplomatic staff. Such a law has become a necessity not only on the grounds set forth in the policy of Chinese exclusion, but because of additional reasons resting in the fact that the assumed virtue of the Japanese, i.e., *their partial adoption of American customs, makes them the more dangerous as competitors.* (emphasis added)

So, it seemed that Japanese were to be excluded both because they were unable or unwilling to assimilate in the United States and because they were successful at achieving very same thing.

The San Francisco meeting coincided with an almost identical mass gathering across the country in Brooklyn, New York, sponsored by the Knights of Labor and other unions, also aimed specifically at the Japanese. The unions demanded amending the Chinese Exclusion Act to include the Japanese in almost the precise terms used by the organizers of the meeting in the West. What made the demand curious was that virtually no Japanese laborers had made the cross-country trek to New York. The unions also proposed a bill that "prohibited any alien from entering the United States to engage in any occupation who did not intend to become a citizen or who intended to engage in any congested occupation or take the place of strikers or locked out workers, or to work for less than the prevailing rate of wages."[12] Since, at that point, no Chinese or Japanese immigrant was allowed to become a citizen, this amounted to total exclusion.

With the Japanese coming into increased focus, community leaders in San Francisco, noting the success of the Six Companies, saw quite clearly that they needed a similar organization of their own. But where the Six Companies aimed to protect the interests of ordinary Chinese by establishing their legal right to function on equal terms with whites without integration into white society, the Japanese Association of America sought to convince whites of their desire to become "true Americans." It was "devoted to raising all of the standards of the Japanese in this country and of genuinely aiding Americanization . . . taking the lead in all movements designed to promote a better understanding between the Americans and the Japanese here, and to inculcate in the hearts and minds of the latter a devotion to and an understanding of the spirit of America."[13]

But the spirit of America, at least on the West Coast, did not include whites welcoming those whose skin color and facial features did not match their own, regardless of how much the newcomers wanted only to adhere to values that whites claimed to value. The Japanese government, hoping to keep the United States as an ally while it built up its military, agreed in July 1900 to issue no additional passports to Japanese menial laborers intending to sail for the United States.[14] With that victory, Phelan, who was largely acknowledged to have spearheaded the effort, would have seemed on the road to higher office, but workers turned out to have more on their minds than Asian immigration.

6 | Workers of the West Unite

Labor unrest in San Francisco had been building for years. The booming recovery from the Panic of 1893 had exploded the demand for workers and, with near full employment, demands for shorter hours and higher wages followed along. The timing could not have been better for labor organizers to convince workers that unions could achieve these goals far more effectively than they could as individuals.

In September 1900, McNab & Smith, one of the city's largest hauling firms, fired members of a newly formed union of teamsters and refused to hire them back unless they quit the group. Michael Casey, the head of the union, which had only a few dozen members, called on all of McNab & Smith's drivers to walk out. Teamsters worked long hours, sometimes seven days a week, for low pay, and so almost one hundred drivers supported the union men. The company hired all the workers back the same day. Word got around, and within weeks more than 1,000 drivers had joined Casey's union. Casey then threatened a full-blown strike if the members did not get a raise in pay and better working conditions. The Draymen's Association, which represented the haulers, decided a standard contract across the industry would prevent competition, and so agreed to a twelve-hour day, with overtime afterward or on Sunday, with a substantial pay increase.

Dockworkers, whose leverage with shippers had been hampered by infighting among the various unions, were the next to press for better conditions. Ten years before, in April 1891, they had experimented in joint action when "the long discussed scheme of organizing the laborers and mechanics employed on the water-front and shipping into one body for the mutual assistance and protection of the members was consummated."[1] The unions, which soon numbered eight, included seamen, longshoremen, and riggers, and called themselves the City Front. Their goals were limited: "No quarrel with capital was proposed or intended, but it was proposed and designed to form and maintain a solid front against rapacious employers and that class of workingmen who are ever willing to bring misfortune upon hundreds in order that they obtain employment." This latter category was almost certainly the Chinese. The group has been largely quiescent during its first decade, but there always existed an ongoing threat of a general strike that could shut down the waterfront completely.

By March 1901, with agitation for more drastic action increasing, the City Front, which by then represented 3,500 men in a variety of unions that worked the dock, voted to support the teamsters in an on-again, off-again strike against the haulers. Although little came of that action, it marked the beginning of increased activism, and, by July, the City Front had grown to thirteen unions representing the full range of waterfront trades—everything from teamsters to longshoremen to firemen to clerks—with approximately 15,000 members.[2] In addition to preparing to press renewed claims in San Francisco, they sent representatives to other West Coast ports to agitate for a militant stance by the unions there.

As the labor movement grew stronger, an Employers' Association was formed in secret to "check the growing evils . . . of strikes and boycotts."[3] Although details of its activities and even its existence were kept from the public, by summer 1901, as many as 300 businesses had joined, each pledging $1,000 to maintain a united front and blunt union strength. With two powerful groups facing off, conflict was inevitable, especially since a series of smaller strikes continued to pop up throughout the city.

On July 20, with a machinists union already two months into a strike, union teamsters refused to handle the baggage of a religious group that had hired Morton Drayage. Morton was an antiunion hauler that had refused to be a party to the contract between the Draymen's Association and the teamsters union. The Draymen's Association, under pressure from Employers' Association, announced that failure to unload the cargo voided their agreement with the teamsters. They fired more than 1,000 union members who refused to unload the cargo.

Michael Casey, who was by then the business agent for the teamsters and president of the City Front issued a statement: "As far as the Brotherhood of Teamsters is concerned, the members are prepared to fight this thing out. We can carry this war for months and will do so if necessary."[4] The head of the Draymen's Association, prompted by the Employers' Association, vowed to resist the union's demand "to the very end," and if the union refused to haul for Morton Drayage "all 1,800 [teamsters in San Francisco] would be discharged."[5]

At first, only the owners of the companies drove the teams, making what few deliveries they could. The union men did not interfere, but nor did they help when one of the owner-haulers needed assistance, which was often. After one frustrating day, however, the owners hired nonunion men to drive the teams. To protect the replacement drivers, the draymen asked that police accompany them on each shipment.

Mayor Phelan, faced with the prospect of violence between fired drivers and the nonunion replacements, was forced to pick a side. The unions liked him for his anti-Asian stance, but members of the Employers' Association were his friends and business associates, men with whom his relationships went back decades. He chose the draymen. Phelan ordered the police to accompany the haulers and protect them against Casey's teamsters, or anyone else that attempted to impede deliveries.

At first, the teamsters chose nonconfrontation and also did not seek to involve other unions, even though "police officers, looking uncomfortable in the high seats of express wagons and mounted officers drawn from the Mission and Golden Gate Park, acted as escorts to nearly every load of freight that was moved yesterday in this city."[6] Casey claimed to have told the Draymen's Association that union workers would return to work and do straight hauling under the previously agreed terms, but would not haul "directly or indirectly" for Morton: "We do not want to see the orchardists of the State suffer, because they are innocent parties to this controversy. We have said time and again that we were willing to haul all perishable freight, such as fruit, either to the commission houses or the canneries, or any other freight that is offered, with the sole exception that it must in no way be connected with the Morton companies."[7] It was even reported that Casey and some of the owners chatted amiably and shared smiles.

The bonhomie did not last forty-eight hours. On July 25, although union leaders insisted the strikers were behaving lawfully, twenty club-wielding police charged the picket line. Four or five union men were badly beaten.[8]

Tensions rose quickly along with the number of strikers. During a confrontation the following night, when one of the policemen raised his club, the pickets closed in on him. Other police once more charged the crowd with clubs, but this time the pickets fought back, hurling rocks. Eventually, more than 1,000 people were on the street, most as spectators watching the melee. By the time order was restored, both police and union men had suffered several casualties.[9]

Within days, the Employers' Association initiated a campaign in which workers, in beer-bottling plants, for example, were given the choice of leaving the union or their jobs. Union leaders responded by threatening a general strike if the Employers' Association refused to negotiate. Phelan offered to act as intermediary, and for a short time both sides seemed willing to be conciliatory. At the end of July, however, the labor organizations had called a full-blown general strike that threatened to bring commerce in San Francisco to a halt: "The president of the Labor Council said, 'We have waited a long time to get things where we could have such an issue as has been made for us. . . . We have things just where we want them.'" And he was not wrong. "The next day the shipping in the harbor was almost completely tied up; the vessels were deserted by their sailors and firemen and could neither take on nor discharge cargoes. There was no activity about the wharfs; the street traffic was again almost entirely suspended, and it was estimated that at least sixty per cent of the business of the city was at a standstill."[10]

Although the standoff lasted for days, the strikers did not attack nonunion replacements and offered to negotiate for higher wages and shorter hours. But the Employers' Association stood firm. They had decided that if they granted concessions at this point, there would be no end to the workers' demands.

Eventually, with the strike dragging on, an odd swap took place—the Employers' Association recruited agricultural workers from outside the city as scab labor, while some strikers, needing to feed their families, went to the countryside to work for the growers. The strikers that remained in the city grew more militant and met workmen arriving in San Francisco with either verbal or physical abuse, preventing many of them from reaching their workplaces. When growers realized they had no real market to which to ship their goods, they sent the city workers home.

With workers growing shorter and shorter of funds, the Employers' Association did not believe the unions could maintain strike discipline, and so refused to even sit and talk with the Labor Council. "The principle involved in this strike may be surrendered but it cannot be compromised," they wrote in an official letter, "and a surrender of it would be the beginning of the end of San Francisco's industrial welfare . . . a conference would be entirely futile and barren of results. It could only inspire in the strikers' delusive hopes of a settlement on their terms, and thus lead them to prolong the struggle. We approve of conferences between individual employers and their own employees as the only legitimate way to settle differences."[11]

The mood on the streets became more fraught. By August, there was widespread violence, wholesale arrests, and even some deaths. Phelan was again forced to choose, and again, after a failed attempt to mediate, he chose the employers. The police details assigned to guard the replacement workers were increased, many pulled from the regular duties patrolling the city streets. Skirmishes between police and strikers became more common. Phelan was denounced as a traitor to the labor movement, and there seemed little chance that he could be reelected that November.

With Phelan an unacceptable candidate, and the strike threatened with collapse if members could not feed their families, a small group of union leaders met to try to win their war with the owners at the ballot box. A number of unions joined up, and they began to formulate plans to run a slate of pro-labor candidates in the November election. In July, after an executive committee meeting, the party spokesman said, "We intend to nominate members of labor unions for all the offices [in the next municipal election] with the possible exception of Mayor. It may be a man on the outside who has always been friendly to the unions may be found who will suit us. In that event, we shall offer him the nomination. . . . We have plenty of men in the labor unions who are competent to conduct the city's business on correct principles and avoid scandals that so often offend the community. There will be no compromise. We shall do our best top win, but if we are defeated, we will all go down together."[12]

But the party remained rudderless. The executive committee announced a convention in September to draw up an official platform and nominate a full slate of candidates, with four delegates assigned from each of the 125 unions in San Francisco, said to represent 50,000 voters. The party asked union men not to vote in the primaries, so that they were eligible to sign petitions for Union-Labor, and also pledged undying support for the City Front in its struggle again the Employers' Association.

The Employers' Association did not take the threat of losing control of city government seriously. They, and almost everyone else, treated the new party as something of a joke with no chance to outpoll either of the major parties.

Almost everyone. One who did not was a man who would become one of the oddest and most unique political bosses in U.S. history.

Abraham Rueff was born in San Francisco in 1864. His father was a successful Jewish merchant, whose wealth allowed his family to avoid at

Abe Ruef. Courtesy of Library of Congress Prints and Photographs Division.

least overt anti-Semitism. Young Abe was a prodigy. He would eventually speak eight languages, including Cantonese, graduate from Berkeley at eighteen with high honors, breeze through law school, and join the California bar at the minimum age of twenty-one.

Ruef (he dropped the second "f") entered politics as a good government zealot. He helped found the Municipal Reform League, from which he intended to launch an anticorruption campaign, for a time trading ideas in correspondence with another young reformer in New York, Theodore Roosevelt. But California, largely controlled by the Southern Pacific Railroad and an oligarchy of industrial barons, was a poor place to be an idealist. San Francisco became the hub of a political machine that controlled both parties and regularly used graft and strong-arm tactics to ensure its continued primacy. Even by the ludicrously high standard of big-city corruption in the late nineteenth century, San Francisco stood out. For years, every incumbent mayor and city Board of Supervisors would be challenged, usually successfully, by a "reformer" such as James Phelan, whose administration would prove even more corrupt than the scoundrels they threw out.

Abe Ruef was not a man to tilt at windmills, and he eventually decided that if he could not improve the political culture, he would dominate it. When he heard of the Union-Labor Party's convention, Ruef, who until that point had been an active and unsuccessful Republican, decided to attend.

What he witnessed was chaos. Sixty-eight unions sent delegations, and their leaders, used to running their own groups, were unwilling to cede authority and were leery of any attempt to create a hierarchical organization. The *Examiner*, which supported organized labor, reported, "Mere suspicion of a slate causes prompt rejection of the committee report on permanent organization amid much excitement."[13] One of the only things everyone present did agree on was "exclusion of all Asiatics."

In the disorganization, Ruef had found the perfect vehicle for personal advancement. Almost immediately, using brains, political savvy, and charm, he took over. He authored a declaration of policy for the group that was "a masterpiece of equivocation designed to gain the support of workingmen without alienating others. It was, in his own words, 'True to every principle of labor, yet conservative.'"[14] A major item of policy, as it must be with every attempt to woo union members, was a strict program of Asian exclusion. To head the ticket and run for mayor, Ruef chose a tall, good-looking, affable family man, Eugene Schmitz, who was a violinist, orchestra leader, and head of the musicians' union. Schmitz had not a scintilla of political experience and up to that point had no intention of acquiring any.

But with Ruef urging and flattering him along, Schmitz proved to be a willing and excellent student. He memorized both the California Constitution and the San Francisco City Articles, and then, at Ruef's elbow, was introduced to dozens of the most important people in the business and political communities. Schmitz was a not natural orator but, since Ruef wrote his speeches, he did have just the right things to say. Still, as the election neared, few gave "Handsome Gene" much chance to be San Francisco's next mayor.

On the streets, the strikers were growing desperate. The City Front insisted they would stay out as long as it took, but there were mutterings that they should make a deal. Even worse, some of the strikers, out of money, had begun to drift back to work. Frustration boiled over on the night of September 28, when "a small body of special officers, afterwards aided by the regular police, was attacked by an armed mob on the chief business street of the city. A pitched battle ensued, and a number of the participants were shot before the mob was routed by the arrival of reinforcements to the other side."[15] The newspapers leapt in to whip up public outrage: "Kearny Street between Market and Post streets, bore every evidence yesterday of the terrible battle fought in the early hours of the morning between a horde of crazed strikers—teamsters, boxmakers, carpenters, sailors and others affiliated with the City Front Federation—and a brave band of five men fighting for their lives. Windows shattered, signs indented, awnings ripped, and buildings furrowed with bullets were the mute evidences of the latest riot that darkens the pages of the history of San Francisco." The police and "special officers," who were in reality hired guns, were praised as heroes. "'I am highly pleased with the stand taken by the special officers this morning,' said Chief of Police Sullivan yesterday. 'It shows that some of them are made of the right stuff and will resist attack. Since the patrol has been established on the waterfront, none of the union pickets will dare venture out after dusk.'"[16]

The Kearny Street battle was a public relations disaster for the unions, which the owners were happy to exploit. The Employers' Association donated $200,000 to the police to increase manpower. The city braced for war: "Houses were barricaded and old weapons that had long done service as ornaments or heirlooms were polished up and made ready for action. Men stayed at home by night and walked the streets heavily armed by day. By this time, however, all signs except the bold bearing of the union leaders indicated to unprejudiced eyes that the struggle was nearing its end, and that the strike had failed."[17]

On the surface, it had. On October 2, a settlement was announced in which the Employers' Association conceded nothing that they had not been willing to give in July. But in a larger sense, the strike would prove to be a turning point in big-city politics.

Phelan, as expected, did not run for reelection. Instead, the Democrats nominated Joseph Tobin, a bland Phelan acolyte. The Republican Party nominated the equally lackluster city auditor, Asa Wells. For workers, there was little to choose between them. Bitter and defeated, a new

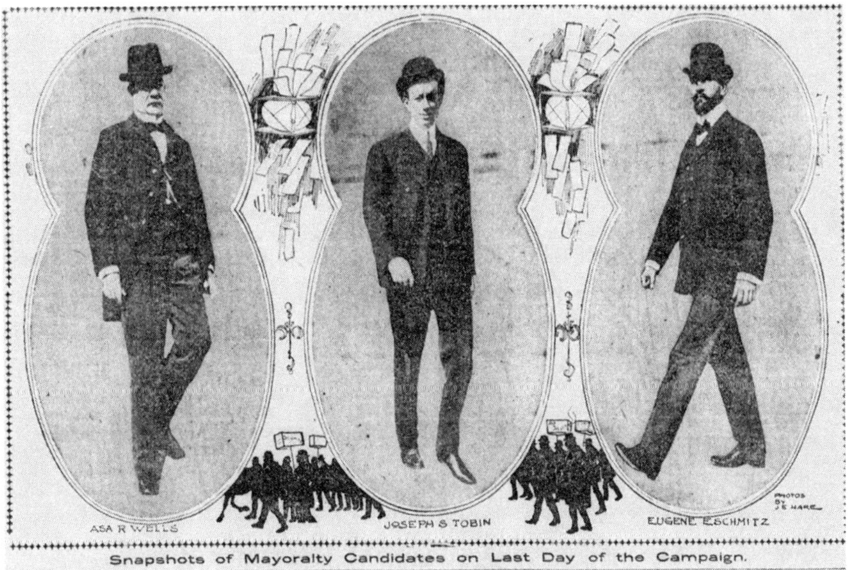

San Francisco mayoral candidates, November 1901.

political party dedicated to workers' rights began to seem attractive, and Abe Ruef was just the man to mobilize the disaffected. At the same time, he might persuade traditional party supporters that a third-party candidacy was just what San Francisco needed to finally put an end to rampant corruption.

Although neither Democrats nor Republicans thought the new party a threat, both did their best to keep Schmitz and the other Union-Laborites from drawing off votes they thought would be theirs. They challenged petition signatures, of which a friendly voting registrar, who "hoped to keep the party off the ballot," disallowed as many as he could. It was not enough but did succeed in keeping the Union-Labor Party from securing a place on the ballot October 10.[18]

The party did not kick off its campaign until October 15, just three weeks before the election. Although "not a finished speaker," "suffering a bit from stage fright," and "nervous and ill at ease," candidate Schmitz nevertheless was wildly applauded at an overflow event at Metropolitan Hall. Schmitz, parroting Abe Ruef, told the crowd of rancorous workingmen just what they wanted to hear. Phelan was "the owner of millions of which he never earned a dollar by work." Tobin, the Democrat, was "the owner of a large fortune by inheritance, which enables him to move in society." Money itself was not objectionable, Schmitz went on, but "its possession should not seemingly be the only qualification for office." The Republican, Wells, was "named by a coterie of the rawest bosses ever aggregated for public plunder."[19]

As election day grew near, it seemed, incredibly, that Schmitz might make it close. He did better than that. When the results were reported, Schmitz had received 21,896 votes, Wells 17,696, and Tobin only 12,644. The *San Francisco Call* reported, "People Rebuke Bosses. Refuse to Swallow Corrupt Programme." Schmitz himself said, "I regard my election as a just and overwhelming rebuke to bossism."[20] In fact, San Francisco had elected a tool of the most corrupt boss of all, and for the next five years Abe Ruef and his cronies, which soon included the once-honest Schmitz, would loot the city on an unprecedented scale.

As local political observer George Kennan wrote in 1907:

> When Mayor Schmitz came before the voters of San Francisco as a candidate for reelection on the Labor-Union ticket, in the fall of 1905, it was perfectly well known to the reading and thinking people of the city that Ruef, the Mayor, and the members of the municipal boards were blackmailers, extortioners, and thieves . . . the administration made a business of selling immunity to gamblers, prize-fight promoters, and keepers of brothels; that the great house of prostitution at 620 Jackson Street was virtually a municipal institution; that the police were giving protection to notorious criminals and taking money therefor that the municipal boards were blackmailing law-breakers and compelling honest men to pay tribute; that the work of the city was given to dishonest contractors who divided their illegal profits with the officials who permitted them to steal; and that, with the exception of the Board of Supervisors, every branch of the city government was shamelessly and almost defiantly corrupt.[21]

Other observers offered that the "blackest deeds of Boss Tweed look as harmless as politics in a woman's club," detailing such incidents as when "the United Railroads bribed the supervisors with the fat sum of $200,000; the city tax-collector ran off with an adventuress and several hundred thousand dollars of the taxpayers' money; houses of ill-fame maintained a fixed schedule of prices by which police officials, from captains to patrolmen, were systematically bribed; gamblers shared their ill-gotten gains with the mayor." Brothels, referred to euphemistically as "French Restaurants," paid handsomely to gain liquor licenses, half of the fees going to Schmitz.[22]

What kept Schmitz and Ruef in power was their unwavering populist appeal to the city's workers. One worker said: "Skilled workmen who before the election of Mayor Schmitz were earning only from three to five dollars a day are now getting from five to seven dollars. As for graft—there has always been graft; but nobody has ever made a howl about it until now, when our administration happens to be in power. Why didn't the capitalist employers say something about it before, when they were getting the plums? Ruef may be making money on the side, but he is taking it from people who can afford to pay; his hand isn't in our pockets." A worker's wife added, "I don't care how much they steal, so long as my husband gets good wages. They're not stealing from us."[23]

With the ascension of labor, anti-Asian activities were ratcheted up since neither party could come back to power without wooing at least some of the workers away from Ruef.

James Phelan, although out of office, called a Chinese Exclusion Convention, during which a resolution was passed, calling "the character and rapidly increasing numbers of Japanese and other Asiatic immigrants a menace to the industrial interests of our people."[24]

During the five years of Abe Ruef's kleptocratic reign, various attempts were made by reformers, most of whom were almost as corrupt as Ruef, to dislodge him, but through three elections, periodic public outrage, and even a grand jury empaneled to investigate corruption, Ruef easily outmaneuvered or outmuscled anyone who dared to challenge him.

It seemed to those few in San Francisco who genuinely wanted change that nothing could be done. They were wrong.

7 | Tremors

On April 19, 1906, the headline under the banner of *The Call=Chronicle=Examiner*, a joint edition of San Francisco's major newspapers, read: "EARTHQUAKE AND FIRE: SAN FRANCISCO IN RUINS." The article described the devastation:

> Death and destruction have been the fate of San Francisco. Shaken by a temblor at 5:13 o'clock yesterday morning, the shock lasting 48 seconds and scourged by flames that raged diametrically in all directions, the city is a mass of smoldering ruins. At six o'clock last evening, the flames, seemingly playing with increased vigor, threatened to destroy such sections as their fury had spared during the earlier portion of the day. Building their path in a triangular circuit from the start in the early morning, they jockeyed as the day waned, left the business section, which they had entirely devastated, and skipped in a dozen directions to the residence portions. As night fell, they had made their way over to the North Beach section and springing anew to the south, they reached out along the shipping section down the bay shore, over the hills and across toward Third and Townsend. Warehouses, wholesale houses, and manufacturing concerns fell in their path. This completed the destruction of the entire district known as "South of Market Street." How far they are reaching to the south across the channel cannot be told as part of the city is shut off to the San Francisco papers. After darkness, thousands of the homeless were making their way with their blankets and scant provisions to Golden Gate Park and the beach to find shelter. Those in the homes on the hills just north of the Haves Valley wrecked section piled their belongings in the streets, and express wagons and automobiles were hauling the things away to sparsely settled regions. Everybody in San Francisco is prepared to leave the city, for the belief is firm that San Francisco will be totally destroyed.[1]

Although San Francisco was not totally destroyed, 28,000 buildings were leveled or burned out, as many as three-quarters of the city's 400,000 residents were left homeless, and 3,000 people died. When the tremor struck, estimated at 7.9 on the Richter scale, not only were aboveground structures damaged, but the city's water mains were destroyed, leaving firemen no means to fight the fires that cropped up

The Call-Chronicle-Examiner

SAN FRANCISCO, THURSDAY, APRIL 19, 1906.

EARTHQUAKE AND FIRE: SAN FRANCISCO IN RUINS

DEATH AND DESTRUCTION HAVE BEEN THE FATE OF SAN FRANCISCO. SHAKEN BY A TEMBLOR AT 5:13 O'CLOCK YESTERDAY MORNING, THE SHOCK LASTING 48 SECONDS, AND SCOURGED BY FLAMES THAT RAGED DIAMETRICALLY IN ALL DIRECTIONS, THE CITY IS A MASS OF SMOULDERING RUINS. AT SIX O'CLOCK LAST EVENING THE FLAMES SEEMINGLY PLAYING WITH INCREASED VIGOR, THREATENED TO DESTROY SUCH SECTIONS AS THEIR FURY HAD SPARED DURING THE EARLIER PORTION OF THE DAY. BUILDING THEIR PATH IN A TRIANGUAR CIRCUIT FROM THE START IN THE EARLY MORNING, THEY JOCKEYED AS THE DAY WANED, LEFT THE BUSINESS SECTION, WHICH THEY HAD ENTIRELY DEVASTATED, AND SKIPPED IN A DOZEN DIRECTIONS TO THE RESIDENCE PORTIONS. AS NIGHT FELL THEY HAD MADE THEIR WAY OVER INTO THE NORTH BEACH SECTION AND SPRINGING ANEW TO THE SOUTH THEY REACHED OUT ALONG THE SHIPPING SECTION DOWN THE BAY SHORE, OVER THE HILLS AND ACROSS TOWARD THIRD AND TOWNSEND STREETS. WAREHOUSES, WHOLESALE HOUSES AND MANUFACTURING CONCERNS FELL IN THEIR PATH. THIS COMPLETED THE DESTRUCTION OF THE ENTIRE DISTRICT KNOWN AS THE "SOUTH OF MARKET STREET." HOW FAR THEY ARE REACHING TO THE SOUTH ACROSS THE CHANNEL CANNOT BE TOLD AS THIS PART OF THE CITY IS SHUT OFF FROM SAN FRANCISCO PAPERS.

AFTER DARKNESS, THOUSANDS OF THE HOMELESS WERE MAKING THEIR WAY WITH THEIR BLANKETS AND SCANT PROVISIONS TO GOLDEN GATE PARK AND THE BEACH TO FIND SHELTER. THOSE IN THE HOMES ON THE HILLS JUST NORTH OF THE HAYES VALLEY WRECKED SECTION PILED THEIR BELONGINGS IN THE STREETS AND EXPRESS WAGONS AND AUTOMOBILES WERE HAULING THE THINGS AWAY TO THE SPARSELY SETTLED REGIONS. EVERYBODY IN SAN FRANCISCO IS PREPARED TO LEAVE THE CITY, FOR THE BELIEF IS FIRM THAT SAN FRANCISCO WILL BE TOTALLY DESTROYED.

DOWNTOWN EVERYTHING IS RUIN. NOT A BUSINESS HOUSE STANDS. THEATRES ARE CRUMBLED INTO HEAPS. FACTORIES AND COMMISSION HOUSES LIE SMOULDERING ON THEIR FORMER SITES. ALL OF THE NEWSPAPER PLANTS HAVE BEEN RENDERED USELESS, THE "CALL" AND THE "EXAMINER" BUILDINGS, EXCLUDING THE "CALL'S" EDITORIAL ROOMS ON STEVENSON STREET BEING ENTIRELY DESTROYED.

IT IS ESTIMATED THAT THE LOSS IN SAN FRANCISCO WILL REACH FROM $150,000,000 TO $200,000,000. THESE FIGURES ARE IN THE ROUGH AND NOTHING CAN BE TOLD UNTIL PARTIAL ACCOUNTING IS TAKEN.

ON EVERY SIDE THERE WAS DEATH AND SUFFERING YESTERDAY. HUNDREDS WERE INJURED, EITHR BURNED, CRUSHED OR STRUCK BY FALLING PIECES FROM THE BUILDINGS AND ONE OF TEN DIED WHILE ON THE OPOPERATING TABLE AT MECHANICS' PAVILION, IMPROVISED AS A HOSPITAL FOR THE COMFORT AND CARE OF 300 OF THE INJURED. THE NUMBER OF DEAD IS NOT KNOWN BUT IT IS ESTIMATED THAT AT LEAST 500 MET THEIR DEATH IN THE HORROR.

AT NINE O'CLOCK, UNDER A SPECIAL MESSAGE FROM PRESIDENT ROOSEVELT, THE CITY WAS PLACED UNDER MARTIAL LAW. HUNDREDS OF TROOPS PATROLLED THE STREETS AND DROVE THE CROWDS BACK, WHILE HUNDREDS MORE WERE SET AT WORK ASSISTING THE FIRE AND POLICE DEPARTMENTS. THE STRICTEST ORDERS WERE ISSUED, AND IN TRUE MILITARY SPIRIT THE SOLDIERS OBEYED. DURING THE AFTERNOON THREE THIEVES MET THEIR DEATH BY RIFLE BULLETS WHILE AT WORK IN THE RUINS. THE CURIOUS WERE DRIVEN BACK AT THE BREASTS OF THE HORSES THAT THE CAVALRYMEN RODE AND ALL THE CROWDS WERE FORCED FROM THE LEVEL DISTRICT TO THE HILLY SECTION BEYOND TO THE NORTH

THE WATER SUPPLY WAS ENTIRELY CUT OFF, AND MAY BE IT WAS JUST AS WELL, FOR THE LINES OF FIRE DEPARTMENT WOULD HAVE BEEN ABSOLUTELY USELESS AT ANY STAGE. ASSISTANT CHIEF DOUGHERTY SUPERVISED THE WORK OF HIS MEN AND EARLY IN THE MORNING IT WAS SEEN THAT THE ONLY POSSIBLE CHANCE TO SAVE THE CITY LAY IN EFFORT TO CHECK THE FLAMES BY THE USE OF DYNAMITE. DURING THE DAY A BLAST COULD BE HEARD IN ANY SECTION AT INTERVALS OF ONLY A FEW MINUTES, AND BUILDINGS NOT DESTROYED BY FIRE WERE BLOWN TO ATOMS. BUT THROUGH THE GAPS MADE THE FLAMES JUMPED AND ALTHOUGH THE FAILURES OF THE HEROIC EFFORTS OF THE POLICE FIREMEN AND SOLDIERS WERE AT TIMES SICKENING, THE WORK WAS CONTINUED WITH A DESPERATION THAT WILL LIVE AS ONE OF THE FEATURES OF THE TERRIBLE DISASTER. MEN WORKED LIKE FIENDS TO COMBAT THE LAUGHING, ROARING, ONRUSHING FIRE DEMON.

Newspaper published as a combined edition the day after the earthquake.

because of broken gas lines.[2] Desperate to halt the spread of the flames, they set off dynamite charges in buildings at the perimeter of the blaze to create firebreaks. It was a disastrous decision. The explosions helped fuel an inferno that raged for four days and left 80 percent of San Francisco, then the nation's ninth-largest city and the largest in the West, in ruins.

But if the destruction was unprecedented, so was the response. Even as the fires burned and refugees streamed through smoldering rubble, the rebuilding of the city began. Within days, three hundred plumbers were repairing the city's waterlines, and millions of bricks and other rubble were being cleared, much of it dumped into the bay. The army was called in to prevent looting—against which a shoot to kill order had been issued by Mayor Schmitz—and help clear the streets. The federal and state governments committed significant funds and logis-

Chinatown in ruins after the earthquake and fire. Courtesy of Library of Congress Prints and Photographs Division.

tical resources to rebuild, not to replicate what was lost, but to erect a new, modern city on the ruins of what had been a slapdash, ill-designed boomtown. Entire neighborhoods were to be redesigned to create as modern and functional a city as existed anywhere in the United States. Such an endeavor, however, would require a good bit of dislocation, and in some cases entire neighborhoods would simply disappear.

One of these was Chinatown.

Home to 14,000 residents crammed into substandard housing in twenty-two square blocks honeycombed with brothels and opium dens before the tremor struck, four days later Chinatown had literally ceased to exist. Its wooden buildings had suffered severe but not irreparable damage in the earthquake only to become perfect fuel for the firestorm that followed. Few white residents cared how many Chinese had died in the conflagration, the number of which would never be known. What white residents did seem to agree on was that Chinatown was a scourge.

The disaster had created many problems for anti-Asians, but it also seemed to have solved one. A few days after the earthquake, on April 23, the *Oakland Enquirer* ran an article titled "Let Us Have No More Chinatowns in Our Cities," which began, "The cities in the immediate vicinity of San Francisco Bay never in the past had such opportunity as now to forever do away with the huddling together of Chinese in districts where it is undesirable, from the standpoint of civilization, to permit the lower and vicious classes of Orientals to congregate."[3]

To make the eviction of the Chinese even more compelling, "it [had] dawned on the establishment of San Francisco that the prime real estate of the city . . . at the absolute epicenter, with its commanding views, was Chinatown."[4] More than a year before the earthquake, the city's *Merchants Association Review* ran an article titled "San Francisco May Be Freed from the Standing Menace of Chinatown," and reported, "Plans have been arranged and a corporation formed to turn the Chinese quarter into a business section and build a new Oriental city on the bay shore."[5] What the article failed to mention was that the corporation, as expected, was controlled by Abe Ruef.

The press played up that the neighborhood had been abandoned. "I took a walk through what had been Chinatown," an *Examiner* reporter wrote. "I did not see a single Chinaman in all the complete ruin of what was once the most populous Chinese quarter in the new world. The yellow men have fled from the place and the only human beings I saw there were two Italians poking about in the ruins of a Chinese curio store. The secrets of the quarter lie buried under tons of brick and mortar."[6]

Chinese leaders were determined to rebuild Chinatown exactly where it had been, but protecting property worth millions to developers in 1906 San Francisco appeared to be an impossible task. That Ruef, Schmitz, and rest of what the press called the "Boodle Boys" would make millions by turning Chinatown white did not raise an eyebrow with most workers and union members.

Still, the Chinese had to live somewhere, so the Ruef crew—this time joined by Democrats and Republicans—decreed that a new Chinatown would be built just outside the city limits in Hunters Point, an isolated spit of land dominated by mud flats jutting out into San Francisco Bay. Newspapers described the area as "desirable," but it was perhaps the least desirable piece of real estate in the entire area.

When the announcement of the Hunters Point scheme was made, only days after the fires had been extinguished, the newly formed Committee for the Relocation of Chinese—chaired by Abe Ruef—was already quietly soliciting offers for the original Chinatown land, which almost certainly included the usual bribes and kickbacks. Some of the land the committee members would buy up themselves. In order to bring the plan to fruition, however, it was paramount that Chinese not be allowed to return. To make certain they were kept away, Schmitz and the citizens' committee proposed temporarily herding all the Chinese into a tent city in the Presidio until they could be permanently herded to Hunters Point.

Newspaper editors fell into line: "What to do with the unfortunate Chinese of San Francisco, a problem which has given the authorities considerable worry during the last few days, has been settled, at least temporarily. Since the destruction of Chinatown, its inhabitants have been living in tents and in even less comfortable quarters on a large tract of land on the north shore of the bay. Knowing the gregarious habits of the Chinese, the citizens' committee and the Mayor feared that if even a few of them returned to their old district and took up quarters, the entire Chinese population would follow, and the problem of moving them, which, has agitated San Francisco for many years would be as great as ever."[7]

The Chinese had no intention of being elbowed out of San Francisco, however, and protests erupted immediately. The Chinese consul filed an official complaint with the city and in Washington, DC. The Six Companies, which newspapers falsely reported had agreed to the plan, announced it would do all it could to thwart the takeover. They vowed to again hire the best white lawyers and use the courts to halt mass evictions. Complicating matters for Ruef and his cohorts was that a small but significant portion of the land in the old Chinatown was owned by the Chinese themselves. Although few of the owners were citizens, there was at that time no prohibition on noncitizens owning and developing property. In addition, the law was such that a landowner could take to rebuilding immediately, with no advance permit requirement.

Not all opposition to Ruef's scheme came from the Chinese. Although San Francisco residents tended to avoid Chinatown, tourists flocked there. In addition, many American firms had discovered a lucrative market across the Pacific. "If the citizens of San Francisco will use the Chinese and drive them away," one businessman observed, "they will flee to other cities and take the Oriental trade from San Francisco. . . . China at present is one of the greatest markets in the world for American goods and it will be greater in time to come, and all nations will be glad to have her trade. . . . It would not be best to San Francisco's interests to isolate the Chinese. It will work against her at the end."[8]

But none of that was likely to be of interest to Ruef and his cronies. If they were to be stopped, a far more politically effective response would be required. The office of the main Chinese newspaper, *Chung Sai Yat Po*, had been a casualty of the fire—printing press and printers' type destroyed—so the editor, Ng Poon Chew, set up shop in Oakland and produced hand-lettered editions, which were gobbled up by refugees. On April 29, Ng presented a three-point plan to reclaim Chinatown, which needed to be "implemented by we Chinese quickly, or we will soon regret it." The first point was, "Hire famous attorneys to represent us as soon as possible," which the Six Companies had already planned to do. The second, "If the Chinese living in Chinatown are also themselves landlords, they should restore their buildings as soon as possible. And there is no need to inform local officials. According to U.S. laws, if the land belongs to the building owner, the landlord has the right to build on his land. Local officials have no right to stop him. The present city officials are [with the anti-Chinese union faction]. If we apply through them, they will try to stop us. So it's better not to go through them." The third was, "If the Chinese rented from the western landlords, the Chinese renters should speak with their landlords as soon as possible and ask them to rebuild and rent them the building. Western landlords like to rent their houses to Chinese because the rent in Chinatown is higher than elsewhere."[9]

The newspaper also made certain the threat level was understood. Three days after publishing its plan to save Chinatown, it wrote, "On the eighth day of this moon, *San Francisco Examiner* reported [that] those who managed the properties of Chinatown said that the lands in Chinatown would eventually be sold to rich westerners to build opulent residences because the hill behind was an effective wind barricade in front was the arresting beauty of the port and the river."[10] The report also noted that whites, which meant Ruef and his associates, were already negotiating to buy land, which was a surprise to no one.

The Chinese, for decades forced into a self-contained community where survival depended on mutual support, responded as a community, and all three strategies were implemented immediately. In the meantime, pressure was increased both in California and in Washington to rebuild Chinatown precisely where had it been before the fire.

The Chinese consul general, vice consul, and secretary of the legation, and representatives of the Six Companies met privately with members of Ruef's committee and formally protested forcing members of the Chinatown community to relocate to any section of the city or its environs not of their choosing: "The Chinese maintain that they have the privilege of building and living next door to any citizen, and while appreciating the advantage to themselves of having a quarter, demand that the quarter be of their own selection." The Chinese consulate, they reminded committee members, was "imperial Chinese property," and no citizens committee was empowered to disturb that location. "This plat of ground," they insisted, "situated in the old Chinatown will form a nucleus about which the Chinese who own their own property in the old quarter may gather unmolested and so in the course of time Chinatown may again arise amid the ruins."[11]

Under normal circumstances, with so much money at stake and with control of the Board of Supervisors, Ruef and Schmitz would have some means to brush aside these impediments, but their attention was divided. Although a grand jury that was empaneled in 1905 to investigate extortion of "French restaurants" (brothels) had been forced to suspend its activities because it could not obtain definitive proof against Ruef or Schmitz, in the wake of the November 1905 elections, in which the Union-Labor Party won complete control of city government, there had been a new push to clean up city hall.

Two of the few prominent San Franciscans who dared oppose Ruef, newspaper editor Fremont Older, who had originally urged James Phelan to run for mayor, and bank president Rudolph Spreckels, journeyed to Washington and persuaded President Theodore Roosevelt to assign U.S. district attorney Francis J. Heney, who was investigating land fraud in Oregon, and former Secret Service operative William J. Burns to mount a campaign against the Ruef machine. Heney was honest and competent, and Burns, who later became known as "America's Sherlock Holmes," and founded the Burns Detective Agency, was brilliant, dogged, fearless, and incorruptible. Spreckels, despite being warned that he would lose most of his society friends and possibly his life, pledged $100,000 to fund the investigation.

In February 1907, Burns and the detectives he hired began ferreting about for evidence against Ruef, Schmitz, and other corrupt city officials that would hold up in court. Although the investigators were theoretically operating in secret, little went on in San Francisco that Ruef did not hear about. That Burns's detectives were highly professional, clearly well funded, and could be neither bought off nor frightened off, was bad enough, but Francis Heney's presence meant that Ruef's old correspondent, now the occupant of the White House, had approved the investigation. Ruef had no intention of totally curtailing his activities, but he could not operate as brazenly as before. Ruef's need to behave with some circumspection was likely what prevented him from being more blatant in the Chinatown swindle, and this gave Chinese leaders the opening they needed to effectively mount a counterattack.

Chinese began to drift back into Chinatown and rebuild, some on land they owned, most on leased properties for which they paid high, often exorbitant, rent. At first, the construction proceeded ad hoc, but Look Tin Eli, the owner of one of Chinatown's most successful tourist attractions, the Sing Chong Bazaar, persuaded other merchants to adopt a bold marketing plan. Born in Mendocino, he spoke perfect English, and had worked his way up in the business world with vision, brains, and guile: "Look persuaded them that an exotic, 'oriental style' of architecture would 'attract tourists' and 'boost business.'" He and other businessmen hired white architects to create what at least white visitors would see as "authentic" Chinese buildings. "Hence, the Sing Chong Building at the northwest corner of California and Grant was distinguished by pagoda-like towers, upturned eaves, and a color scheme of bright red, green, and gold."[12] Other buildings were similarly designed, and within months of the earthquake's devastation, construction was well underway.

Chinatown, it seemed, would remain exactly where it was.

For Union-Labor Party supporters, to say nothing of the speculators who intended to capitalize on the Hunters Point move, being bested by the Chinese was expensive and humiliating. For Ruef, with Burns's detectives doggedly gathering evidence against him, the timing could not have been worse. For the first time since he had come to power five years before, some of his closest associates began to question his leadership, and they expressed their doubts in a tangible and very public manner.

To make matters worse, Burns was discovering a depth of corruption that shocked even the most cynical graft-hardened San Franciscans. George Kennan wrote:

> In the summer of 1906, after the earthquake and fire, [Chief of Police] Dinan and a large part of the police force went into the business of blackmailing looters and dealers in half-burned junk stolen from the ruins of the city. The property destroyed or injured in the great conflagration was valued at four hundred million dollars, and a considerable part of it consisted of

> brass or copper, which, even in a defaced or melted form, was salable. In the early summer, hundreds of looters began to dig in the ruins of the burned buildings for valuable metals and for merchandise that had not been wholly consumed. It was the business of the police, of course, to prevent robbery of this kind and to protect, as far as possible, the property-owners; but, instead, Dinan and a large number of his subordinates gave protection to the looters, blackmailed the junk-dealers, and shared the profits of both.[13]

In late summer, Mayor Schmitz decided that an extended working vacation in Europe might be in order, and he announced he would leave at the end of September and be gone two months. Schmitz denied his absence had anything to do with the discovery by Burns's men of papers in an earthquake-damaged safe of a liquor distributor that detailed a scheme in which he would share kickbacks with police officials on every ounce of whiskey to sold to San Francisco saloons. Saloons were required to renew their liquor licenses every three months, and without the kickbacks, their applications would be denied. The distributors' attorney, Ruef, would be paid a hefty monthly fee to ensure that all ran smoothly.

Schmitz's denials were scoffed at, and his trip received less than rave notices in the press: "Mayor Schmitz, the tool of Ruef, is in Europe and local newspapers are quoting well known citizens, who express the belief that he will never return. A humble fiddler less than six years ago, Schmitz is now traveling in regal style, dining with princes and entertained abroad by kings of finance."[14] The *Examiner* wrote, "He finds himself somewhat in the position of Mark Twain, who, in the middle of a romantic story, got his hero and heroine into such inextricable difficulties that he left the reader to work out the plot for himself. But the Mayor has solved this problem. He is going to Europe at once."[15]

The most damaging defector from the Ruef/Schmitz cabal was District Attorney William Langdon. Shifting in the prevailing wind and fully aware that Hearst's political ambitions would require him to abandon Ruef, Langdon solicited the support of Hearst's newspapers in a prospective run for governor. Because Francis Heney and William Burns had finished their business in Oregon and come to San Francisco to personally supervise the investigation, Langdon was prevailed on to dismiss the Ruef stooge who was serving as his second-in- command and appoint Heney as assistant district attorney.

With the reformers closing in and Mayor Schmitz's return uncertain,

Ruef was desperate to find a way to deflect public attention, a means to arouse his supporters to the same level of fervor they had exhibited during the strikes that had been the Union-Labor Party's springboard to power. "In the municipal administration," a Japanese professor wrote, "were a group who did not care to have a great searchlight of publicity thrust upon the city. They sought to shift the focus of the world's attention upon some other object."[16]

Anti-Asian racism had worked perfectly in the past, and so would be trotted out once again. With Chinese no longer an option, the Japanese would become the object of choice.

8 | Gentlemen . . . and Ladies

To mount his attack on the Japanese, Ruef was sufficiently savvy not to further disrupt a fragile postearthquake economy, and so he chose an institution that would have great propaganda value but little tangible effect—schools. On October 11, as talk of a new grand jury began to circulate, the San Francisco School Board ordered Japanese and Korean children to attend the "Oriental School," a segregated public elementary school previously reserved for the Chinese. They used as justification a state law that, after the 1896 *Plessy v. Ferguson* separate-but-equal decision by the Supreme Court, permitted—but did not mandate—the segregation of "Mongolian" children into their own schools.

The School Board had made little attempt to hide the racist intent of school segregation. In a 1905 order, which had not previously been acted on, they wrote: "Resolved that the Board of Education is determined in its efforts to effect the establishment of separate schools for Chinese and Japanese pupils, not only for the purpose of relieving the congestion at present prevailing in our schools, but also for the higher end that our children should not be placed in any position where their youthful impressions may be affected by associations with pupils of the Mongolian race."[1] Enforcing the order when they did, more than a year later, "enabled Schmitz and Ruef to make martyrs of themselves at a time when their other activities should have received the universal condemnation of the city."[2]

The initiative was almost laughably transparent as the number of children affected was only ninety-three out of a total school population in the tens of thousands. Board member Aaron Altmann, an artist from a wealthy family—and Abe Ruef's son-in-law—who had studied painting in Paris before being appointed by Mayor Schmitz to the Parks Commission, then moving to the School Board, was said to have made a thorough study of the issue, but details of the study were never forthcoming. Japanese leaders responded to charges that Japanese children—all ninety-three of them—were overburdening the schools by pointing out that although twenty-three schools had been destroyed in the earthquake, "on July 23, 1906, the schools were opened with an attendance of 25,000. After a tour of inspection, the president of the

Board of Education announced that there was very little overcrowding. He said nothing about the dangers of the Japanese."[3]

But facts had little to do with the decision. The Japanese were chosen because they could be demonized even more so than the Chinese, not because of their failures, but rather because of their success.

Japan's progress had not slowed in the decades following former president Grant's visit. Their industry, educational system, railroads, and agricultural production had all been modernized and were the equal of many Western powers. Especially their military. The samurai ethic had merged with modern weapons and warships to present a serious threat to even the most advanced world military powers.

Of which Russia was not one.

Japan had already soundly defeated China in 1895 and gained control of the Korean Peninsula as a de facto colony when it found itself at diplomatic loggerheads with Russia as to the status of Manchuria and the northern part of Korea. Japan attempted to be conciliatory, but Russia refused to negotiate. European powers were cognizant of Japan's progress, but defeating the sclerotic Qing dynasty was one thing, and Asians besting Europeans quite another.

It was a fatal underestimation. Russia's army and navy were led by often lazy and incompetent aristocrats and staffed by conscripts who lacked incentive to do anything but serve their time and remain alive. Procurement had been shoddy, often little more than a conduit for well-placed princes, counts, dukes, and businessmen to channel expenditures into their private coffers.

After negotiations broke down, Japan began the hostilities by launching a surprise attack on the Russian fleet at Port Arthur, Russia's warm-water Pacific port, only declaring war a few convenient hours later.[4] The conflict lasted for eighteen months, culminating with a rout of the Russians on land at Mukden in February 1905 and the obliteration of their fleet at Tsushima Strait in May. Finally, Tsar Nicholas II, who had resisted calls to end war, unwilling to believe mighty Russia could be defeated by an inferior race, offered to negotiate peace. Japan agreed, and both sides chose President Theodore Roosevelt as mediator. In the treaty that ensued, the Japanese gained full control of Korea and Manchuria, and a lease of Port Arthur. TR won the Nobel Peace Prize, but his failure to support the reparations that Japan initially insisted on created bitter feelings, and charges of favoritism among the Japanese.

With the defeat of Russia, no one in the world, least of all Roosevelt,

San Francisco Examiner cartoon showing a shadow over California.

could possibly deny that Japan was now a world military power. The Japanese made no secret of their desire for further expansion, which many on the West Coast viewed as a direct threat. It did not take much to rouse the populace to the specter of hordes of bloodthirsty Japanese soldiers and sailors descending on America's Pacific Coast, and this had already been exploited in speeches and in newspapers. As early as September 1905, William Randolph Hearst's *San Francisco Examiner* had run a cartoon depicting a Japanese soldier casting a shadow across the Pacific and over California under the heading "And Now?"[5] The segregationists could also exploit the continued efforts by the Japanese to assimilate, as they could be portrayed as worming their way into white society for nefarious ends. Finally, there were fewer than 3,000 Japanese in San Francisco, and likely only about 100 Koreans, so they were unlikely to mount the sort of spirited defense that had the Chinese.[6]

Choosing a despised but seemingly powerless target seemed just the sort of gesture that would reassure white supremacists that the Ruef political machine was the guardian of their interests. But if Ruef thought school segregation would replace the scandal in the headlines, he had miscalculated. Word of the school segregation initiative ended up being buried in the back pages of San Francisco newspapers. The initiative was barely mentioned in the *Examiner*, and in the *Call* it rated only a third of a column on page 11, and then another short piece on page 9 of the October 18 edition, after the order had been carried out: "President Altmann of the Board of Education announces that all of the Japanese children attending the schools have finally been ejected from the buildings where white children were in attendance." The article claimed, "Since the April disaster the Japanese have attended the primary and grammar schools in large numbers, crowding out the American pupils." This was blatantly untrue, of course, unless dozens could be considered large numbers. On another point, the *Call* was more accurate: "The Japanese clung on, tenaciously and did not leave promptly. They were segregated, however, one by one, until at the present there are none in attendance."[7]

Although the segregation of Japanese elementary school students seemed not all that important to most San Franciscans, it turned out to be extremely important to the Japanese and set in motion a series of events that would reverberate for decades.

Immediately after Aaron Altmann announced the segregation plan, the secretary of the Japanese Association of America (JAA) filed a formal protest to the School Board but was just as quickly rebuffed. The JAA then sent word of the order to newspapers in Japan, which treated the board's action as a national rebuke. One wrote: "Stand up, Japanese nation! Our countrymen have been humiliated on the other side of the Pacific. Our poor boys and girls have been expelled from public schools by the rascals of the United States, cruel and merciless like demons. At this time, we should be ready to give a blow to the United States. Yes, we should be ready to strike the Devil's head with an iron hammer for the sake of the world's civilization. . . . Why do we not insist on sending ships?"[8]

Stoked by public anger, the government called in the U.S. ambassador, Luke Wright, and furiously protested this stain on Japanese honor. On October 21, Ambassador Wright telegraphed Secretary of State Elihu Root that the nation that had just vaulted itself into the category of international naval power had been grievously insulted by the United States. "The reported exclusion of children from the schools has given the deepest offense," he wrote, "as Japanese schools are open to foreigners." But, finding a potential negotiating point that would have great significance later, Wright added, "I believe it possible that Japanese authorities can be induced quietly to check the importation of Japanese coolies into the United States."[9]

The School Board had not bothered to give notice to state or federal officials, and so Wright's telegram had come as a surprise in Washington. Learning what had prompted it and hearing of the Japanese reaction, Roosevelt, who had backed the effort to prosecute Ruef and Schmitz and knew exactly why the segregation directive had been issued, reportedly "went into a rage, moved to sue the Board of Education, threatened to send in troops and directed Secretary Root to cable the American ambassador in Tokyo to give assurances to Japan."[10] Root replied to Wright on October 23, "The United States will not for a moment entertain the idea of any treatment of the Japanese people other than that accorded to the people of the most friendly European nations."[11]

TR then dispatched Secretary of Commerce and Labor Victor Metcalf, a native Californian and former congressman, to San Francisco to investigate and, if possible, diffuse the situation. Metcalf wrote a grim report to Roosevelt on November 28, in which he noted that state law clearly allowed segregation, it was unlikely that the action violated any treaty with Japan, and the government could not expect any softening of the board's position: "After my conversation with the President of the Board of Education and his legal advisor, I judge it hopeless to look for any modification or repeal on the part of the board of the obnoxious resolution."[12]

With Japan growing more incensed and reports circulating in Europe that it was willing to go war over the insult, Californians played up the threat that Japanese in United States were an advance guard. In early December 1906, California congressman Everis Hayes told a reporter, "The Japanese immigrant is not an immigrant in the ordinary sense of the word. . . . They came to learn our weaknesses and defects so as to turn that knowledge to their own advantage. Before Japan went to war with China, she had an army of spies and observers in Manchuria. The Japanese knew more about the Russian army than the Russians themselves. They are doing the same thing now in the United States."[13] Shortly afterward, Hearst's *Examiner* ran a front-page banner headline, "Japan Sounds Our Coasts. Spies of the Emperor Plat Monterrey Bay. Brown Men Have Maps and Could Land Easily." The agents of this perfidy, according to the *Examiner*, were "innocent looking Japanese fishermen . . . little brown fellows who affected an unfamiliarity with the English language [but] rigged up mysterious apparatus for dredging abalone" off the coast of Santa Cruz.[14]

TR thought such reports were nonsense and made certain his feelings were known in an address to Congress: "The overwhelming mass of our people cherish a lively regard and respect for the people of Japan. . . . To shut them out from the public schools is a wicked absurdity, when there are no first-class colleges in the land, including the universities and colleges of California, which do not gladly welcome Japanese students and on which Japanese students do not reflect credit. . . . Throughout Japan, Americans are well treated, and any failure on the part of Americans at home to treat the Japanese with a like courtesy and consideration is by just so much a confession of inferiority in our civilization."[15] He even suggested at one point that Japanese immigrants should be allowed to become naturalized citizens.

A few days after the president's address, the conclusions of Metcalf's final report, which the president would present to Congress and were deemed "sensational," leaked out. Metcalf detailed nineteen incidents of violence against the Japanese, including the murder of a Japanese bank president, found absolutely no justification for the segregation order, and asserted that "complaints of the Japanese, while based on the alleged violation of treaty rights in the matter of equal treatment, were probably prompted by maltreatment of Japanese residents of San Francisco by members of labor unions and other organizations who objected to their presence as workers on the Pacific Coast . . . Some of these facts will not be to the liking of those who have been engaged in what an administration official today characterized as 'an effort on the part of the labor unions to drive the Japs from the country.'"[16]

The *Examiner* was quick to pounce on the report, running as its lead story, "Metcalf Sides with the Japanese," which described union leaders as being "irate" over the report. Pro-union forces in San Francisco were, in fact, livid at being accused of what they had actually done, and they vowed to resist any attempt to turn them from their patriotic duty. Aaron Altmann, feigning innocence, was "extremely bitter" and denounced Metcalf for going "out of his way to mix the school matter with the labor situation." Altmann added that "under no circumstances should Metcalf have in any way connected the attitude of the Board of Education in segregating the Japanese and Chinese pupils with anti-Japanese and

Korean League."[17] For a champion to right this terrible wrong, Altmann and the labor unions turned to an old ally who would press their case under extremely unusual circumstances.

International tensions simmered, but Schmitz, Ruef, and their cronies found themselves in increasingly desperate straits. Langdon, whose civic zeal had increased proportionally with his distance from his former allies, had empaneled a grand jury to seek indictments against Ruef, Schmitz, the entire Board of Supervisors, and sundry other Boodle Boys. The grand jury's first action was to recommend that the police chief be suspended, not an auspicious beginning for the ruling political machine. On October 22, the day Heney officially took up his post in the district attorney's office, with Burns at his side, newspapers reported, "'You may say,' declared Burns last night with an emphasis that bespoke certainty, 'that we are going to get the crooks.'"[18]

For Ruef, the only way to head off indictments seemed to involve taking over the district attorney's office, removing Heney, and getting Burns and his detectives on the earliest train out of town. For two days, rumors circulated that Acting Mayor Gallagher, also a target of the investigation, was about to do just that. On October 25, the rumors proved correct: "With unparalleled audacity Abe Ruef ordered the suspension from office of District Attorney Langdon late yesterday afternoon, had himself appointed in Langdon's place and straightway dismissed Francis J. Heney, who had been selected as Langdon's deputy for the purpose of sending to the penitentiary the grafters who have been preying upon the city of San Francisco."[19] After his appointment, Ruef publicly vowed to continue the investigation into widespread corruption—for which he would have been his own best witness—and empanel a grand jury of his own.

Heney's response ran as a banner above the story: "With the fullest sense of the responsibility resting upon me, I name among such corrupt and criminal officials Mayor Schmitz, Acting Mayor Gallagher, and each and every one of the eighteen members of the Board of Supervisors. I have the evidence to prove these allegations and at the proper time and place, as the law prescribes, District Attorney Langdon and myself, as his assistant, will lay it before the new Grand Jury. It is to prevent such exposure of their infamy that Ruef, Gallagher, and the Supervisors, in their panic fear of the felon's cell, have taken this utterly illegal step."[20]

The *Examiner* devoted the first two pages to the scandal, leading with "Abe Ruef, in a desperate attempt to head off indictment and a revelation of the graft of his creatures . . . appointed himself to the position of District Attorney of San Francisco." The paper included a statement from Langdon denying Ruef's right to remove him, and promising, "As District Attorney, I shall pursue this investigation to the end."[21]

Ruef's tenure in office lasted less than a day. The following morning, a judge issued an injunction blocking Langdon's dismissal, and he and Heney were back in court questioning witnesses before the grand jury. Also in the courtroom were a bevy of glowering corrupt police officers and other physically imposing Ruef minions, making it clear that handing down indictments against the wrong people could have severe and painful consequences.

But the pendulum had swung too far for the threat of strong-arm tactics to stop it. A suddenly aroused citizenry demanded that justice be done, and even some unions, including bricklayers and masons, repudiated Ruef, Schmitz, and the others who had been largely responsible for their ascension in city politics. On November 2, the president of the public works board spent forty-five minutes in Heney's office, after which Heney was said to have in his possession evidence that building permit graft had netted Ruef and Schmitz $1 million.

One by one, Ruef's underlings were dragged into the grand jury room, the public eye, or both, and one by one they announced their commitment to civic responsibility and cooperated with the investigation. On November 5, Ruef was dealt a fatal blow when his candidates for judgeships were soundly defeated at the polls, beaten by men who promised to aid in the downfall of the Ruef machine.

Finally, on November 16, Abe Ruef and Mayor Eugene Schmitz were indicted for extortion. Ruef surrendered himself at the offices of his attorney and was taken into custody, and was released a short time later after posting $50,000 bail. Schmitz, who had defied predictions and decided to return home, learned of the indictments as his luxury liner, *Patricia*, was steaming into New York Harbor. He too posted bail and vowed to continue to discharge his responsibilities as mayor, one of which would be to attempt to deflect public anger to the Japanese. Schmitz attended meetings, spoke to workers' groups, and took up the cause of keeping the United States white and pure with renewed zeal. On December 10, for example, he addressed a mass meeting sponsored by the Japanese and Korean Exclusion League, held at the aptly named Dreamland Pavilion, the theme of which was "No Japs in Our Schools."

Ruef tried to leave the city but was stopped by a suddenly competent police force. He then prompted his allies in the state legislature to introduce a bill mandating a change of venue, which would have also freed the accused on a technicality. That failed also. The city descended into near anarchy: "Jurors were bribed; Fremont Older . . . who led the campaign against the boodlers, was kidnapped; a gunman was hired to murder him, and only the ruffian's loss of nerve saved Older's life. Francis J. Heney was shot while in court by an ex-convict who was a juryman on a former Ruef trial, and whom Heney had exposed."[22]

During this campaign of chicanery and terror, to the surprise of many city officials, the defendants, and likely some of the jurors, the trials of both men limped along. The international crisis that Ruef had precipitated, however, moved at more hurried pace. On February 2, 1907, Ambassador Wright sent a chilling communication to President Roosevelt: "A letter just received from one of the shrewdest and most experienced observers I know, a man who sees and talks with leading men in England, Germany, France and elsewhere, informs me that there seems to be a settled opinion among those considered the most far-sighted that Japan will, ere long, attack the United States." Although Wright did not consider such an attack imminent, he did urge decisive action to head off the threat. "This may be all wrong—quite likely it is—but it seems to me that no opportunity should be neglected to avert Japanese ill-feeling, especially as a collision would lead to very unpleasant immediate results, no matter what the remote results might be."[23] Roosevelt, one of the few American politicians to have had extensive contact with the Japanese, was more aware than most that ill feeling could have an unpleasant upshot.

Two days after Ambassador Wright sent his communiqué, on February 4, 1907, an eight-man contingent, led a by the still-under-indictment Mayor Schmitz, his two daughters in tow, embarked for Washington to meet the president. The invitation from TR had been to School Board members only, but Schmitz had shoehorned himself in to head the delegation. There were some who thought his presence ill-considered: "The relations between the Mayor and the President are none too friendly, it is said. . . . The President was quoted by a member of the California delegation recently as referring to Schmitz as the 'bassoon player.'" But Schmitz had not only politics but also his own freedom to consider, and that of his mentor: "Abe Ruef, who had the last word with Schmitz at the steps of the Overland Limited, said he thought the board would refuse to admit the brown children to any except the Oriental school if such a compromise was sought in Washington."[24]

Wright's message arrived on February 6, a day before Schmitz and his party got to Washington. Someone likely told the mayor that the city's action had placed the nation on the brink of war, because before his meeting with Roosevelt, he told reporters, "We have come here with open minds to hear what the President has to say. . . . It is not true that I said in Chicago that we would not yield under any circumstances." (It was true.) "It would be foolish to come 3000 miles to attend a conference if we had already made up our minds to reject any proposal that might be offered to reach a satisfactory adjustment of pending questions. All I wish to say is that we will not stand on technicalities if it can be shown by exercising a spirit of compromise we can reach results which will be for the general welfare of the whole country." He added that he also welcomed the opportunity to tell the president he was not a bassoon player.[25]

Roosevelt was unlikely to have overestimated Schmitz's cooperation—the only thing between San Francisco's mayor and a jail cell was the continued support of the working class, and that would evaporate if he was seen to have been intimidated by the president. But Schmitz had also come armed with a proposal. If the United States and Japan would enter into a treaty that excluded Japanese "coolies," San Francisco might see fit to readmit age-appropriate segregated students who were not U.S. citizens. (Citizens could be segregated according to *Plessy*, and some other students were older than their grades because of a lack of English language skills.) But Schmitz and the board members insisted they would need assurances that the Senate would ratify such a treaty and that Congress would enact laws to put it into effect, assurances that the president could not provide. But Ambassador Wright had indicated previously that Japan would find those very terms acceptable, so Roosevelt instructed his ambassador to determine whether the Japanese would commit to them.

Word was sought from across the Pacific, but the president of the United States was forced to welcome an accused felon to the White House and participate in serious discussions on how to diffuse a serious international crisis precipitated by a gratuitously racist act. Schmitz left the February 9 meeting feeling quite good about his position. "Nothing has been decided on and no proposition is pending," he said to reporters. "Nothing will be settled, if it is settled at all, until Monday or Tuesday, when another conference will be held. . . . The meeting was entirely friendly, but I am not prepared to say whether the result is satisfactory, nor am I prepared to say it was unsatisfactory." Schmitz added that he was willing to either receive proposals or make them.[26] One can only speculate on the self-control the volatile Roosevelt was forced to exhibit being forced to seriously negotiate with a "bassoon player" whom he considered nothing more than a common grafter.

When Roosevelt had received indications that Japan was amenable to an agreement that would trade emigrating laborers for schoolchildren, and that Schmitz and the School Board would abide by the terms as well, he decided to bypass what might be an uncertain treaty ratification process and come to an "understanding" with Japan on his own. He would need Congress's help, but what he had in mind would pass both houses easily.

On February 19, Schmitz announced an agreement between himself, Roosevelt, Secretary Root, and the members of the San Francisco School Board, "that all children of alien races, under 16 years of age, who speak the English language, may be admitted to the white schools. Special schools or classes are to be established for children of alien birth who are deficient in the elements of the English language." The report included a proviso that Schmitz, "without quoting the President," had "received assurances that the immigration of Japanese laborers will cease."[27]

Congress did its part. A clause, written by Root, was added to the pending Immigration Act of 1907, which was otherwise to preclude immigration by "idiots, imbeciles and prostitutes," which stated, "That whenever the President shall be satisfied that passports issued by any foreign government to its citizens to go to any other country than the United States, or to any insular possession of the United States, or to the Canal Zone are being used for the purpose of enabling the holders to come to the continental territory of the United States to the detriment of labor conditions therein, the President may refuse to permit certain citizens of the country issuing such passports to enter the continental territory of the United States from such other country or from such insular possessions, or from the Canal Zone."[28] This was not a treaty, did not address immigration directly from Japan—which in theory but not always in practice was not issuing passports to laborers—or even bind TR to take action, but it was sufficient to mollify Schmitz and the anti-Asians, at least temporarily. Schmitz returned home victorious, just in time for the opening of his trial for extortion.

On March 14, as Ruef's extortion trial was beginning, Roosevelt kept his end of the deal by issuing Executive Order 589, which refused entry to any passport-holding Japanese immigrant attempting to enter the country through a third-party state. Although he had assured Schmitz that the Japanese government was amenable to the arrangement, TR had, in fact, not solicited their agreement. Nonetheless, forty-three Japanese children reentered San Francisco schools, and tensions between the two nations were defused while both turned to hammering out a deal.

After extensive negotiations, in which Roosevelt informed Japanese officials that another exclusion act was possible if they did not compromise, Japan agreed to not issue any further passports to laborers headed either for the United States or Hawaii, except in the case of the "laborers who have already been in America and to the parents, wives, and children of laborers already resident there."[29] Since the "Gentlemen's Agreement," as it was called, was not an official treaty or formally signed document, but merely an exchange of diplomatic notes, Roosevelt was able to initiate the arrangement without submitting it to Congress, and even without making the precise terms public.

On cursory examination, the plan seemed to work. In 1907, the last year before the Gentlemen's Agreement took effect, 30,000 Japanese, almost all male laborers, had entered the United States. In 1909, when the program had fully taken effect, only 2,432 Japanese immigrated to the American mainland, and 5,004 left the country.

But the Gentlemen's Agreement turned out to have a major loophole. Because almost all Japanese immigrants had been male, the ratio of men to women in 1907 was more than 7 to 1. In 1900, there had been only 985 Japanese women in the United States, only 410 of whom were married. By 1910, the number of married women had increased to 5,581—almost all after 1907—and by 1920 had ballooned to 22,193.[30]

The reason for the explosion in married Japanese was that the Gentlemen's Agreement did not restrict passports granted to wives who had been married before it went into effect. Anyone married subsequently could enter the United States. As with the Chinese, the inability to find a wife had been one of the reasons Japanese workers had returned home.[31] Many got married in Japan and, leaving their wives there, returned to the United States to work, as had Wong Kim Ark returned to China to visit his wife and child. Any child born of these cross-Pacific marriages would be a citizen of the country in which he or she left the womb. But no longer could Japanese workers who left the United States return there, so the wives would need to come to America. Any children born after they arrived would therefore be United States citizens, as would members of subsequent generations.

Arranged marriages were common in Japan, often involving husbands and wives who did not know each other, and so, using go-betweens on either side of the Pacific, Japanese men in the United States sent pictures of themselves to Japan—usually photographs taken when they were much younger or photographs of someone different altogether. Japanese women who wanted to come to the United States would choose a potential husband from these photographs, send back photographs of themselves, and then participate in a marriage ceremony performed in Japan without a groom. Eventually, almost 10,000 of these "picture brides" would arrive during the next decade.

Many of the women were "genuinely shocked to see their husbands. Sometimes the person was much older than he appeared in his photograph. As a rule, husbands were older than wives by ten to fifteen years, and occasionally more. Men often forwarded photographs taken in their youth or touched-up ones that concealed their real age. . . . Suave, handsome appearing gentlemen proved to be pockmarked, country bumpkins."[32] Not only were their new husbands older and more haggard than the photographs they had seen, but the men were also generally a good deal poorer and less successful. Custom was strong, however, and all but a few of the women chose to remain with their new husbands. With these marriages came children. Many children: "At the turn of the century, there were only 269 children; by 1910 the number had grown to 4,502; and by 1920 it had multiplied more than sixfold to 29,672."[33] And so, a measure to limit the Japanese population on the West Coast vastly increased it. Even worse for the nativists, since those children were birthright citizens, they would have the very rights that the anti-Japan faction was attempting to deny to their parents. Thus most families became a mix of the native-born—called "Nisei"—and immigrants—"Issei."

The effect was profound and far from what was intended. Nisei children became the vehicle by which the Japanese were transformed from itinerant laborers to would-be "Americans" as noncitizen parents saw their future entwined with their citizen children: "The entry of women into immigrant society was integral to the process by which Japanese immigrants sank roots in American soil."[34]

Another consequence of family life was a movement out of the cities and into the countryside. Many worked for white farmers or growers, but some purchased small farms for themselves. This worked to the advantage of individual Japanese who could afford their own land, but it also further diffused a community that would need to act in concert as anti-Asian activities ramped up. One of the targets would be the very land that Japanese farmers had purchased.

9 | This Land Is (Not) Your Land

Although Abe Ruef, Eugene Schmitz, and the Boodle Boys had been neutered by Heney and Burns—Ruef ended up going to prison, and Schmitz's conviction was overturned on a technicality—anti-Japanese activities did not cease, but simply acquired a new set of champions. One was Democrat James Phelan, who would use the Japanese to resurrect his political career and result in his election to the Senate in 1914. With Phelan's inspiration, Democrats made racism a cornerstone of their program, and they were the only party to officially call for Japanese exclusion in its platform. But also leading the racist charge on the West Coast was a group otherwise identified with political reform, trust-busting, philanthropy, muckraking, pure food and drugs, and women's rights—the Progressives.

One of the cornerstones of the Progressive movement was blunting monopolistic control of the economy by a few massive, interlocking financial and industrial cartels. To achieve this, Progressives sought to increase competition, albeit with controls to prevent the formation of new trusts. This, they believed, would lower prices and increase quality of goods and services that otherwise were at the mercy of plutocrats, such as J. P. Morgan, Andrew Carnegie, and John D. Rockefeller. Increased competition and the diffusion of industrial control would also benefit workers, especially organized labor, which would be facing off against smaller, less powerful foes when demanding increased pay or better working conditions. The movement was often identified with Theodore Roosevelt, but he was far less antagonistic to big business than he pretended.

In California, that formula was slightly different. Progressives wanted increased competition among employers, but union leaders were equally determined to eliminate competition in the labor market. Once more, the target became the Japanese, and, as always, the issue was couched in faux-sociological terms: "Progressives in California believed that economic self-preservation was closely united with racial preservation. It was believed that, if the Japanese were allowed to make economic inroads, it would be only a matter of time before they would make racial inroads. Intermarriage and propagation of their race would impair the Anglo-Saxon racial purity so important to the Progressives' concept of economic leadership."[1]

From 1908 on, bill after bill was introduced in the California and Washington state legislatures to restrict the property, contract, and civil rights of resident Japanese immigrants. In January 1909, for example, California lawmakers introduced bills to force alien landowners to give up their lands in five years if they had not achieved citizenship, limit land leases to one year, reimpose school segregation for Japanese children, and implement a "municipal segregation ordinance which would give cities the power to confine Japanese and other Orientals in ghettoes."[2] Each enjoyed widespread support: "Had California been an independent republic . . . most of the anti-Japanese bills introduced into its legislature would have passed without difficulty."

But not one of them was enacted into law, nor would any other anti-Japanese bill for four more years.[3] Anti-Japanese activists had acquired a new set of opponents, most in Washington, DC, but some among the very Californians they had most hoped to attract. In addition, white supremacists were at a disadvantage because, except for the West Coast, few cared about the Japanese "invasion" at all and could not understand why Californians in particular were making such an issue of it.

Opposition in Washington, first under TR, then William Howard Taft, was based on the same diplomatic issues that had marked the school segregation controversy. Japan took insults quite seriously, and, after the defeat of the Russians, a cadre of militarists insisted that a rising world power should not feel at all averse in engaging the American navy as well. Japan was also a rising economic power and becoming an increasingly important trading partner. TR had learned from the school segregation incident that anti-Japan sentiment was largely a political convenience based on overblown or manufactured arguments. He was unsparing in his condemnation of the "idiots" in the California legislature, "those infernal fools" whose behavior was "worse than the stupidity of the San Francisco mob."[4] He was, therefore, determined to sidetrack any initiative by state governments to undermine the interests of the nation at large.

Although Taft had been elected president in November 1908, he would not be sworn in until March 4, 1909. For the measures introduced in California that January, Roosevelt, although he would be soon leaving office, and Elihu Root directly engaged California governor and fellow Republican James N. Gillett, predicting dire diplomatic consequences if the state contravened the Gentlemen's Agreement, especially since Japanese immigration had been net negative the year before. They likely did not emphasize that among the Japanese who had arrived, many were women who would doubtless spawn even more native-born children. Gillett agreed to withdraw his support and the measures died.

Opposition to discriminatory legislation had other roots within California. On December 7, 1908, "half a thousand of San Francisco's leading businessmen pledged the city to hold a great world's exposition in celebration of the opening of the Panama Canal."[5] The fair, according to the organizers, was "destined even in its inception to be more vast in scope and more magnificent in detail than even the Chicago Columbian exposition of 1893 or any world's fair before or since," and would open in either 1915 or 1916. San Diego had also wanted to host the celebration, but San Francisco's business elite pledged to raise $1 million just to get the planning started—and receive official recognition from Washington—a number that would balloon tenfold. A miffed San Diego was ultimately forced mount a smaller, competing, unofficial fair.

As the plans progressed, so did the ambitions and the audacity of its organizers. The Panama-Pacific International Exposition would announce to the world San Francisco's return from devastation and that the city had retaken its place among the nation's, even the world's, elite. Millions would come to see its attractions: a four-acre walk-through replica of Yellowstone National Park, a six-acre Grand Canyon, and a five-acre working model of the Panama Canal. The actual Liberty Bell would be brought on loan from Philadelphia. The Ford Motor Company would set up an assembly line and, for three hours a day, build an automobile every ten minutes. Fairgoers would watch hula dancers, ride a miniature railway or a submarine, and sit in a compartment on a swing arm that propelled those inside to and fro over the grounds. There would even be a forty-three story "Tower of Jewels" decorated with more than 100,000 pieces of polished colored glass called "novogems," imported from Europe and strung on wires. Fifty colored spotlights would shine on the tower each night, making it visible in every corner of what was now known as "The Jeweled City." Although nations from around the globe would participate, one of the most important exhibitions, the organizers decided, would be from Japan.

Why the Japanese pavilion was so important was not clear, but likely it was based on the fascination with Japanese culture that prevailed in most of the United States, and even, to the nativists' irritation, in areas where Japanese immigrants were reviled. But whatever the reason, those Californians who had risked the state's prestige, and a good bit of their own money, on the exposition's success were none too keen to see the chances diminished by what they deemed a silly crusade against a few thousand workers and farmers.

Anti-Japanese forces were dealt another blow in 1911 when the Taft administration negotiated a commercial and navigation treaty with Japan. The treaty was strongly favored by business interests, which viewed Japan as a strong and potentially dynamic market for American goods. When nativists saw that there was no provision to restrict "coolie immigration," which would have embedded the terms of the Gentlemen's Agreement in the law, they vowed opposition. Still, the president was a Republican, as were the senators from both California and Washington. Although Democrats, such as James Phelan, were free to say anything they pleased, Republican senators were under enormous pressure not to embarrass their party by voting against ratification. In addition, Hiram Johnson, who succeeded James Gillett and took office January 3, 1911, aspired to higher office. Opposing a president of his own party was not the best way to gain support. Johnson's ambition was an effective lever: "To insure the maintenance of cordial relations between the United States and Japan, [Taft] had Secretary of State Philander Knox maintain correspondence with Johnson during the early months of Johnson's first term, reminding him that it was essential to refrain from allowing any legislation—be it anti-land or exclusion legislation—to enacted against the Japanese."[6]

The treaty was signed on February 11, 1911, and the terms were precisely what white Californians had feared. The first clause stipulated: "The citizens or subjects of each of the High Contracting Parties shall have liberty to enter, travel and reside in the territories of the other to carry on trade, wholesale and retail, to own or lease and occupy houses, manufactories, warehouses and shops, to employ agents of their choice, to lease land for residential and commercial purposes, and generally to do anything incident to or necessary for trade upon the same terms as native citizens or subjects, submitting themselves to the laws and regulations there established."[7]

Other clauses guaranteed freedom of navigation and commerce, protected Japanese homes and business from arbitrary search, and limited tariffs. The breadth of the agreement and rights granted to Japanese, both immigrants and commercial traders, could not seem to have been worse, but not guaranteed was the right to purchase land, an omission that would become significant two years later.

A ratification vote was scheduled less than two weeks after the draft was submitted to the Senate. California Republicans were desperate to find some contrivance that would allow them to support both their party and Japanese exclusion. On February 21, the Japanese ambassador, in lofty tones, offered them one: "In proceeding this day to the signature of the treaty of commerce and navigation between Japan and the United States, the undersigned Japanese ambassador in Washington, duly authorized by his government, has the honor to declare that the Imperial Japanese government is fully prepared to maintain with equal effectiveness the limitation and control which they have for the last three years exercised in the regulation of the emigration of laborers to the United States."[8] Although there was some grousing in the West about trusting to the "honor" of the Japanese government, the western senators agreed, almost certainly with relief, not to oppose ratification of the treaty.

White supremacists, enduring a string of defeats in their crusade to eliminate Japanese infestation, needed to find a better target. They soon settled on land ownership. Johnson told Philander Knox that he was doing his best to thwart discriminatory legislation, but it was "increasingly difficult because of the growing antagonistic reaction of white Californians against Japanese increased land holdings."[9] Phelan, as he often did, enunciated this antagonism in a note to Democratic presidential candidate Woodrow Wilson in 1912:

> The Japanese have invaded the central valleys of California. Take, for example, one highly productive fruit growing valley known as the Vaca Valley. There, the Japanese, refusing to work for wages after the first year or so, bargained for a share of the crop, and finally ousted in many instances the tenant farmers by offering the landowner larger returns, and in some instances acquired the property by purchase. The white man is thus driven off the land to move farther away. The village stores, churches, and homes suffer and in many instances are left without patronage or occupants. In other words, the Japanese are a blight on our civilization, destructive of the home life of the people, driving the natives to the city for employment.[10]

Phelan's dire forecast was no more accurate than the prediction that ninety-three Japanese students would hopelessly befoul San Francisco's schoolchildren: "In 1913, out of a total population 2,500,000, the Japanese numbered, by a liberal estimate, 50,000. Of approximately 27,000,000 acres of unimproved land in the state, the Japanese owned 12,726 acres in 1912, much of which they had reclaimed themselves."[11] Other statistics show a slightly larger, but still minuscule, Japanese presence in California's agricultural sector: 1,816 farmers who owned 16,449 acres or leased an additional 80,000 acres from white owners.[12] An additional 30,000 Japanese worked as laborers on white-owned farms, generally for the largest landowners.

Still, few in the Democratic Party, certainly not Woodrow Wilson, questioned Phelan's assertions, and Wilson's nomination became a turning point. If he won the presidency, not only would he be the first Democrat in sixteen years to hold the office, but he would have done so with help of a man whose bigotry against Asians matched Wilson's bigotry against African Americans.

Wilson's task was made easier when the Republican Party split with the conservative traditionalists backing Taft and the insurgents breaking off to form the Progressive Party. Roosevelt, who had hand-picked his good friend Taft to be his successor in 1908, had grown disillusioned with him and attempted to wrest the nomination. When that failed, he and the Progressives mounted their own presidential campaign with TR their nominee for president and Hiram Johnson for vice president.

But if the Republican Party split was a benefit, Wilson had acquired a powerful enemy who was anything but. William Randolph Hearst, who had trumpeted warnings of the coming Japanese invasion, had parlayed a sizable inheritance from his father, George, once a United States senator from California, into a huge newspaper fortune, emphasizing lurid headlines, human-interest stories, and an only nodding acquaintance with facts. Hearst, who would later become extremely conservative, at that point considered himself a supporter of workers and the common man, the backbone of his readership, but he knew them only as abstractions. Politically, he identified with the Progressives, a party he wished to run and use as a springboard to becoming California governor or even president, neither of which sat well with Roosevelt, the actual leader of the party, who himself aspired to a return to the White House.

Hearst, as had Phelan, saw the Japanese as the perfect foil for his ambitions, and during the school segregation crisis the *Examiner* ran front-page articles almost daily warning against an invasion. In addition to reporting that the Japanese fleet was steaming across the Pacific, the *Ex-*

William Randolph Hearst. Courtesy of Library of Congress Prints and Photographs Division.

aminer wrote that coolies were actually Japanese soldiers in disguise, that forty-man army units were drilling secretly at night in Hawaii, and that Japanese both in Hawaii and on the mainland had secreted large caches of rice and ammunition. That not one of these stories had a shred of evidence to back them up bothered Hearst not one bit. Whether or not Hearst believed what his newspapers were reporting—and, like Phelan, he is likely to have convinced himself that at least some of it was true—he thought Wilson too weak and professorial to face down the threat.

At its core, however, Hearst's antipathy for Wilson was personal: "Hearst, as a college student who preferred pranks to studies, was expelled from Harvard during his junior year; Wilson, who valued studies as preparation for service, had spent years distinguishing himself as a scholar and university president. Hearst had a 'monumental anti-British bias'; Wilson a great appreciation of things British. Hearst was noisy, rough, and self-aggrandizing in his political campaigns; Wilson, restrained, even reluctant. Hearst preferred the term 'striking' to describe his style of journalism; Wilson considered it disreputable. If these differences were insufficient to alienate the two men from one another, Wilson had snubbed Hearst by declining to meet with him in 1911."[13]

Whether his motives were political or personal, Hearst set his enormous resources in a campaign to deny Wilson the Democratic nomination. His researchers easily found potent ammunition. In addition to overtly racist views of African Americans, Wilson had little regard for immigrants from Southern and Eastern Europe; he did, however, have a favorable, albeit paternalistic, view of the Chinese. In his five-volume *History of the American People*, when comparing the "multitudes of men of the lowest class from the south of Italy and men of the meaner sort out of Hungary and Poland, men out of the ranks where there was neither skill nor energy nor any initiative of quick intelligence," Wilson had asserted, "the Chinese were more to be desired, as workmen if not as citizens, than most of the coarse crew that came crowding in every year at the eastern ports." Although Wilson granted the Chinese had "many an unsavory habit, bred unwholesome squalor in the crowded quarters," he insisted "it was their skill, their intelligence, their hardy power of labor, their knack at succeeding and driving duller rivals out, rather than their alien habits, that made them feared and hated and led to their exclusion at the prayer of the men they were likely to displace should they multiply."[14]

If Wilson were to overcome Hearst's attacks and win the Democratic nomination, he did not feel he could afford to lose the West, and speaking favorably of Asian workers made that almost a certainty. James Phelan, who favored Wilson but feared his position on Asians would make him unelectable, sent a telegram to the chairman of the Democratic National Committee: "Has governor spoken against oriental coolie immigration? Charged here volume five history he favors same. Should declare against coolies as inassimilable and destructive to republican government and white labor. Answer."[15]

Eventually Phelan communicated with Wilson directly and sent him a position statement that Wilson released under his own name, with Phelan endorsing it as if Wilson had crafted it himself:

> In the matter of Chinese and Japanese Coolie immigration, I stand for the National policy of exclusion (or restricted immigration). The whole question is one of assimilation of diverse races. We cannot make a homogenous population out of people who do not blend with the Caucasian race. Their lower standard of living as laborers will crowd out the white agriculturist and is in other fields a most serious industrial menace. The success of free Democratic institutions demands of our people education, intelligence, patriotism; and the State should protect them against unjust and impossible competition. Remunerative labor is the basis of contentment. Democracy rests on the equality of the citizen. Oriental Coolieism will give us another race problem to solve and surely we have had our lesson.[16]

Wilson won the Democratic Party nomination and subsequently the presidency in November 1912. Despite his new aversion to the Japanese, he lost California to Roosevelt, but it was only by 174 votes out of more than 670,000 votes cast, the best result by a Democrat in California since 1892. Taft, running on the traditional Republican line, was not on the ballot. He would eventually be awarded a plum consolation prize when he was appointed to the Supreme Court by Warren Harding in 1921, where he would be as undistinguished as a chief justice as he was as president. Hiram Johnson, TR's running mate, complained that the Japanese exclusion question cost the Progressive Party "at least ten thousand votes." Whatever the vote count, Phelan and his fellow Democrats were buoyed by the result, convinced they had a winning issue in a restrictive alien land law. With Wilson in the White House, they no longer need contend with interference from Washington.

Their target was small—only 331 Japanese-owned farms occupying 1 acre out of every 8,000 devoted to agriculture—but for racists, this was merely the germ of an infection that would multiply and overwhelm white society. Rather than playing down Japanese devotion to self-sacrifice and hard work, these were cited as the very reasons that the Japanese would ultimately overpower whites. California attorney general Ulysses Webb would later argue before the Supreme Court: "The fundamental question is not one of race discrimination [but] . . . of recognizing the obvious fact that the American farm, with its historical associations of cultivation, environment and including the home life of its occupants, can not exist in competition with a farm developed by Orientals with their totally different standards and ideas of cultivation of the soil, of living and social conditions. If the Oriental farmer is the more efficient, from the standpoint of soil production, there is just not much greater certainty of an economic conflict which it is the duty of statesmen to avoid."[17]

That Japanese workers also seemed a good deal less compliant than the Chinese—on more than one occasion they had refused to pick ripe fruit unless they were given a raise in pay—was more proof of the Japanese menace. Although opposition remained among business leaders, fair organizers, and some large farmers who employed Japanese workers, populist sentiment had become overpowering.

In the session of California legislature that began one week after Wilson's inauguration on March 4, 1913, two bills depriving Japanese noncitizens of the right to lease or own land were introduced immediately. Reaction in Japan was intense. The *Examiner* reported that if the bills passed, "official sources" warned that Japan would withdraw support for the Panama-Pacific Exposition, and in Japan itself, "a crowd of approximately 20,000 Japanese in Tokyo cheered wildly as a member of the Diet demanded the Japanese fleet to be sent to California to protect Japanese nationals and Japan's honor."[18]

Other than expressing his disapproval to Hiram Johnson, however, Wilson did nothing to derail the legislation. He would have been unable to pressure the Progressive dominated California legislature as had Republicans Roosevelt and Taft, but he was also reluctant to antagonize the western states: "He certainly did not attempt to use the federal courts, especially the Supreme Court, to challenge the California law; nor did he take the issue to the people or Congress and thus force federal domination upon California."[19] Instead, he told the Japanese ambassador that, whatever his personal feelings, the federal government could not overrule state law and that the United States remained eager for cordial relations with Japan.

California was determined to pass a restrictive land law, but legislators were aware that they must avoid a direct provocation. Militarists in Japan, although a minority, had not ceased agitating for an armed response. Any new law also needed to sidestep the antidiscriminatory provisions of the 1911 treaty. For that, legislators turned to Attorney General Ulysses Webb and Francis Heney, who, fresh from dismantling the San Francisco political machine, decided that politics would be a nice alternative to being shot in a courtroom. With his eye on the Senate seat coming vacant in 1914, which for the first time would be awarded by popular vote, Heney, along with Webb, drafted:

> Sec. 1. All aliens eligible to citizenship under the laws of the United States may acquire, possess, enjoy, transmit and inherit real property, or any interest therein, in this State, in the same manner and to the same extent as citizens of the United States, except as otherwise provided by the laws of this State.
>
> Sec. 2. All aliens other than those mentioned in section one of this act may acquire, possess, enjoy and transfer real property, or any interest therein, in this State, in the manner and to the extent and for the purposes prescribed by any treaty now existing between the Government of the United States and the nation or country of which such alien is a citizen or subject, and not otherwise and may, in addition thereto, lease lands in this state for agricultural purposes for a term not exceeding three years.[20]

The law also stated that corporations formed by "aliens ineligible for citizenship" would be treated the same as individuals, and land purchased in violation of the law would revert to state ownership. Technically, the Japanese had never been specifically declared "ineligible for citizenship," as had the Chinese in 1882, but Webb and Heney assumed they would be so judged since they were neither "white" nor "African."

In public, the bill's proponents insisted that their motives were based purely on economics and not race, but Webb would later admit, in a speech before the San Francisco Commonwealth Club in August 1913, that this was not the case: "The fundamental basis of all legislation upon this subject, State and Federal, has been, and is, race undesirability. . . . [The 1913 law] seeks to limit their presence by curtailing their privileges which they may enjoy here; for they will not come in large numbers and long abide with us if they may not acquire land."[21]

In the debates in the state legislature, James Phelan once again took the lead, paying particular attention to opposition from the Panama-Pacific organizers. He "warned the committee that the Japanese are as clever in diplomacy as they are able in agriculture and manufacturing. . . . [He] insisted that independent action on the part of California will not jeopardize the success of the Exposition. The Japanese are as anxious to seize the opportunity which the Exposition offers them as

California is to have their co-operation. 'The future of California,' said Mr. Phelan in conclusion, 'is of far greater importance than the success of this Exposition. And in saying this I do not believe for a moment that in enacting this land legislation you will jeopardize the success of the Exposition.'"[22]

In the end, the bill easily passed both houses. Although Wilson sent Secretary of State William Jennings Bryan to dissuade Hiram Johnson from signing it into law, Johnson, with presidential aspirations of his own, was unmoved. In August 1913, the law went into effect.

Questions as to its legality were raised almost immediately. From the first, Japanese leaders claimed that not only was the law in violation of the 1911 treaty, but also of the Fourteenth Amendment to the Constitution. Some legal scholars agreed, arguing that the classifications "aliens entitled to citizenship" and "aliens not entitled to citizenship" were "artificial and arbitrary," a contrivance to prevent the Japanese from purchasing land: "Can persons within the jurisdiction of the state be put into a class by themselves because, for any reason whatever, they cannot become citizens and thus subjected to special legislation imposing burdens not imposed upon other persons?"[23]

Since the text of the Fourteenth Amendment guaranteed equal protection to any "person," not just to any "citizen," the answer to that question would seem to be no: "The California law will in all probability be declared void, because to uphold it would limit the protection of the Fourteenth Amendment to citizens and to those eligible to citizenship. To hold otherwise would mean a new departure for the Supreme Court and the way would then be opened up for making classifications based upon the possession, or lack of possession, of other political privileges."[24]

Legal issues pertained not only to the Fourteenth Amendment but, Webb's and Heney's assumptions notwithstanding, also potentially to the question of how race would be defined in the United States. Soon after the law passed, a prescient, unsigned article appeared in a southern law journal: "The real danger lies in Japan asserting and proving that its citizens are entitled to naturalization under the 'privileges' of the Naturalization Act. Are they of Mongolian descent?"[25] The author cited the case of "one Akhay Kumar Mozumdar, a Hindu of high caste, a native of Calcutta, India, and a Yogi philosopher," who was ruled eligible for citizenship in U.S. district court in Spokane, Washington. In that case, the judge wrote:

The Court of Palms and the facades of the Palace of Education and the Palace of Liberal Arts, Panama-Pacific International Exposition, San Francisco, 1915. Courtesy of Library of Congress Prints and Photographs Division.

> In the original naturalization act, the expression "free white persons" was doubtless primarily intended to include the white emigrant from northern Europe with whom the Congress of that day was familiar, and to exclude Indians and persons of African descent or nativity. Beyond this perhaps Congress had no definite object in view. It could not have foreseen the vast immigration problems with which the Government is now confronted, or the difficulties which might hamper and harass the Courts in the administration of the law. But whatever the original intent may have been, it is now settled by the great weight of authority, at least that it was the intention of Congress to confer the privilege of naturalization on members of the Caucasian race only. It is likewise true that certain of the Indians belong to that race, although the line of demarcation between different castes and classes may be dim and difficult of ascertainment. . . . The testimony in this case satisfies me that the applicant has brought himself within the provisions of

> the naturalization acts and he will be admitted to citizenship accordingly, upon the taking of the oath prescribed by law.[26]

Mozumdar was "the first of his race" to be granted citizenship, and the government chose not to appeal. And so, "a high-caste Hindu of pure blood" who has "always considered himself a member of the Aryan race" was "entitled to naturalization as a white person," on anthropological grounds. Although a Japanese plaintiff would have difficulty making the same argument, the question of just who would be considered white under the law had entered the jurisprudence.

No Japanese would bring suit questioning whether he was an "alien ineligible for citizenship" for some years. There seemed better ways to attack the 1913 law. Like the Gentlemen's Agreement, there were practical loopholes that could be exploited without the investment of time, money, and the uncertainty of outcome that a court challenge would entail.

Although there was outrage in Japan, James Phelan was proved correct. Not only was there was no war, but the Japanese mounted a four-acre pavilion at the Panama-Pacific International Exposition, which began in March 1915, and both the fair and the pavilion were enormous successes.

10 | A Home of One's Own (Children)

The 1913 law turned out to be only marginally effective and loosely enforced. The language used was sufficiently vague to be filled with loopholes, which enterprising Japanese found not difficult to exploit: "Japanese farmers were able to place land in trusts and guardianship for their American-born children, form agricultural land-holding corporations, put land in the name of friends and American-born relatives or enter into three-year leases that were simply renewed for another three years at lease's end."[1] Rather than decrease, Japanese landholdings in California rose from 17,035 acres owned, 89,466 acres leased, 50,400 acres sharecropped, and 37,898 acres contracted in 1910 to 74,769 acres owned, 192,150 acres leased, 121,000 acres sharecropped, and 70,137 acres contracted for in 1920.

Although California authorities, especially Attorney General Webb, did not announce that they would more or less allow skirting of the law, there are two likely possibilities why they did so. The first is that despite all the public pronouncements by men such James Phelan—who was indeed elected to the Senate in 1914, albeit with only 31 percent of the vote, defeating both Francis Heney, running as a Progressive, and a mainstream Republican—the Japanese threat to white farmers was largely a fantasy. In fact, white farmers who leased land to Japanese tenants or sold to Nisei nominees did so at prices a good deal higher than they could get from other whites, and the sharecropping arrangements were equally favorable. The second was Japan's entry into World War I on the side of the allies. Although the United States would not enter the war until 1917 and was technically neutral before that, the Japanese proved to be of enormous value to the Allies, especially Great Britain, even deploying a fourteen-ship flotilla in the Mediterranean to help ensure that shipping could continue free of the U-boat menace. The last thing Anglophile Woodrow Wilson wanted was to have to explain to the British why the United States insisted on provoking a valuable ally in the war with the Axis.

The exigencies of U.S. foreign policy did not deter the Germanleaning Hearst, however. On October 10, 1915, the *Examiner* ran a two-page spread in its Sunday supplement, "Japan's Plan to Invade and Conquer the United States," replete with "The Humiliating Terms of Peace Which Japan Intends to Force on a Beaten United States." The "terms" included giving up the Philippines and Honolulu, waiving all restrictions on Japanese immigration, unlimited fishing rights, ending land-owning restrictions, and the payment of reparations. The source was reported to be Japan's most popular book, produced by its "Powerful and Official National Defense Association," but was actually the product a right-wing crackpot militarist.[2]

Whether even Phelan, Webb, and the other Anti-Japanese believed such nonsense is not clear. Nor can there be certainty as to whether these men, and some women, perceived a genuine threat from the Japanese in the United States, or if they were simply forced to perpetuate a tale they were aware was largely fanciful because they had staked their careers on it. What is certain was that their irritation grew as Japanese landholdings did. Whatever their true feelings, the anti-Japanese were none too pleased when, in February 1917, both houses of Congress overrode President Wilson's veto to enact a new, extremely restrictive immigration law that exempted the Japanese.

The impetus of the Immigration Act of 1917 was not Asians entering from the west, but rather Slavs and southern Europeans entering from the east. Wilson in a message to Congress in 1915 had denounced "hyphenated Americans," who, he said, "have poured the poison of disloyalty into the very arteries of our national life."[3] While the bill was being debated in Congress, Madison Grant, a conservationist who had saved any number of species of plant and animal life from extinction and helped found both the American Museum of Natural History and Bronx Zoo, published *The Passing of the Great Race or The Racial Basis of European History*. The book took Social Darwinism one step further and postulated that the "Nordic" races, the highest order of humans, were being "polluted" by lesser subraces and must protect themselves and human existence through strict segregation and controlled breeding. Part of the eugenics movement, Grant developed a large and enthusiastic following, which would eventually include a young Austrian trying to harangue his way into German politics, Adolph Hitler.

The eugenics movement was founded by Charles Darwin's brilliant half cousin. Francis Galton, a prodigy, was reading at two, and by the time he was six, he had learned a good bit of Greek and Latin, was quoting Shakespeare, and solving advanced math problems. He studied medicine, traveled extensively, and eventually made important contributions to such diverse disciplines as meteorology and criminology, in which he developed the first system for fingerprint classification.

Galton was obsessed with classification. After the publication of his cousin's work on natural selection, Galton undertook a study of various human traits that he used to develop a theory of heredity and selective breeding that he called "eugenics." Unlike Herbert Spencer, Galton relied on hard data, but did not realize that conclusions are often determined by assumptions—and his were faulty. Still, the notion that the human species could be improved by a rigorous program of selective breeding, suffocating inferior traits to create better humans, had enormous appeal, and eugenics societies sprung up around the world.

Eugenics soon split into two related approaches—positive and negative. Positive eugenics, on which Galton had focused, encouraged the superior humans to breed with other superior humans to produce yet more superior humans. Negative eugenics, which was the popular in the United States, was aimed at preventing deterioration of the gene pool by preventing inferior humans from breeding with superior humans, and, if possible, preventing them from breeding at all.[4]

The best way, of course, not to have inferior breeding is not to have inferior breeds, and so the eugenics movement was soon the underpinning of the push for restrictive immigration laws, aimed in particular at Mediterranean Europe and Slavic nations. In 1910, Charles Davenport, a biologist who had been a zoology professor at Harvard before turning his attention to *Homo sapiens*, founded the Eugenics Record Office at Cold Spring Harbor on Long Island, New York, to collect massive amounts of data on family histories and "genetic profiles," with the goal of finding a means to weed out inferior traits. One of Cold Spring Harbor's major benefactors was John Harvey Kellogg, who invented Kellogg's Corn Flakes. Although Davenport's methods were ludicrously flawed, he provided what was by then a vibrant and powerful American eugenics movement with reams of data.

In 1917, that data was put to use to draft what would be the first of three increasingly stringent immigration laws. And so, the 1917 law included an enormous list of those prohibited admission into United States. It included "idiots, imbeciles, feeble-minded idiots, epileptics, insane persons, persons of constitutional psychopathic inferiority, alcoholics, paupers, professional beggars, vagrants, persons afflicted with tuberculosis or with a loathsome or dangerous contagious disease, persons mentally or physically defective, such physical defect being of a nature which may affect the ability of such alien to earn a living, polygamists, anarchists, or those who were against the organized government or those who advocated the unlawful destruction of property and those who advocated the unlawful assault of killing of any officer, prostitutes," among others. Many of these categories were catchalls and gave officials at ports of entry wide latitude in deciding who was allowed to enter and who was excluded. This included doctors or surgeons who could certify an immigrant medically unfit without the need to conduct a serious examination, or any examination at all. The law also increased taxes paid by newly arriving immigrants over the age of sixteen to $8.[5]

The reason Wilson vetoed the bill, however, was the inclusion of a literacy test that required immigrants to demonstrate basic reading comprehension in either English or their native language, a brainchild of Senator Henry Cabot Lodge (R-Mass.), who had been attempting to restrict immigration since 1895. Wilson had successfully vetoed two previous attempts to include a literacy test, as had Presidents Cleveland and Taft before him. This time, with "effective discipline exercised by the American Federation of Labor and the readiness of Congress to yield to the propaganda and demands of a minority of public opinion with an overestimated batch of votes behind it," Congress voted the bill into law. Wilson denounced the requirement: "It is not a test of character, of quality, or of personal fitness, but would operate in most cases merely as a penalty for lack of opportunity in the country from which the alien came."[6]

What so disturbed the West Coast anti-Japanese, however, was the "Asiatic Barred Zone," which prohibited immigration by "natives of any country, province, or dependency situate on the Continent of Asia west of the one hundred and tenth meridian of longitude east from Greenwich and east of the fiftieth meridian of longitude east from Greenwich and south of the fiftieth parallel of latitude north, except that portion of said territory situate between the fiftieth and sixty-fourth meridians of longitude east from Greenwich and the twenty-fourth and thirty-eighth parallels of latitude north, and no alien now in any way excluded from, or prevented from entering the United States shall be admitted to the United States."[7] A quick look at an atlas revealed that those coordinates exempted Japan and the Philippines.

Japan was omitted, according to bill's sponsors, "at the request of

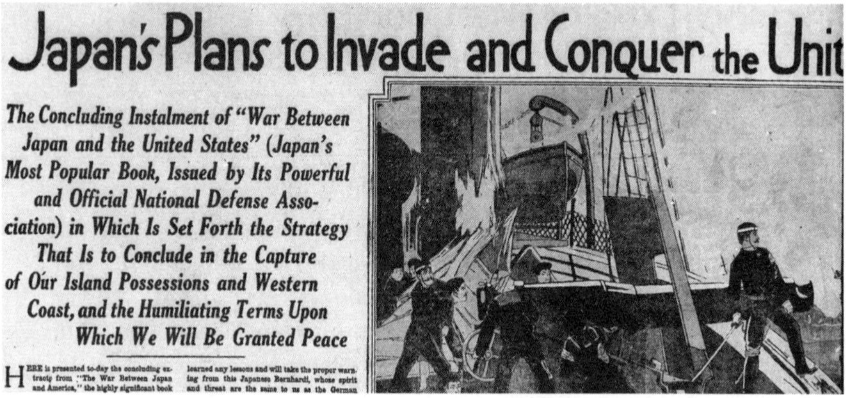

Japan's Plans to Invade and Conquer the Unit

The Concluding Instalment of "War Between Japan and the United States" (Japan's Most Popular Book, Issued by Its Powerful and Official National Defense Association) in Which Is Set Forth the Strategy That Is to Conclude in the Capture of Our Island Possessions and Western Coast, and the Humiliating Terms Upon Which We Will Be Granted Peace

HERE is presented to-day the concluding extracts from "The War Between Japan and America," the highly significant book learned any lessons and will take the proper warning from this Japanese Bernhardi, whose spirit and threat are the same to us as the German

San Francisco Examiner "investigative" article predicting a Japanese invasion.

the State Department because the immigration of Japanese labor is now forbidden by a 'gentlemen's agreement' between the two nations, and the Japanese embassy objected to having Japan discriminated against specifically while the Japanese government was carrying out this agreement faithfully."[8] This was blatantly untrue, since Japanese diplomats in Washington objected to the wording of the bill every bit as much as western senators. James Phelan had tried to introduce an amendment ensuring that no Japanese immigrant previously barred would be admitted under the new regulations, but the language was softened so as not to offend the Japanese.

But Phelan and the other western congressmen were also under enormous pressure to vote to override Wilson's veto. Eugenics advocates were pressing the case that without such stringent legislation, the very survival of the Nordic races was at stake. And, although the Japanese could not be included because the United States' entry into the war seemed more and more likely, westerners were assured that the measures already in place would be sufficient to prevent an upsurge in immigration. Phelan, who had voted against the original because of insufficient control over Japanese immigration, gave way on the override and, doubtless grumbling all the way, voted to enact the bill into law.[9]

Although neither he nor Phelan were on the record as saying so, Ulysses Webb would also have certainly resented Japan, ally against Germany or not, being coddled as the immigration bill wended its way through Congress. For whatever reason, in mid-1916, during the run-up to both state and presidential elections that November, after almost three years of allowing the 1913 California land law to be openly flaunted, Webb finally decided to use his office to ratchet up the pressure.

Although the first state action was ironically against a Chinese noncitizen whose native-born partner in a land lease had died, that case was more technical than political and received little notice outside the courtroom in which it was decided. The next state suit, however, would cause quite a stir indeed.

On December 14, 1915, Fulton Gunnerson sold his house at 3356 Lemon Street in Riverside, California, for $1,500. The real estate agent, a man named Noble, accepted payment from the buyer, Japanese-born Jukichi Harada, but the title deed was drawn in the name of his three American-born children, the oldest of whom was nine. (His marriage, therefore, predated the picture bride era.) Harada, who owned a successful restaurant named after his hero, George Washington, paid in full without needing a mortgage. He later stated "that he had no intention of doing anything but make a gift of the property to the children," and that both Gunnerson and Noble had been fully apprised of that.[10] There was no mention of Jukichi Harada anywhere in the deed, either as a co-owner, trustee, or beneficiary in case of the children's death. Rather, whichever of the children survived would inherit the property.

The Haradas' new home was in a desirable section of the city, and they were the first Japanese family to move there. Harada explained "that he had lost one child while living in a rooming house, and determined to obtain a home for them where there was room for them to be out of doors and where they would be conveniently located with reference to the Sunday school and public school which they attended."[11]

The 1911 treaty had given all Japanese the right "to own or lease and occupy houses" wherever Americans enjoyed a similar right. Harada's neighbors did not agree. They took "every means to oust the Haradas from the community," including hiring a local lawyer and former state senator Miguel Estudillo to offer to buy the house back for $2,000. When Harada refused, "fifteen residents signed a petition to have [them] removed beyond the tracks." When the petition failed, the residents must have put pressure on Noble, the real estate agent, because he wrote a letter to Ulysses Webb asking whether "Jap children" could own land. Webb wrote back that they could.[12] After considering the case, despite his personal view that the Haradas had acted within the law, Webb decided to try to seize their home.

With none of the three children "aliens ineligible for citizenship," Webb's only option was to demonstrate that Jukichi Harada somehow had a fiduciary interest in the property, despite the absence of his name on the title. Even if Webb were successful in that endeavor, he would have to then demonstrate that even though the Harada house was covered by the treaty, the land underneath was not. For some reason, Webb decided not to attempt to separate the land from the dwelling and relied strictly on the assertion that the transaction purchasing the home was a sham and elder Harada was the true owner of the property.

Webb's case was fatally weak. In general, a person who paid for something in the name of another would be considered a trustee under California law, but a specific exception was made for parents giving an unencumbered gift to their children. Jukichi Harada, since he was also not listed as a beneficiary, had legally set himself outside the transaction. Webb tried to argue that because the entire family would occupy the house, the father was the actual owner, but there was nothing in the law to support that either.

Harada's lawyers, both of whom were white, filed an extensive brief that effectively undercut Webb's arguments as to ownership of the property. They also claimed that the law itself violated the 1911 treaty, a far less certain avenue since landownership had been omitted from the treaty, but whether a Japanese noncitizen could own the land on which a legally purchased building sat was less clear. Finally, although it was tangential to the particulars of the case, they also included a point that would become salient in a few years:

> The question of whether a Japanese person is not eligible to citizenship in the United States is one that has never been decided by the Supreme Court of the United States. . . . Natives of Japan are . . . classified as "Mongolian," or members of the yellow race, and whether such classification be correct or incorrect . . . the classification certainly seems to be arbitrary, and when we consider the intelligence of the citizens of Japan residing in this country, and also the prominent, powerful and respected position which the Empire of Japan occupies amidst the great powers of the world, it seems a travesty upon justice to deny the privilege of citizenship to the Japanese. . . . The legislature of the State of California, however, without a guiding decision from its supreme court, has jumped to the conclusion . . . that Japanese persons are among those ineligible to citizenship under the laws of the United States.[13]

Webb opted to try the case personally, which may have indicated either that he thought his position was stronger than it seemed to be or that the judge, Hugh H. Craig, would simply refuse to rule for a Japanese family that had intruded into a white neighborhood. During the initial trial in December 1916, before Judge Craig, in which Webb's co-counsel was the same Miguel Estudillo who had represented Harada's neighbors, "the Japanese counsel from Los Angeles sat at Harada's side making notes of the procedure," and "the courtroom was crowded with Japanese."[14] One of Harada's lawyers, W. A. Purington, cited *Wong Kim Ark* and claimed the same birthright citizen guarantees apply to native-born children of noncitizen Japanese.

Estudillo replied that if the judge ruled for the Haradas, the land law would be useless. Japanese aliens would be entitled to own land throughout "on exactly the same terms as native Californians," which was blatantly untrue. "Property," he warned, "can be purchased in the name of Japanese children, farmed by their parents or rented to other Japanese for agricultural purposes." Estudillo then exclaimed, "There is nothing to prevent the state of California from becoming Japanized!"

Craig did not rule for more than four months, and when he did, it was only to deliver a partial verdict: the 1913 Alien Land Law did not conflict with 1911 treaty and therefore the state of California had the right to forbid ownership of land to "aliens not eligible for citizenship." Craig based his ruling on the omission of landholding in the treaty, which represented to him the clear intent of those who drafted the treaty and acceptance by those who signed it of the creation of that exception.[15]

From there, a good deal of legal jockeying ensued, which prevented a final judgment from being issued until September 1918. Attorney General Webb turned out to have been correct the first time. Although Judge Craig had ruled the Alien Land Law did not violate the California constitution, he found for the Haradas in language that could only be seen as a rebuke to the attorney general:

> The argument of counsel for plaintiff has been directed almost solely to a discussion of the relation of Jukichi Harada to this property, but has lightly passed over the interests of these children, who are defendants. They are American citizens, of somewhat humble station, it may be, but still entitled to the equal protection of the laws of our land. Their parentage has nothing whatever to do with their rights to hold property. That depends

> on their status as American citizens. . . . Before any controversy arose, before the deed was drafted, before the opinion of the attorney-general was received, he told Noble he wanted to buy the property for his children. He disclaimed any interest in it when he filed his answer herein, and when on the witness stand under oath, he said over and over that it was the children's property. He has never said anything else about it. These are matters in the record. Counsel for plaintiff are too well versed in the laws to believe for one moment that a resulting trust could exist or be enforced in the face of those reiterated disclaimers on the part of Jukichi Harada, all of which are matters of record. He does not own nor can he ever own or hold any interest in fee in this property while the law remains as it is. If this is true, there is no violation of the Anti-Alien Land Law and its purpose is accomplished.[16]

If that were not bad enough, Craig added, "The actions of Harada were precisely what the actions of an American-born father would have been. . . . He would have paid the purchase money, he would have provided for the improvements, he would have attended to the negotiations and would have taken care of the papers. It can be confidently stated, that the children of American parents could not have their title attacked under such circumstances. . . . If this is true, such a theory can not obtain here, as the political rights of American citizens are the same no matter what their parentage."

Judge Craig added one more comment, which must have been particularly rankling to Webb, coauthor of the law: "If an embarrassing or unfortunate situation results by reason of the limitations of the statute, the remedy is not to be sought in the courts, for they cannot deny to American citizens the right to own or hold an interest in land under our laws as they now exist."

Webb fumed for a bit and then filed for a retrial, which Judge Craig denied in January 1919. Feeling wronged, he was sufficiently upset to threaten to again file for a retrial, this time claiming judicial misconduct. Eventually, he thought better of it and let the matter drop.

Jukichi Harada and his family remained in the house on Lemon Street until May 1942, when they were forced into internment. Both Harada and his wife died in captivity, while their youngest son, Harold, fought with the famed 442nd Regimental Combat Team. After the war ended, their daughter Sumi returned to Riverside to live in the home that was so much more than walls, floors, and a roof. She used the house to provide shelter for other internees who had returned from unjust imprisonment to try to rebuild their shattered lives.

The Alien Land Law was not repealed until 1951.

In 1991, Harada House was designated a National Historic Landmark.

11 | The Golden West

With a combination of the Harada case, the increase in both Japanese population and landholdings, and the end of World War I, 1919 precipitated a turning point for Issei and Nisei on the West Coast.

Although the first two resulted in direct action to further limit the rights of Japanese noncitizens, the third created a backdrop to provide white racists increased justification for their initiatives. Before the war, Japan was considered a rising naval power in the Pacific, but many in the United States and Europe did not deem the defeat of the decrepit Russian navy as proof of Japan's prowess. Despite the drumbeating in the Hearst and McClatchy newspapers, few in Washington considered that Japan could seriously menace the United States. Both President Roosevelt and President Taft had been eager to engage in whatever diplomacy necessary to defuse talk of a sea war with Japan, and each also believed there had been a certain amount of bluster in the Japanese threats. By the war's end, however, it had become clear that Japan had become a legitimate military power with imperialistic ambitions that it had both the will and means to achieve.

At the beginning of war, after it had aligned itself with Great Britain, Japan had succeeded in ousting the Germans from Tsingtao, and chasing the German navy from the South China Sea. But Japan had not joined the Allies merely to help out. In January 1915, in secret, the Japanese government presented to China "Twenty-one Demands," which, if all had been agreed to, would have turned China into a vassal state. Korea had been dealt with similarly in 1910. China, fresh off a revolution that had ousted the Qing dynasty, was saddled with a fragile government and an empty treasury and seemed unable to resist.

The demands were in five groups. The first two affirmed that Japan would be the dominant foreign power in Shandong, southern Manchuria, and parts of Mongolia. The third required China to acknowledge Japanese partnership in a key iron, coal, and steel industrial complex. The fourth prohibited China from conceding any coastal or island territories to any foreign power other than Japan. Each of these was simply a confirmation of goals Japan had already attained. The fifth, however, the most controversial, was new. It instructed China to allow Japanese appointees to take effective control of China's government, industry, and military. Finally, Japan warned of severe consequences if China made the communication public.

The two nations negotiated for three months. China, in no position to resist militarily, finally leaked the demands to the Western allies. Both Great Britain and United States condemned the initiative and exerted diplomatic pressure on Japan to rescind the ultimatum. Japan held to the first four groups, which was merely face-saving since they were a restatement of the status quo, but withdrew the fifth. In the end, the Twenty-one Demands achieved little other than warning Europe and the United States that Japan was determined to create its own sphere of influence where Western powers had previously enjoyed total sway.

For the anti-Japanese faction in the United States, Japan's expansionism reaffirmed that of which they had spent almost two decades trying to persuade Washington. For newspaper magnates McClatchy and Hearst, it justified all the lurid warnings about Japanese warships poised off the coast of California and Hawaii, which demonstrated the extreme peril of allowing those of Japanese ancestry to live and move freely in the American West. Of course, all this fearmongering was based on the assumption that Japanese immigrants and even their American-born children felt their primary allegiance was to Japan and not the United States.

One odd side effect of Japanese ambitions in China was a softening of anti-Chinese propaganda. Prohibited from both immigration and citizenship, content to live in their own enclaves and endure, even welcome, segregation, the Chinese became a more benign presence, and even in some cases an object of sympathy for the manner in which their country was forced to endure humiliation at the hands of the Japanese. Of course, the humiliation foisted on China by the Western powers was overlooked. Korea too could be depicted as a victim of Japanese barbarity, made easier since there were so few Koreans in the United States.

After the war, the attacks on the Japanese began in earnest. In an attempt to influence the peace talks and gain independence, Koreans had engaged in peaceful protests, which were repressed harshly by the Japanese, and thus made perfect fodder. Japanese occupiers were portrayed as brutal, sadistic, and merciless, which to some significant degree they were. On April 3, 1919, for example, the *Examiner* ran a story about rival publisher V. S. McClatchy's trip to Korea, in which McClatchy wrote, "In the streets of Seoul, Mrs. McClatchy and myself saw girl students suspected of inciting rebellion against Japanese rule, led through the streets by armed Japanese soldiers. The girls, some of them hardly more than children, were bound in couples by their thumbs, the lashing being tied so securely that any attempt to pull apart would have dislocated their thumbs. About their necks were leather thongs, drawn tightly into the flesh so that an attempt to escape would have meant strangulation."[1] McClatchy was no stranger to hyperbole, but accounts of Japanese mistreatment of Korean civilians were widespread, most from unimpeachable sources. The article also noted that the "stories of brutality sustained" the characterization of Japan by James Phelan as the "Germany of the Far East."

Phelan had been forced to limit anti-Japanese diatribes during war, but he was up for reelection in 1920 and intended to ride race hatred to another six years in Washington. His campaign slogan was "Keep California White," which was printed along with his picture on placards and in newspaper advertisements. Almost the moment the war ended, he announced his intention to pursue exclusionary laws at both the national and state levels. In Sacramento on March 31, 1919, while peace terms were being negotiated in Paris, Phelan told a McClatchy reporter, "During my investigations into the Japanese situation, I find a general feeling of apathy in the public mind due to a lack of knowledge of the conditions. I find the best way to get recognition of a condition, the best way to get action on the part of the men in power, is to make a noise." Phelan promised to make that noise because, likening the Japanese to cockroaches, he said, "Publicity is something they do not like; the operations of the Japanese and their propagandists will not bear the scrutinizing light. They are exceedingly crafty, working in the dark, and when the light is directed upon them, they scamper to cover."[2]

He promised to propose a series of laws to eliminate Japanese landholding, close off further immigration, and otherwise make life so difficult for the Japanese that they returned to their homeland. It either had not occurred to Phelan, or he did not care, that for the vast majority of Japanese, the United States was their homeland. They had come to the United States for the same reasons as his forebears—freedom, opportunity, and a better way of life.

But granting Japanese in United States a measure of humanity was not going to get him reelected, so Phelan continued to play to the racist gallery, abetted by the other white supremacists in state and local governments, labor unions, and media barons Hearst and McClatchy.

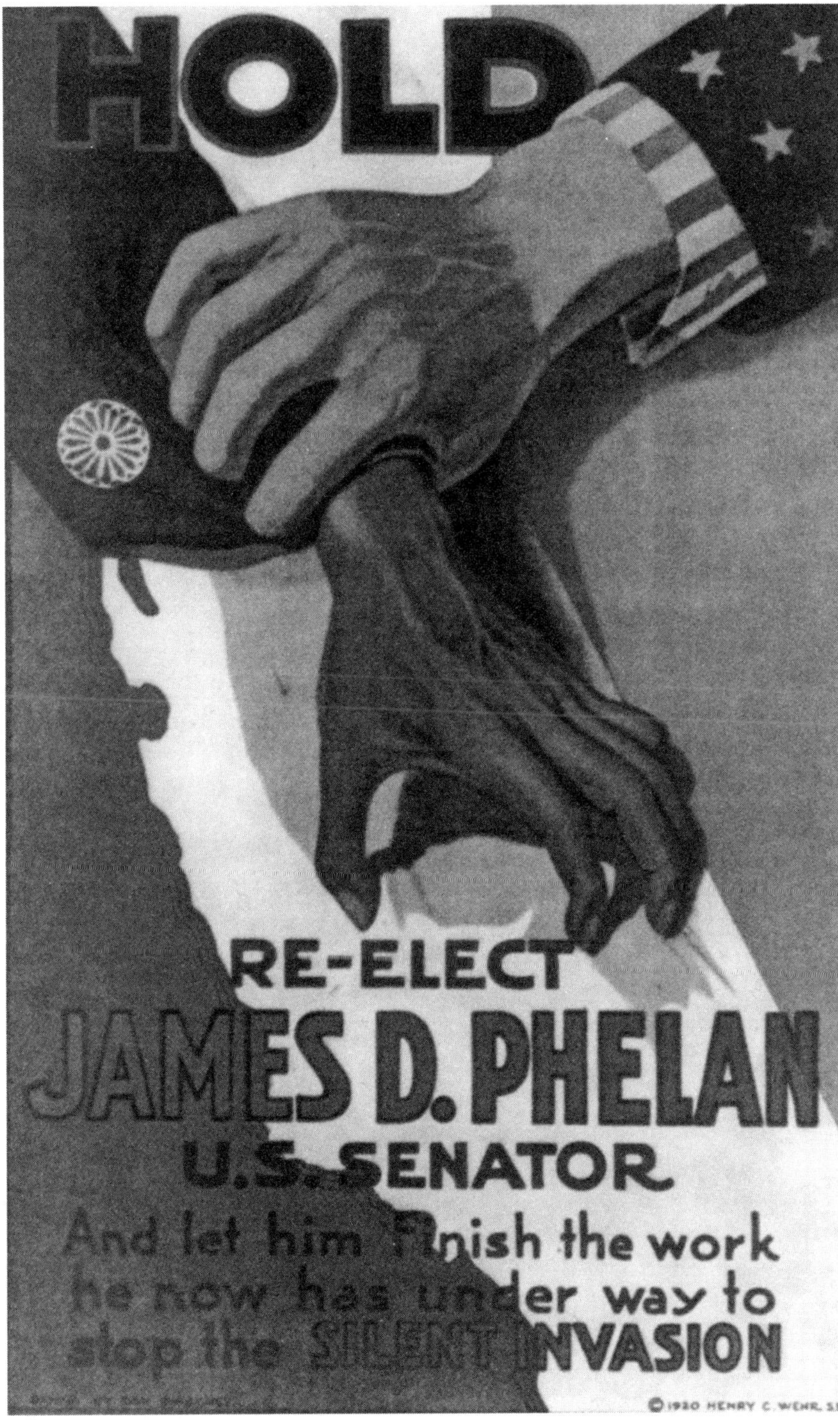

James Phelan poster for his reelection campaign in 1920, showing the hand of Uncle Sam grabbing wrist of a Japanese American reaching for a map of California. Courtesy of Library of Congress Prints and Photographs Division.

A number of civic and fraternal organizations were also on the ramparts of exclusion, none more important than the Native Sons of the Golden West, "perhaps the influential pressure group in the State."[3] The group was founded in 1875, "embracing only the sons of those sturdy pioneers who arrived on this coast prior to the admission of California as a state," and was followed the next year by the Native Daughters of the Golden West.[4] The groups were divided into "parlors," with a Grand Parlor being the ruling body. Boasting a roster of the most powerful, wealthiest, and admired figures in the state, the Native Sons and Daughters were dedicated to honoring and preserving California's heritage, and in their monthly publication, the *Grizzly Bear,* members extolled the virtues individuality, community spirit, and hard work.

But the Native Sons and Daughters were also dedicated to keeping California "as it has always been and God himself intended it shall always be—the White Man's paradise," and almost every issue of the *Grizzly Bear* contained disparaging articles about first the Chinese, then the Japanese. Although no one said so publicly, both the organization and the names given were reminiscent of the Ku Klux Klan.[5] Prominent members in 1920 included Eugene Schmitz, Aaron Altmann, many of the Boodle Boys, Ulysses Webb, and, of course, Phelan. In 1919, an up-and-coming young politician recently discharged from the army, Earl Warren, joined the group.

They did not attempt to hide their racism. In 1942, the grand historian of the Native Sons, Peter Conmy, produced a pamphlet, *The History of California's Japanese Problem and the Part Played by the Native Sons of the Golden West in Its Solution,* in which he detailed some of the group's history in promoting Japanese exclusion: "Official Native Son interest in the problem began in 1907. In that year Grand Treasurer John E. McDougald introduced a resolution in the Grand Parlor calling for the exclusion of all Orientals. The resolution does not mention Japanese. The fact, however, that the Chinese were already excluded left the import of the action to be the exclusion of the Japanese. The reason ascribed in the preamble supporting the resolution was economic inability of Orientals to adjust to American wage levels."[6] A resolution the following year requested that President Roosevelt deploy the United States fleet in the Pacific to repel an imminent Japanese attack. Other items were visceral appeals to racism. "Would you like your daughter to marry a Japanese?" asked the *Grizzly Bear.* "If not, demand your representatives in the Legislature vote for the segregation of whites and Asiatics in the public schools."[7]

Conmy made specific reference to the Harada ruling: "One of the factors which contributed greatly to the exclusion movement was a decision by the California Supreme Court holding that a Japanese might purchase land intended as a gift for his child to be given to the child when he attained his majority, and that in the meantime the parent might be appointed guardian of this future interest of his child."[8]

Although the Native Sons and the other groups opposing the Japanese worked energetically, they often drowned each other out. Phelan and McClatchy decided nativists needed to speak with one voice. In September 1919, under McClatchy's aegis, with the full support of his supposed competitor Hearst, one hundred of northern California's most prominent citizens met in Sacramento to form what the *Examiner* labeled "An Anti-Jap League." One of the speakers, State Assemblyman Ivan Parker, told the group, "The state is beginning to feel the menacing advance of the Japanese [who] control 65 percent of the vegetable crop of the Sacramento Valley." State Controller John Chambers, who would compare the Japanese to rodents in his *Annals of the American Academy of Political and Social Science* article, added, "The menace of the yellow race is greater than the menace of the worst agitators of Europe who are now among us. If the government at Washington will not protect us against this peril, then we of necessity must protect ourselves."[9]

During the ensuing months, the organizers of the Sacramento meeting solicited support from groups sympathetic to their cause, always stressing that one powerful group would be more successful in gaining passage of the legislation they sought, both state and federal, than a splintered cacophony. It took some months for initiative to coalesce around a single set of goals, but on September 2, 1920, McClatchy's *Sacramento Bee* finally announced in a page 1 headline, "Japanese Exclusion League of California Formally Organized." The league joined together the Native Sons and Daughters, the newly founded American Legion, the California Federation of Labor, the Federation of Women's Clubs, the California State Grange, the Farm Bureau, and the Loyal Order of Moose. Although California state senator James Inman was elected president and Phelan was prominently featured, McClatchy would be the league's most powerful figure. "The body will seek passage of an Anti-Alien Land Act at the November election and also inaugurate nation-wide propaganda to work for the control of the Japanese problem," McClatchy's *Bee* reported.[10] Similar groups were formed in other western states to end immigration from Japan and Mexico and to force immigrants from those nations to leave the United States.

The Exclusion League published a five point program: (1) cancellation of the Gentlemen's Agreement; (2) exclusion of the picture brides; (3) rigorous exclusion of Japanese as immigrants; (4) confirmation of the policy that Asiatics shall be forever barred from American citizenship; and (5) amendment of the Constitution providing that no child born in the United States shall be given the rights of a citizen unless both parents are of a race eligible for citizenship.[11] These were all issues for the federal government tackle, however. Their immediate priority was to place a referendum on the November 1920 ballot to create a new state alien land law that would close the loopholes in the 1913 act. They sought to prohibit even short-term leases of land to aliens ineligible for citizenship, bar stock companies owned by those ineligible for citizenship from acquiring agricultural lands, and prohibit Japanese noncitizens from acquiring land through inheritance.

The league, abetted by the state's major newspapers, propagandized furiously and successfully. Despite protests from Japanese diplomats in Washington, the ballot initiative was approved in every county in the state and passed by a margin of more than 3 to 1. The new law put a stranglehold on Japanese farmers, and the Japanese American Association stated the day the results were announced that they would continue "the great fight . . . against the lawless and unreasonable anti-Japanese measure . . . on behalf of Japanese residents, on behalf of Japanese-American friendship, on behalf of justice and humanity."[12] They vowed to contest both the prohibition against Japanese naturalization and the constitutionality of the law, which they saw as in violation of the Fourteenth Amendment. The *Examiner* reported on Japanese intention to test the law in the courts with its usual understatement: "Having made an unavailing fight Tuesday to defeat the measure at the polls [for] which considerable gold from Japan was hurried across the Pacific, the unwelcome Orientals now are scheming to invoke the courts to compel their reception here upon equal terms with whites."[13]

The endorsement of the land law did not save James Phelan, however. Ohio senator Warren G. Harding, a Republican running for president on a platform that featured opposition to Woodrow Wilson's League of Nations, crushed his Democratic opponent, Ohio governor James M. Cox, and dragged Senate candidate Samuel Shortridge along with him, but the Senate race was a good deal closer. Phelan was forced to content himself with a statement expressing satisfaction that the anti-Japan Law passed. Although Phelan would never again hold public office, his efforts to promote Japanese exclusion would not flag.

The Japanese American Association made good its vow to test the new land law in court, first by attacking the most fundamental precept of anti-Japanese policy.

12 | The Heart of an American

Takao Ozawa was born in Kanagawa, Japan, on June 15, 1875, and immigrated to San Francisco in 1894. He learned English and enrolled at Berkeley High School, from which he graduated in 1903, just prior to his twenty-eighth birthday, having completed the "scientific course."[1] The previous year, he had filed a petition of intent to seek citizenship. Although the Chinese had been specifically excluded from naturalization in 1882, the Japanese had not been, and in dozens of cases, most in the East, an immigrant from Japan had become a U.S. citizen. After high school, Ozawa attended the University of California at Berkeley for three years, but left before graduation and moved to Honolulu. He got married, had five children, obtained a clerical or sales job working for an American sugar company, and by all accounts lived an exemplary life.[2]

In September 1914, Ozawa, armed with his petition of intent, filed an application for citizenship at the federal district court office. He was one of the first of Japanese descent not born in Hawaii to do so. The clerk at the court, Augustus Murphy, refused the application, citing section 2169 of the *U.S. Revised Statutes,* which stated that the Naturalization Act "shall apply to aliens, being free white persons, and to aliens of African nativity and to persons of African descent." Ozawa returned a few weeks later, accompanied by two white character witnesses, and refiled his petition.

Murphy queried officials in Washington who instructed him to accept the application and let the matter be decided in court.[3] In January 1915, the case was assigned to the distinguished seventy-year-old judge Sanford Ballard Dole, a member of one of Hawaii's most prominent families. Dole had been a counselor to Queen Lilioukalani, then president of the Republic of Hawaii, and then its first territorial governor. He had been appointed to the federal bench in 1903 by Theodore Roosevelt. His cousin James, the "Pineapple King," founded the Hawaiian Pineapple Company, now Dole Foods. Dole had a reputation for fairness, but nonetheless prized his standing as a member of Hawaii's white elite.

Takao Ozawa's case was heard on January 29, 1915. During the hearing, Ozawa, who acted as his own attorney, "underwent a lengthy examination by Judge Dole on points relating to American government." Dole asked Ozawa if he were a samurai, to which Ozawa replied he was not but his brother in Japan was. "I am pure Japanese," he said, "but my heart is American." Ozawa also told the judge that in the event of war between Japan and the United States, he would fight "under the Stars and Stripes." In another exchange, Dole asked if the Japanese regarded themselves as "Mongolians." Ozawa replied, "Some of the scholars say that the Japanese are not Mongolians, but are a mixture of Malay and other races." At the conclusion of the hearing, Dole announced, "He is all right, the only question being that he is a Japanese.'" From there, he adjourned the hearing without coming to a decision.[4]

After a series of postponements at Ozawa's request, so that he could obtain more material to present his case, the hearing resumed on June 9, 1915. Ozawa, again representing himself, filed a lengthy brief.[5] In it he asserted, "There is not a special law prohibiting Japanese from naturalization. And also there is not one supreme court decision against Japanese from naturalization. So that during the last 20 years, 50 Japanese were naturalized." He submitted a list of fourteen of those cases as well as the federal courts that approved the applications.[6]

But the thrust of Ozawa's argument was the description of just how American he and his family were:

> I neither drink liquor of any kind, nor smoke, nor play cards, nor gamble, nor associate with any improper person. My honesty and my industriousness are well known among my Japanese and American acquaintances and friends; and I am always trying my best to conduct myself according to the Golden Rule. So I have all [the] confidence in myself that as far as my character is concerned, I am second to none. . . . In name, General Benedict Arnold was an American, but at heart he was a traitor. In name, I am not an American, but at heart I am a true American. I set forth the following facts that will sufficiently prove this. (1) I did not report my name, my marriage, or the names of my children to the Japanese Consulate in Honolulu; notwithstanding all Japanese subjects are requested to do so. These matters were reported to the American government. (2) I do not have any connection with any Japanese churches or schools, or any Japanese organizations here or elsewhere. (3) I am sending my children to an American church and American school in place of a Japanese one. (4) Most of the time I use the American language at home, so that my children cannot speak the

> Japanese language. (5) I have lived continuously within the United States for over twenty-eight years. (6) I chose as my wife one educated in American schools . . . so it is my honest hope to do something good to the United States before I bid a farewell to this world.[7]

Ozawa made substantive points as well, the most important being that according to prevailing science he was a member of "one of the four white races." The Chinese also were, but they had been explicitly barred from citizenship in 1882, whereas the Japanese had not. He posited that the Naturalization Act of 1790 had barred only Africans from citizenship, because the term "white" had been used only to differentiate it from "black."

He used some odd imagery to press his point: "Whenever we speak of white eggs, we mean the eggs having white shells. Hence the term 'white' does not indicate any quality of eggs. . . . On the other hand, when we speak of 'fresh white eggs,' we mean newly laid eggs . . . that is, of good quality. Similarly in the term 'white person,' the word 'white' designates the color of the person, but not quality. On the other hand, the term 'free' indicates the good quality of the person. . . . If it was the true intent of the congress to exclude all races except white persons, a limiting word 'only' should have been used in place of 'free.'"[8]

Ozawa also made an ominous prediction if his petition were denied, which received a good deal of attention: "What will the United States gain by humiliating the Japanese whom our Uncle Sam assisted to become one of the five great powers? She will only create bitter feelings in the minds of the Japanese, thus transforming a good friend into an enemy. . . . The final result will be the greatest war between the European and Asiatic peoples. . . . On the other hand, if the United States treats Japan fairly . . . Japanese will surely respect American people as never before. Peace between the United States and Japan will forever continue."[9]

The U.S. district attorney, J. Wesley Thompson, had a simple reply to all of Ozawa's arguments—none were based on the law. This was not entirely true—"white" had in fact not been defined in the 1790 law. Thompson did file an addendum stating Ozawa was morally unfit for citizenship because he threatened war between the Japan and United States, which confuses "threaten" with "predict," but might also be seen as an indication that Thompson thought he might lose.[10]

That was a prospect made even more frightening when a rumor

begin circulating in late October that, because of an order from the attorney general's office, Judge Dole's decision would be final and not subject to appeal. An adverse decision then, one granting Ozawa citizenship, would set precedent and "let down the bars" to Japanese aliens in Hawaii and on the mainland. A former U.S. district attorney, Robert Breckens, claimed that two years before such an order had come in writing and was in the files; the district attorney in office at the time, Jeff McCarn, denied that such an order existed, but refused to allow reporters access to his files. The prospect of unfettered Japanese naturalization caused such a stir, however, that a few days later Judge Dole was forced to publicly refute the notion that his decision could not be appealed. He observed that the only way his ruling could be binding was if it were sustained by the Supreme Court. In addition, he pointed out that the decision of one district court judge was not even binding on other district court judges. Another judge could issue a decision opposite of his and each would be operative in its own jurisdiction until the Supreme Court decided which of the two should stand. He added that the case was so important that he was determined to give it the appropriate study and reflection. He need not have bothered. He retired on December 16, 1915, the Ozawa case still undecided.

Dole was replaced by Charles Clemons, who had been born in Vermont, attended Yale and Yale Law School, and then moved to Honolulu to practice law in 1902. Unlike Dole, Clemons was first-generation and had arrived in Hawaii with the large population of Japanese immigrants already in place. Whether his own immigrant status would make Clemons more sympathetic to Ozawa's application was not immediately apparent, but the prospect was worrisome to the exclusionists. In addition, it was not clear whether Taft's attorney general, George Wickersham, had actually issued an order that naturalization decisions were not to be appealed. Just two weeks after Clemons was assigned the case, the acting U.S. district attorney, Horace Vaughan, declared that if the judge ruled for Ozawa, he "will take immediate steps with a view to having the court's order in the case cancelled." Vaughan, however, "was noncommittal as to the grounds on which he would base an action to have the order cancelled."[11]

Although a decision was promised at the end of January, Judge Clemons did not issue his ruling until March 25. The day before the verdict was rendered, "a prominent Japanese" told reporters, "It would give the able Japanese in Hawaii who are thorough believers in the United

States, first, last, and for all, an opportunity to further show their interest in things American. It would show to America that the Japanese who have come here to live and who expect to die here to be thorough citizens, willing to do their part to make for a better and greater nation."[12]

They would not get the chance. The next day Judge Clemons ruled for the government.

The decision was based neither in ethnology, which Clemons admitted was an indistinct science—though he did note the weight of evidence would indicate that Japanese were not white—nor in the "moral or intellectual" qualifications of the applicant, but simply on previous court decisions, in particular *Ah Yup*, all of which classified "Mongolians," in which he included the Japanese, as not "white." He rejected Ozawa's contention that referred to the quality of the applicant, ruling instead that it was merely a differentiation from "slave" or "prisoner." Clemons did not comment on the morality or its "inconsistency with ideals of American government." But he concluded, "The remedy lies with Congress and our alien friends should through their friends, or directly, seek that branch of the government, and if they show such devotion to the United States and its constitution as this petitioner has shown in his twenty years of complete surrender to our customs and institutions, his petition should not fall on deaf ears."[13]

As is apparent from the naïve last sentence, Clemons was relieved to have dispensed with the case.[14] Just five days later, in an interview, Clemons advised Ozawa not to attempt to prompt legislative action until the question had been decided by the Supreme Court: "In connection with any special efforts of the friends of these people to secure favorable action by Congress, it would be of decided advantage to them to forestall any such conjunctive questions."[15] Since the chances of congressional legislation authorizing Japanese naturalization were nil, Clemons advice to wait for the Court to decide was the only default alternative. Ozawa intended to press that alternative; this time he would have help.

Judge Clemons's decision was reported on extensively, nowhere more so than on the West Coast. Japanese American societies on the mainland had hoped for a favorable ruling, but sent word in June that they wished to aid Ozawa in appealing the decision. With alien land laws making it difficult for Japanese aliens to own farms, the prospect of it being made more difficult still, the right to citizenship had become vital. Particularly vexing to the Japanese was being described as "Mongolian," which they insisted had no firm scientific basis and was seen as a contrivance to end-run the strict wording of the Naturalization Act.

In early August, representatives of a number of these societies met in Vancouver to "discuss ways and means of encouraging and assisting" Ozawa in mounting an appeal.[16] They were successful, because one week later, Ozawa announced his intention to appeal, and also that he would be represented by an all-white law firm. To fund the appeal, which would begin in circuit court in San Francisco, $5,000 had been raised, half by the Japanese societies, half by a sympathetic American pastor, Doremus Scudder, who would soon leave for a ministry in Tokyo. One source of opposition to Ozawa's mounting an appeal was the Japanese government, which was reported to have felt the time was not right for Japanese aliens to press for citizenship, but officials did go into specifics as to their reasoning.[17]

The appeal was presented to the Ninth Circuit Court in San Francisco on June 1, 1917. Ozawa's attorney traveled to the mainland, but Ozawa did not. The hearing was predictably brief. The three-judge panel said the question was too significant for them to rule on and passed it on to the Supreme Court. From there, the case, already front-page news, acquired even more notoriety. Newspapers reported that to plead for Ozawa before the nine justices the Japanese Associations of the Pacific Coast would approach no less than former president William Howard Taft, and pay whatever fee Taft required. Former secretary of state Elihu Root and former Supreme Court justice Charles Evans Hughes were two others the associations were said to have solicited. (Ozawa, who had studied up on naturalization law, was also said to have wanted to represent himself, but was dissuaded.) Taft declined, and was forced to deny he had accepted a $30,000 retainer.[18] Although Root and Hughes were also not retained, the Japanese Association succeeded in engaging former attorney general George Wickersham to represent Ozawa before the Court. Wickersham, a past president of the Japan Society, had a long history with the Japanese community and was sympathetic to their cause. That he took the case for only $1,000 is indicative of he eagerness to participate. With Wickersham as counsel for the plaintiff, any small possibility that the Court could simply brush away the appeal evaporated.

Wickersham, however, could not compel the case to be heard quickly. The government had no intention of prosecuting such an incendiary issue while the war was in progress, but even afterward they were in no hurry to have it heard. Wickersham returned from a trip to Europe in March 1919, when the arguments were scheduled, only to find out that it been put off until the fall at the request of the solicitor general. "The reason for the postponement cannot be learned," reports read, "it is considered, however, that the action of the Supreme Court has some relation to the [peace conference] in Paris, where the problem relating to racial discrimination is being taken by delegates from the Allied Nations."[19] Argument was postponed once more at the request of the government in October 1919, and then again in the spring 1920, by which time alien land laws had been enacted in California and Washington State.

The government continued to stall, and it was not until the fall term 1922, with anti-immigration fervor rife in Washington, that *Ozawa v. United States* was finally heard. By that time, the argument that Japanese were white had undergone some refinements. Ozawa "has traced the history of Japan for some thousands of years, carrying it back to the Ainu tribe, and no less a person than James M. Beck, solicitor general of the United States, has expressed the belief that that particular part of the Japanese race has the distinct mark of the Caucasian."[20] Wickersham also argued that the Japanese had not been specifically excluded by either the 1790 law or any of the laws subsequently enacted to amend it, especially the legislation enacted in 1906. In fact, that the 1882 Exclusion Act had taken pains to specifically prohibit the Chinese from naturalization was proof that the 1790 law had not applied to any Asian, an argument Ozawa had put forth in his brief.

Wickersham did not choose to raise Fourteenth Amendment issues, even with *Yick Wo* as precedent. There is no record as to why he avoided a constitutional challenge, but he was experienced before the Supreme Court, and sufficiently acquainted with the new chief justice, his old boss, Taft, who had had declined to represent Ozawa two years earlier, so he must have decided an equal protection argument would be futile.

Arguments began on October 3, 1922, and took two days. From there, it was only six weeks before the Court issued an opinion and the decision was unanimous. Takao Ozawa, the "quiet little man, working in an obscure clerical position, delving in the library at night," who had "ruled his whole life and the life of his family with one fixed aim in view," to become a citizen of the United States, would be denied that right.[21]

Justice George Sutherland wrote the opinion. He had joined the

George Sutherland. Courtesy of Library of Congress Prints and Photographs Division.

Court just weeks before. Sutherland, born in Great Britain, was an immigrant, albeit from one of the "desirable countries" in northern Europe.

After dispensing with technicalities—one that the 1906 law conflicted with the 1790 Naturalization Act, one in the wording of the *Revised Statutes* in 1873—Sutherland took up the argument that the term "white" in the 1790 law was used only to differentiate it from "black." He chose the broad interpretation, one that inferred objectivity: "The provision is not that Negroes and Indians shall be excluded, but it is, in effect, that only free white persons shall be included. The intention was to confer the privilege of citizenship upon that class of persons whom the fathers knew as white, and to deny it to all who could not be so classified. It is not enough to say that the framers did not have in mind the brown or yellow races of Asia. It is necessary to go farther and be able to say that, had these particular races been suggested, the language of the act would have been so varied as to include them within its privileges."[22] Although to postulate that had Congress and President Washington been aware of the Japanese they would have been excluded was not injudicious, for Sutherland, who generally ruled strictly by language, what today would be referred to as "textualism," inferring intent when there was no means of confirmation was a departure from principle.

That left the same problem Clemons had faced. What was the definition of "white?" If it were appearance, then Ozawa's argument of having paler skin than many of those qualified for naturalization would have merit. If it were a scientific classification, Sutherland would need to choose selectively from a number of theories, because few serious ethnological studies used broad and general terms, such as "white," "black," or "yellow," as defining traits. Even Blumenbach and his descendants had not defined boundaries on their ethnological classifications, so whether "Mongolian" applied to the Japanese was not specified. Nor could Sutherland simply say that the Japanese were not white because they "looked different," even if that was what he thought, which he well may have.

To avoid chromatic difficulties, Sutherland dismissed skin tone as a proper yardstick: "Manifestly the test afforded by the mere color of the skin of each individual is impracticable, as that differs greatly among persons of the same race, even among Anglo-Saxons, ranging by imperceptible gradations from the fair blond to the swarthy brunette, the latter being darker than many of the lighter hued persons of the brown or yellow races. Hence, to adopt the color test alone would result in a confused overlapping of races and a gradual merging of one into the other, without any practical line of separation."

That left science: "Beginning with the decision of Circuit Judge Sawyer in *In Re Ah Yup*, the federal and state courts, in an almost unbroken line, have held that the words 'white person' were meant to indicate only a person of what is popularly known as the Caucasian race. . . . We see no reason to differ." Among the cases Sutherland felt no need to differ with were *In re Mozumdar, In re Singh, and In re Ellis*. In the first two, "Hindus," as all East Indians were then described, were allowed to become American citizens because science classified them as Caucasian. In the third, federal district court judge Charles Wolverton ruled that "a Syrian, a native of Palestine and a Maronite," was also entitled to be naturalized because Middle Easterners were also Caucasian and thus white as defined in the 1790 law.[23]

But not science entirely. Sutherland added, "The determination that the words 'white person' are synonymous with the words 'a person of the Caucasian race' simplifies the problem, although it does not entirely dispose of it. Controversies have arisen and will no doubt arise again in respect of the proper classification of individuals in borderline cases." He did not, however, delineate the criteria that would establish whether or not a case was "borderline," apparently leaving it to legal authorities, in this case himself, to make that determination,

That subjectivity was enough to disqualify Takao Ozawa: "The appellant in the case now under consideration, however, is clearly of a race which is not Caucasian, and therefore belongs entirely outside the zone on the negative side." Ozawa would not be allowed citizenship. Sutherland did feel the need to append a disclaimer. "Of course," he noted fatuously, "there is not implied—either in the legislation or in our interpretation of it—any suggestion of individual unworthiness or racial inferiority."[24]

The Court's decision made headlines across the nation. Most newspapers simply recounted the decision, but Hearst's *Examiner* opened its page 1 story, "Two decisions that will go far toward checking the 'yellow peril' that menaces the country in general, and the Pacific Coast in particular, were handed down by the Supreme Court."[25] Both Ulysses Webb and James Phelan were overjoyed, Webb proclaiming that alien land laws had been saved, and Phelan exulting that previous naturalizations, including those of Japanese who had served in the American military—which he had not—would be rescinded.[26]

But no commentary on the case was more trenchant than "Race Lines and Color Lines: An Editorial Inspired by the Ozawa Case," written by Charles Clemons, the judge who had denied Ozawa's plea in district court. "It is absurd, of course," the judge wrote, "that a man must be either 'white' or 'of African nativity . . . (or) of African descent,' as the statute reads, in order to become a naturalized American citizen. It is absurd because there is really no such thing as 'white' person. The nearest ever get to cuticular whiteness is, as every undertaker knows, when we have ceased to count as voters; in other words, when we are in our coffins. . . . After a century or more of the United States as a haven of the 'downtrodden and oppressed' of the world, we are so mixed racially that the statutory rule of eligibility to citizenship by naturalization has become unworkable; at the least the courts are in despair as to it workability." Once again, Clemons called on Congress to foment a "radical cure of this international ill," without seeming to realize that he could have taken a step in just that direction by putting his thoughts of the absurdity or racial classification in his decision. "How hypocritical," he concluded, to claim to be an enlightened people "while retaining so much prejudice against the mere racial 'color' as such!"[27]

That it might have been equally hypocritical to base his decision denying an obviously qualified applicant for citizenship on a word he felt had no meaning did not seem to have occurred to him.

13 | What Meets the Eye

In the first Supreme Court decision to attempt to come to a constitutional definition of "white," George Sutherland had—more or less—relied on science to make the term synonymous with "Caucasian." There were, of course, those "borderline cases," and although Sutherland had made no attempt to define the term, based on his opinion, certain darker-skinned groups did not fall amiss of his borderline category. Sutherland had cited district court rulings in *Mozumdar* and *Singh,* to buttress his argument, and in each of those cases, pigmentation had not conflicted with classification. Those precedents seemed to bode well for another "Hindu" applicant, Bhagat Singh Thind, whose case came before the Court only weeks after the *Ozawa* decision was handed down.

Thind was a Sikh, born in Punjab, India, in 1892. He attended college in India, but after reading Emerson, Whitman, and Thoreau, he immigrated to the United States. He arrived in Seattle on July 4, 1913, before he could have fallen under the prohibitions of the 1917 Immigration Act.[1] Thind initially worked in lumber mills in Oregon to support himself, but moved to San Francisco and, as had Takao Ozawa, attended the University of California at Berkeley. In July 1918, he enlisted as a private in the U. S. Army, the first turbaned Sikh to serve. His unit remained in Camp Lewis, Washington. In December 1918, just after the war ended, Thind, by then an "acting sergeant," received an honorable discharge, his character described as "excellent."[2]

At the same time as his enlistment, Thind applied for naturalization in Seattle as a "high caste Hindu of full Indian blood." One week before his discharge in December 1918, his application was approved. He was sworn in as a United States citizen wearing his army uniform. Four days later, however, while still in the military, his citizenship was revoked at the request of a local Immigration and Naturalization Service official on the grounds that he was not a "free white person."

Thind persisted, applying again in Oregon the following May. He was again granted a certificate of citizenship over the objection of the same Immigration and Naturalization Service examiner who had opposed his citizenship in Seattle. The government filed suit seeking to once again annul the certificate on the ground that Thind was not a "white person"

Bhagat Singh Thind in uniform. Courtesy of David Thind.

and not lawfully entitled to naturalization. This time there was an additional complaint, that Thind was a member of an Indian nationalist group, the Ghadr Party, some of whose leaders advocated armed revolt and terrorism to oust the British from India. The word "Ghadr" itself implies violent uprising in Hindi.

There was no question that many Ghadrites, like the Irish Republican Army, were prepared to use any means available to fight the British. Some in the group were recruited by Germany during the war, armed, and sent to foment insurrection in India. The expedition was a disaster, resulting in nothing but long prison terms and executions. In the United States too, the Germans recruited militant Indian nationalists, most Punjabis like Thind, to plan attacks against the British. Called the Hindu–German Conspiracy, twenty-nine Ghadrites and Germans were convicted in San Francisco in 1918 and sent to prison for violating American neutrality laws. Thind, however, denied that he countenanced such behavior, and produced his army discharge papers to prove his commitment to the United States. The examiner was overruled and Thind was ruled eligible for citizenship.

The government sued, seeking to annul Thind's citizenship, once more solely on racial grounds. The trial took place in September 1920 in federal district court in Oregon before veteran judge Charles Wolverton. During the trial, government attorneys again raised the political issue. Thind freely admitted a past association with the Ghadr Party, his friendship with its founder, Har Dayal, whom he had met at Berkeley, and who had fled the United States for Berlin in 1914, and his commitment to an independent India, but denied that he would participate in or even tacitly support violent acts. Judge Wolverton was told that British Intelligence had keeping surveillance on Thind as a pro-German, anti-British conspirator, but had no proof beyond sharp rhetoric that Thind had or would participate in violent acts. Thind strongly denied the accusation, and insisted his willingness to serve in the military and fight against Germany if called on to do so further undercut the British Intelligence reports.

In his decision of March 28, 1921, Judge Wolverton did not give the intelligence reports much stock: "The testimony in the case tends to show that, since his entry into this country, the applicant's deportment has been that of a good citizen, attached to the Constitution of the United States." Of what Wolverton termed "his alleged connection with what is known as the Gadhr party," Wolverton wrote that Thind "stoutly denies that he was in any way connected with the alleged propaganda of the Gadhr Press to violate the neutrality laws of this country, or that he was in sympathy with such a course. He frankly admits, nevertheless, that he is an advocate of the principle of India for the Indians, and would like to see India rid of British rule, but not that he favors an armed revolution for the accomplishment of this purpose."[3]

But the judge added, "Were his allegiance to the laws and customs of this country dependent upon his protestations alone, I should not be inclined to give them credence. They are, however, strongly corroborated by disinterested citizens, who are most favorably impressed with his deportment, and manifestly believe in his attachment to the principles of this government . . . . I am impressed that his deportment here entitled him to become a citizen, unless it be that he is debarred from citizenship under the naturalization and immigration laws of Congress."

With political objections not germane, it was then necessary to determine if Bhagat Singh Thind was "white," for which Wolverton relied on precedent: "I am not disposed to discuss the question of first impression, whether a high class Hindu, coming from Punjab, is ethnologically a white person within the meaning of Section 2169 of the Revised Statutes as amended. I am content to rest my decision of the question upon a line of cases." Wolverton cited a number of examples, of which *Mozumdar*, oddly, was not included. He also excluded *Ellis*, where he had been the sitting judge. He concluded that although there were "decisions to the contrary . . . they are not in line with the greater weight of authority." Dismissing any application of the 1917 law or the Chinese Exclusion Act, Wolverton ruled, "It must be concluded that Bhagat Singh is entitled to naturalization."

The government appealed to the Ninth Circuit Court of Appeals, but that court, as it had in *Ozawa*, declined to rule and referred the case to the Supreme Court. Once again, the grounds for the appeal were racial—the government's brief contained no mention of the Ghadr Party.[4] Ethnology in the 1920s had remained an inexact science, if indeed it was a science at all, and both sides submitted dense briefs to the Court that were detailed, authoritative, and, though neither side would admit it, totally subjective.

Thind's brief sought to provide evidence that "high caste Hindus"—to differentiate them from the lower classes—had "Aryan" origins and therefore according to the law he was Caucasian and therefore "white." "It may be assumed," the brief read, "that the terms 'Caucasian' and 'white persons' are synonymous." That, Thind contended, was what Sutherland had ruled in Ozawa, except for those "borderline" cases, which should be interpreted as being the exception rather than the rule.[5] In addition, of course, as Sutherland had cited two cases of Hindus who had been justly ruled Caucasian, thus seemingly eliminating them from the borderline category. The brief, therefore, spent twenty pages demonstrating that Bhagat Singh Thind was Aryan/Caucasian, and further contended that the law should be interpreted in the way it was written and apply equally to everyone, not according to whim.

The government also stressed Justice Sutherland's qualification of the "Caucasian-means-white" rule with the notion of "borderline cases," of which, they contended, Thind was "ethnologically" an example. The brief admitted that there was "little ground for challenge" to Thind's Aryan origins or that Aryans likely were Caucasian, but "the decision in Ozawa did not establish a sharp line of demarcation but rather a more or less debatable ground, leaving individual cases to be determined as they arose."[6] In other words, according to the government, the Court had left itself free to make up the rules as it went along. The remainder of their argument went to intent, that in using the phrase "free white persons," the founders had intended to limit citizenship to those who looked and acted in a manner with which they felt comfortable and to exclude any race or ethnic group they believed could not "assimilate" into white, European-based American society. As damning as this construction might have been, it was also likely correct, but hardly the image the United States, even in 1923, wished to put forth to the world.

The only question, then, seemed to be whether the Court would be bound not only by precedent, but the precedent he had set just months earlier.

It was not.

The decision was handed down on February 19, 1923, George Sutherland once again speaking for a unanimous Court. He began by quoting his *Ozawa* opinion as to Congress's motive in drafting the 1790 law: "The intention was to confer the privilege of citizenship upon that class of persons whom the fathers knew as white, and to deny it to all who could not be so classified. It is not enough to say that the framers did not have in mind the brown or yellow races of Asia. It is necessary to go farther and be able to say that, had these particular races been suggested, the language of the act would have been so varied as to include them within its privileges."[7] Sutherland once again avoided noting that with nothing in congressional records to indicate motivation, *proving* intent was impossible. In *Ozawa*, he had dismissed a likely possibility that Congress meant "white" only to differentiate it from "black," and he did so again here. Postulating that had those who enacted the law thought about the Japanese, or Hindus, they would have specifically excluded them thus became a contrivance the Court could use to define whiteness as it so chose.

As such, Sutherland dismissed Thind's primary assertion while at the same time confirming it: "The conclusion that the phrase 'white persons' and the word 'Caucasian' are synonymous does not end the matter. It enabled us to dispose of the problem [Ozawa] as it was there presented, since the applicant for citizenship clearly fell outside the zone of debatable ground on the negative side." Then with a healthy dollop of disingenuousness, he added, "In the endeavor to ascertain the meaning of the statute, we must not fail to keep in mind that it does not employ the word 'Caucasian,' but the words 'white persons,' and these are words of common speech, and not of scientific origin."

Sutherland went on to expound on how the word "Caucasian" had lost the very scientific definition he had given it three months earlier: "'Caucasian' is a conventional word of much flexibility. . . . What we now hold is that the words 'free white persons' are words of common speech, to be interpreted in accordance with the understanding of the common man, synonymous with the word 'Caucasian' only as that word is popularly understood." Sutherland seemed to have forgotten the Court's own *Ozawa* precedent in which he cited a number of cases to demonstrate that, regardless of popular understanding, dark skin was itself not an bar to citizenship.

But not until three paragraphs from the end did Sutherland get to what the decision was actually about: "The children of English, French, German, Italian, Scandinavian, and other European parentage quickly merge into the mass of our population and lose the distinctive hallmarks of their European origin. On the other hand, it cannot be doubted that the children born in this country of Hindu parents would retain indefinitely the clear evidence of their ancestry." It was not sufficient, it seemed, for a United States citizen to *look* white—he or she was also required to *act* white.

There is the view that the two cases were consistent, that Sutherland used the "commonly understood" definition of "white" in both, but that dismisses the Court's racism too lightly. Distilling the verbiage, George Sutherland ruled that Takeo Ozawa could not become a United States citizen no matter how light his skin, because science said he was not white, and Bhagat Singh Thind could not become a United States citizen no matter what science said, because he did look white.

In addition, Sutherland's *Thind* opinion has recently come under scrutiny as a political rather than a wholly racial decision: "The paucity of arguments and evidence in the Court's opinion in *Thind*, combined with distortions of the arguments and evidence that are included in the opinion, suggest the conclusion reached by many Asian Indians that the decision was a political one influenced by British pressure to restrict the activities of Indian independence activists."[8]

But if the denial of Thind's naturalization was based even in part on his political activities, why go through the charade of pretending it was solely color-based and not mention political considerations at all? The Court could easily have disqualified him for citizenship on narrow political grounds, leaving the earlier decisions undisturbed, and thus avoided having to place one leg on science and the other on sensory input. In the end, any interpretation circles back to the same conclusion. Justice Sutherland and the Supreme Court used arbitrary and self-serving standards, be they scientific or political, to determine what they wanted the law to be.[9]

In another sad upshot, the *Thind* ruling voided the naturalization of A. K. Mozumdar and others of East Asian origin. Mozumdar unsuccessfully appealed the revocation of his citizenship but nonetheless remained in the United States until his death in 1953, having become a lecturer and spiritual leader, touting the power of positive thinking, popular with Hollywood celebrities.

Thind never gave up. In 1935, the United States enacted a law that overturned the naturalization ban for aliens who had served in the American military. Thind applied once more, and in March 1936, he returned to district court, this time in New York. For the third time, he was ruled eligible to become a U.S. citizen. By this time, he was "Dr. Thind," a well-known spiritual leader with followers across the country. With the law now objectively on his side, the government did not object.

In 1940, citizen Thind married Vivian Davies in a Presbyterian church in Toledo, Ohio. He would eventually lecture to more than 5 million people, working tirelessly up to the day of his death in 1967, leaving behind his widow and two sons.

14 | Turning the Soil

At the same time the citizenship cases were working their way through the legal system, challenges to the alien lands were proceeding.

Washington territory had created the model for anti-Asian land laws in 1886, when the legislature enacted a bill that prohibited landholding by aliens ineligible for citizenship. As was true of all anti-Asian laws, it was on its face race-neutral but, since the Chinese had been prohibited from becoming citizens after 1882, the target was clear. There had been a number of initiatives that same year, including one that would not allow aliens ineligible for citizenship to run laundries, but they failed because of the probability they would run afoul of the Fourteenth Amendment.[1] State officials began to worry that the 1886 law might not survive a court challenge and so, three years later, when Washington attained statehood, they replaced it with a constitutional provision that restricted the prohibition to aliens who had not legally declared their intention to become United States citizens. Technically, a Chinese could make such a declaration, but barred by the Exclusion Act, it would not be accepted.

As in California, in the years after 1900, as the Japanese population grew, they replaced the Chinese as the main target of anti-Asian bigotry. The Japanese population in Washington rose from 5,617 in 1900 to 12,929 in 1910, to more than 15,000 in 1920, which was a higher percentage per capita than in California. Although the number of Japanese farmers was relatively small, "the Japanese, through his skill and effort, had won an important place for himself in the agricultural market."[2]

Also as in California, however, the constitutional provision in Washington had sufficient loopholes to render it largely ineffective. Japanese farmers could either lease land from whites or purchase land through shell corporations owned on paper by white trustees, usually the purchaser's attorneys. To close the loopholes, Washington enacted an alien land law in 1921 modeled after the California law of 1920.

In order not to discourage desirable foreign nationals—Europeans—from investing in the state, the law did "not include lands containing valuable deposits of minerals, metals, iron, coal or fire clay or the necessary land for mills and machinery to be used in the development thereof and the manufacture of the products therefrom." But for all other land, leases to aliens were not permitted, nor shell corporations, nor land held in trust for Nisei by alien parents. Although the test was still "an alien who had not declared, in good faith, his intention of becoming a citizen," rather than simply "an alien ineligible for citizenship," with the *Ozawa* district court ruling still in force, Japanese were not eligible for citizenship and therefore could not apply in good faith. The Supreme Court decision in 1922 merely made that ineligibility permanent.

Violation of the provision prohibiting leasing land to aliens was punishable by forfeiture of the land and up to one year in jail. In July 1921, soon after the law was enacted, Frank Terrace and his wife, Elizabeth, along with N. Nakatsuka (no other name was given) brought suit to prevent Lindsay Thompson, Washington's attorney general, from enforcing that provision since Terrace wished to lease a part of his land to Nakatsuka. The suit was financed by the Northwest American Japanese Association and was brought in federal rather than state court, since the challenge was to be on Fourteenth Amendment grounds.

Judge Edward Cushman, who would hear the case, was an associate of congressman Albert Johnson, a former McClatchyesque newspaper publisher, outspoken anti-Semite, white supremacist, and sponsor of what would become the most restrictive immigration law in U.S. history. Cushman, to no one's surprise, refused to issue the injunction, and, in his opinion, dismissed constitutional questions out of hand as well as any conflict with the 1911 commercial treaty.

On July 25, 1921, only days after hearing the case, Cushman issued his opinion. He first denied Nakatsuka's eligibility: "Nakatsuka not being eligible to citizenship under the law as it now stands, even if such complainant had filed, or sought to file, a declaration of intention to become a citizen, he could not—considering the present uniformity in the decisions—fairly be said to have done so 'in good faith.'"[3] As to the conflicting with the treaty, Cushman, using California as a model, wrote, "The lasting impression created by the [treaty] language is that it was intended to withhold the right to own or lease agricultural lands."

In dismissing the Fourteenth Amendment challenge, Cushman resorted to the same circular logic that Washington had employed with the "good faith" test: "The United States might have excluded all of the subjects of Japan; but rather chose to admit them, withholding the right to lease agricultural lands, thereby recognizing the right of the state to prohibit it, or regulate it. That purpose is not to be defeated by allowing the citizen landowner the broad construction of his rights under the Fourteenth Amendment for which contention is made. The citizen landowner may sell to whom he pleases; but he may not sell to one who is rightfully forbidden the right to buy." He added, citing the Slaughterhouse Cases, "the primary purpose of which was the enfranchisement of the slaves," ignoring that the amendment read "persons" and not "citizen."

Terrace and Nakatsuta appealed to the Supreme Court, which heard the case in April 1923. They claimed a denial of due process and equal protection guarantees of the Fourteenth Amendment, and secondarily, that the Washington law interfered with treaty obligations: "The prohibition of the act is contrary to the due process clause of the Fourteenth Amendment, because it is, is effect, a prohibition of the right of an alien to engage in one of the common occupations of life. The applicability of the due process clause to the right of the citizen landowner is no less clear. The Terraces acquired this property prior to the passage of the act, at a time when it might lawfully be leased to a Japanese, but the act now prohibits this by severe penalties. Their right to use their property in a lawful way, and enjoy its fruits, has been proscribed."[4] For precedent, they used *Buchanan v. Warley*, a 1917 case in which a white homeowner had won the right to sell to a Black family in Louisville, Kentucky, despite a city ordinance prohibiting sales to Blacks in neighborhoods in which whites were a majority. The Fourteenth Amendment had been applied not to the denial of equal protection to the Black family, but rather to the denial of the right of the white seller to dispose of his property as he wished.

Washington's reply was that the case had nothing to do with equal protection of the laws, but rather the right of the state to protect its citizens from foreign infestation. "This course of legislation indicates a uniform popular view that the public welfare is directly affected by the alien ownership of realty. It is particularly noteworthy that the most drastic action in this regard has been taken by those States in which there are found large bodies of aliens who are not permitted by Congress to become naturalized. Presumably, this legislation is the result of experience and of a more intimate knowledge of local conditions than the Court can obtain by the exercise of its judicial knowledge."[5]

And the risk was manifest. "In the field of agriculture, the American and Oriental cannot compete. The possible result of such a condition would be that in the course of time, in certain sections of the country, at least, all lands might pass to these classes of aliens. The people of the

State would then be entirely dependent for their very existence upon alien races who recognize to the State or Nation no other obligations than those forcibly imposed."

On November 12, 1923, by a 6–0 vote, the Court agreed. Pierce Butler, writing for the majority, advanced, with false naïveté, the argument that the law had not targeted specific races: "Appellants' contention that the state act discriminates arbitrarily against Nakatsuka and other ineligible aliens because of their race and color is without foundation. All persons of whatever color or race who have not declared their intention in good faith to become citizens are prohibited from so owning agricultural lands. Two classes of aliens inevitably result from the naturalization laws—those who may and those who may not become citizens. The rule established by Congress on this subject, in and of itself, furnishes a reasonable basis for classification in a state law withholding from aliens the privilege of land ownership as defined in the act."[6]

As a result, "The Terraces, who are citizens, have no right safeguarded by the Fourteenth Amendment to lease their land to aliens lawfully forbidden to take or have such lease. The state act is not repugnant to the equal protection clause and does not contravene the Fourteenth Amendment."[7]

This argument of "facial neutrality" had first been used with great effect by southern whites to deny fundamental rights to Blacks, most significantly the right to vote. Two cases decided the same day, March 1, 1880, set the standard. In the first, *Strauder v. West Virginia*, the Court ruled that since West Virginia explicitly forbade Blacks from serving on juries, Taylor Strauder's murder conviction must be overturned on Fourteenth Amendment equal protection grounds. Immediately afterward, however, in *Virginia v. Rives*, the Court ruled that even though Blacks almost never managed to be chosen for jury pools, since no specific prohibition was written into Virginia law, the conviction of two Black brothers must be upheld. Southern states got the message: as long as they did not announce their decision to discriminate, even transparently discriminatory legislation would pass legal muster, as it has ever since.[8]

With the "facially neutral" Washington law so upheld, the Court turned its attention to California. The same day the Court issued the opinion in *Terrace v. Thompson*, it ruled in *Porterfield v. Webb* that a similar provision of the 1920 California law was neither in violation of the 1911 treaty nor the Fourteenth Amendment. That the California law was broader in that it made no distinction between ineligible aliens who voiced an intention to become citizens and those who had not was not a tangible distinction. Pierce Butler again the wrote the opinion and was joined by the same justices who had concurred in *Terrace.* He merely referred to the earlier case as controlling in this one.

On week later, November 19, 1923, the Court decided two more challenges to the California law. In *Webb v. O'Brien,* the justices, aligned exactly as in the previous cases, overturned a district court ruling that a sharecropping arrangement was not an employment contract, but rather gave the lessee, a Japanese man named Inouye, "a capable farmer," an interest in the land "substantially similar to that granted to a lessee."[9]

Under the terms of the contract, Inouye would keep half the crop, and was able to live on O'Brien's land and provide housing for anyone working for him. O'Brien had won in district court because cropping contracts had not been specifically included in the 1920 law. Ulysses Webb had immediately appealed, claiming that although Inouye had not attained a legal interest in the land, the cropping contract amounted to the same thing. This reasoning, asking the Court to rule on substance rather than language, was precisely what the justices had refused to consider in dismissing Fourteenth Amendment challenges.

The standards, however, were different when the Japanese were the beneficiaries of language. Butler wrote, "The term of the proposed contract, the measure of control and dominion over the land which is necessarily involved in the performance of such a contract, the cropper's right to have housing for himself and to have his employees live on the land, and his obligation to accept one-half the crops as his only return for tilling the land clearly distinguish the arrangement from one of mere employment."

The fourth case, *Frick v. Webb,* concerned the last of the contrivances that the Japanese employed to avoid alien land laws: establishing a corporation in which a Japanese alien would be a shareholder. The syllabus read, "Frick is the owner of 28 shares of the capital stock of the Merced Farm Company, a corporation organized under the laws of California, that owns 2,200 acres of farm land in that state. Frick desires to sell the shares to Satow, and Satow desires to buy them. By the complaint it is alleged in substance that the appellees have threatened to and will enforce the act against appellants if Frick sells such stock to Satow."[10] Once again, Pierce Butler writing for the same majority, concluded the state may "forbid indirect as well as direct ownership and control of agricultural land by ineligible aliens. The right 'to carry on trade' given by the [1911] treaty does not give the privilege to acquire the stock above described. To read the treaty to permit ineligible aliens to acquire such stock would be inconsistent with the intention and purpose of the parties. We hold that the provision of section 3 above referred to does not conflict with the Fourteenth Amendment or with the treaty."

The reaction among anti-Asians was predictable. Ulysses Webb called *Porterfield*, "most gratifying and a great victory for California." V. S. McClatchy added that the decision had been "confidently expected by those instrumental in promoting such legislation, as not only legal but fair to all parties interested and absolutely demanded as a national safeguard." He added that such groups as the American Legion, the American Federation of Labor, the Grange, and the Sons of the Golden West "urged the coming Congress to enact legislation excluding hereafter as immigrants or permanent residents all aliens ineligible to citizenship under our laws."[11]

Not everyone was as enamored with the Court's judgment. Preeminent Columbia University law professor Thomas Reed Powell, writing shortly after the decisions were handed down, published a detailed analysis of the cases without racial overtones or commentary.[12] Even strictly as jurisprudence, Butler's reasoning did not hold up. Of particular note were the Washington and California laws' focus on agriculture, as if farming represented an especially onerous threat to the American way of life:

> An increase in the number of Japanese farmers does not disfranchise the citizens whom they displace. . . . These judicial affirmations of the "obvious" need to be supplemented by some demonstration or assertion that ineligible aliens and nondeclarant eligibles are more of a menace on the land than in the factory, shop and kitchen. Such assertion appears a little later when Mr. Justice Butler observes that "the quality and allegiance of those who own, occupy and use the farm lands within its border are matters of highest importance and affect the safety and power of the state itself." Again we are not told why. One sees readily that allegiance has a close relation to matters within the scope of national authority, but its peculiar relation to fruit raising is less evident.[13]

Powell added, "The state is a community as well as a political entity, and interest in and work for the welfare of the community are not precluded by exclusion from political power as they are not ensured by possession of political power. Foreign allegiance is a bird of different feather, but foreign allegiance is not California's line of demarcation. Moreover, it is hard to see how from any distinctly state point of view foreign allegiance is of more significance on the farm than in the mine or factory."[14]

Finally, Powell found the Court's acceptance of California's and Washington's assertion that aliens ineligible for citizenship are somehow more dangerous than aliens who are: "If Mr. Justice Butler is justified in saying that "reasons supporting discrimination against aliens who may but who will not naturalize are obvious," he sets something of a task for himself when he comes to the discrimination against those who cannot become citizens in favor of those who can but do not choose to do so. His monition on the menace of those who have not renounced allegiance to a foreign power makes it hard to justify the favor extended by California to those whose recusance is voluntary."

Whatever the legal merit of Justice Butler's arguments, their political value to the anti-Asian movement was incalculable. The four decisions taken together crushed any chance for Japanese farmers to carve out a place for themselves in Western economies, and thereby perhaps erode some of the blind prejudice directed toward them because they were too good at what they did. Japanese-owned lands shrunk from 74,769 acres in 1920 to 41,898 acres in 1925, a decline of 44 percent; leased lands decreased from 192,150 to 76,397 acres, a decline of 60 percent.[15]

The effect, therefore, was as great as that of the Ozawa decision, and although James Phelan had lost, "Keep California White" seems to have won.

15 | Slamming the Door

V. S. McClatchy's entreaty to Congress for direct action on exclusion had not fallen on deaf ears. Led by Washington Republican Albert Johnson, the nation would move to virtually close the valve on immigration for a better part of the world's population.

The literacy test in the 1917 law had not been as effective as planned in barring "undesirables," especially those from southern and eastern Europe, so nativists and their eugenicist allies had moved to find a more effective means to bar offending races and ethnic groups. In 1921, the United States had for the first time established immigration quotas based on nationality. The law, called the Emergency Quota Act, was a reaction to swarms of refugees fleeing the widespread destruction and economic collapse that war had caused across Europe, and cataclysms such as the Russian Revolution and the Armenian genocide. The new wave of immigrants skewed sharply to southern and eastern Europe, which eugenicists decried as polluting the country's Nordic ideal. Another result was a vast increase in the supply of labor at the very moment that the U.S. economy was winding down from a wartime footing, certain to arouse opposition by organized labor: "A devastated Europe was portrayed as a region filled with potential immigrants who would take any work in America, potentially depressing wages and taking jobs from Anglo-Saxons."[1]

The 1921 law, sponsored in the House of Representatives by Johnson, who was at one point elected the honorary president of the Eugenics Research Association, capped the number of immigrants admitted yearly from any nation at 3 percent of the number of residents already living in the United States from that nation as of the 1910 census. Both the numerical limits and the quota system for establishing those limits were new to immigration law. Johnson and his allies wanted more, but "a coalition of powerful industrial leaders and steamship owners lobbied well enough to prevent the 1921 law from being even more restrictive."[2] The formula, as it was meant to, favored countries in northern Europe, Great Britain, and Scandinavia, whose history of immigration to the United States was longer and their numbers consequently greater. Professionals and other highly trained immigrants were exempted from the quota.

As with other discriminatory legislation, enforcement of the 1921 law did not always go smoothly. The biggest problem was figuring out just who should be admitted when they landed in the United States, usually in New York City. Immigrants pouring out of steamships had not been precleared at their ports of embarkation, so the officials at the ports of entry were forced to try to keep quota statistics on a running count. When a country's quota was exceeded, anyone else trying to gain entry was deported, which sometimes resulted in families being split.

In addition, although the law was marginally successful in weeding out "undesirables," nativists came to realize that immigration from southern and eastern Europe had so vastly increased since 1890 that 3 percent of the 1910 population was unacceptably high. And so once more Albert Johnson, this time joined by another Republican, Pennsylvania senator David Reed, introduced legislation to solve the embarkation problem, lower the rate to 2 percent, and move the operative census back to 1890.

The new law would be both more restrictive and more rigorous. It would also make enforcement a good deal easier. As the *Columbia Law Review* noted in 1925, "Perhaps the greatest reform achieved by the Act is the shifting of control of quotas from domestic ports to our consular offices abroad. . . . A consular officer may issue an immigration visa to an 'eligible' applicant upon his compliance with certain formalities. However, the number of visas which may be issued annually in any country is limited to the annual quota for that nationality. Furthermore, no more than ten percent of the annual allowance of visas is to be issued in any calendar month. Thus, no eligible immigrant is permitted to leave his home country unless certain of entry on arrival in the United States."[3]

There were other refinements that were "expected to give effect to the policy of limitation adopted by Congress, without the friction and inhumanity which characterized its predecessor."[4] Excepted from the quota were unmarried children under eighteen years of age, the wife of a resident citizen, previously admitted immigrants returning from temporary visits abroad, or those born in Canada or an independent Latin American republic, with their wives and unmarried children under eighteen years of age. Ministers of any religious denomination, college professors, and those over the age of fifteen coming to the United States for their schooling were also exempt from the quota. Within the quota, preference would be given to mothers, fathers, wives, and children of American citizens and farmers. There was, of course, the usual laundry list of those who could not enter the United States under any circumstances, expanded from the usual mental, physical, and moral deficiencies to include a wide range of political undesirables.

Once again, organized labor, spearheaded by an immigrant, Samuel Gompers, head of the American Federation of Labor (AFL), had lent crucial support to the bill as a vehicle for restricting cheap labor. Gompers tried to portray those who favored an intentionally unfair quota system as victims. "The report of the [AFL's] legislative committee," newspaper reports read, "declares that the Johnson immigration bill, providing for a two per cent quota and the admission of families of foreign-born citizens, is being 'maliciously attacked in foreign countries, by their nationals in the United States' and by 'unfair and greedy corporations.'"[5]

Although Congress was for the most part casting their gaze across the Atlantic, V. S. McClatchy, James Phelan, and Ulysses Webb went to Washington, DC, to make certain the nation's legislature turned to face the Pacific as well. McClatchy buttonholed senators and congressmen, accusing the Japanese of violating the Gentlemen's Agreement by continuing to send "picture brides" across the Pacific. He insisted the Japanese could not assimilate, had an "astronomical birth rate," and with their growing landownership were "as menaces to California's Anglo-Saxon civilization." "They come here specifically and professedly for the purpose of colonizing and establishing here permanently the proud Yamato race," McClatchy warned. "He singled out the Japanese among other races ineligible to citizenship, as a population who 'naturally make more dangerous competitors in an economic way.'"[6] McClatchy and his followers would also have preferred the law provide for a means to evict Japanese noncitizens already in the United States, but the legal problems were seen to be insurmountable.

McClatchy, Phelan, and Webb were given a warm welcome by nativist congressmen, who included an "aliens ineligible for citizenship" exclusion in the bill. Amid furious protests by Japanese diplomats, however, President Calvin Coolidge, who had taken the office when Warren Harding died in August 1923, had announced his opposition to Japanese exclusion. He feared both for the safety of American missionaries in Japan and militancy of the Japanese.

McClatchy, bearing letters of support from the AFL, the Native Sons, the American Legion, and the Grange, retorted, "Immigration is a domestic question which this government should regulate without sugges-

On the Issue of Americanism There Can Be No Compromise

The Seattle Star

7TH LATE EDITION

Weather

VOLUME 22. SEATTLE, WASH., TUESDAY, MAY 18, 1920. TWO CENTS IN SEATTLE

HUSBAND SHOT THRU HEART

CALL MATTHEWS PRO-JAP

AS IT SEEMS TO ME

DANA SLEETH

"SUICIDE" IS WIFE'S VERSION TO POLICE

Climbs Over Porch and Crawls Into Her Room Thru Window

Hoarding of Wealth Probe Is Proposed!

WASHINGTON, May 18.—A resolution to investigate the relation between high prices of necessaries and concentration of wealth was introduced in the senate today by Senator David I. Walsh, of Massachusetts. The investigation, under the resolution, would be made by a committee of five senators, and the president would be requested to give the committee access to income tax returns of corporations.

1,000 FAMILIES ARE HOMELESS

Missouri River Sweeps Over

TACOMAN KILLED BY HIS STEPSON

Phil B. Friedman Slain Dur-

VETERANS HERE SEND PROTESTS TO WILSON

Fear Pastor in Capital May Influence President for Brown Men

Dr. Mark A. Matthews, pastor of First Presbyterian church, and personal friend of President Wilson, is denounced as pro-Jap in resolutions passed by Theodore Roosevelt Post, Veterans of Foreign Wars, here last night.

Good News:

Women Take Credit

Frisco Clothes Cheaper.

WORKERS DEMAND DEATH OF BIGAMIST

Murderer of Wives Is Now Locked Up in San Quentin Prison for Life

PORT COSTA, Cal., May 18.—Demanding that "Bluebeard" Watson be surrendered to them, and declaring they would lynch him, 60 stevedores crowded the station here when the train bringing the famous prisoner arrived from Los Angeles early today.

The prisoner was locked in a compartment on the train.

Slayer Assigned for Labor in Jute Mill

A McClatchy newspaper headline attacking anyone who sympathized with the Japanese.

tion or interference from any foreign nation." McClatchy "quoted the state board of health as saying that if existing conditions continue, ultimately the Japanese will exceed whites in California."[7] This, of course, was total balderdash. The Japanese represented such a tiny percentage of the population of California that even if the birth rates were as McClatchy suggested—which they were not—it would have taken several centuries for them to overtake whites. Including Japanese in the quota system, McClatchy told the congressmen, would be insufficient "because it would be an abandonment of the principle of exclusion of aliens ineligible for citizenship and a discrimination in favor of the Japanese."[8]

The House was sympathetic with the Californians and overwhelmingly passed a bill that replaced the Gentlemen's Agreement with total exclusion. An amendment to maintain the Gentlemen's Agreement was defeated in the Senate 76–2.[9] The senators, who debated the amendment behind closed doors, claimed to have rejected the amendment because the protests by the Japanese ambassador, Masanao Hanihara, amounted to a threat of retaliation and they would not be bullied. Two days later, the Senate affirmed exclusion 71–4. From there, the draft bill went to a conference committee to hammer out the details.

As the final version was being drafted, Senator Reed expounded on what was to be the great achievement of eliminating what he called the "hyphen vote": "With the new system in force, we will hand down the America of today for future generations with a citizenship unchanged in personal characteristics. The immigration of the last three decades was changing our national characteristics. . . . The proposed new law will enable us to take our make-up as it is and continue it unchanged from new racial influences. . . . It is my belief that if immigration is sharply restricted for fifty years, we will have developed a distinct American type."[10]

Coolidge did his best to have Japanese exclusion eliminated from the final bill, which was certain to sail through Congress, even summoning Senator Reed to the White House to urge moderation. When that failed, Coolidge proposed extending implementation until 1925. He again stressed the appeals from Christian groups not to put their missionaries at risk by antagonizing the Japanese. Senators from both parties denounced the proposed extension, charging that "subterfuge had been employed to upset the expressed decision of Congress and that this was a move toward the surrender of the nation's right to deal with a 'strictly domestic' question."[11]

Coolidge was defended on the floor of the Senate by, of all people, Senator Reed, who said, "It is a matter of lively concern to the Christians of the United States that they carry the cause of Christianity to other lands," and that they "are concerned at the rough-shod way in which Congress has acted." Reed added, "I take the blame for what I have done because I was partly responsible. I offered the amendment favoring the exclusion." Although Reed said he would do it again, he was willing to stand by the president and put off implementation until the following year.[12]

In a surprise move, the conference committee did just that, extending the date of implementation from July 1924 to March 1925. The impact would be small. Even Albert Johnson in the House agreed that the delay would result in fewer than one hundred additional Japanese immigrants entering the United States. But the western states were furious. They wanted exclusion without delay. They assailed Coolidge for usurping congressional authority and demanded that the original date be reinstated. Both houses agreed and voted overwhelmingly to restore the July date. The bill, with the exclusion provision intact, passed both houses on May 15, 1924: in the House 323–71 and in the Senate 69–9.

From there, Coolidge had little choice but to sign the bill into law. He would be running for his own full term in the November elections, and antagonizing the western states with the empty gesture of a veto might well cost him the election. And so, on May 24, 1924, Coolidge signed the Johnson–Reed Act, marking the high point for eugenics-based race prejudice in the United States. After decades of lobbying, with African Americans living under Jim Crow rule in the South and herded into ghettos in the North, white supremacists achieved their most coveted goal, and the Japanese joined the Chinese as the only ethnic groups specifically named as unfit to enter the United States.

16 | Banzai and Baseball

The Johnson–Reed Act had the desired effect in choking off new Japanese immigration. From 8,801 in 1924, the number of Japanese entering the country fell to 723 in 1925, and would not exceed 1,000 in any year until after the end of World War II.[1] Still, largely as a result of Nisei children, the population of Japanese in the United States had almost doubled since 1910. It would eventually top out in 1930 at almost 140,000, half of which were Nisei.[2] In addition, the first generation of American-born Japanese were getting older, a good number already their teens, and like current DACA children, identified solely as Americans.

Still, although they were "were more likely to speak English than Japanese, more likely to practice Christianity than Buddhism, and more likely to prefer 'American' food, sports, music, and social mores than those of Japanese tradition," Nisei children also lived in homes where "the traditional Japanese world [was] maintained." Despite the tradition of total respect for ones elders, Nisei "overwhelmingly identified themselves as Japanese Americans, not as Japanese in America."[3] They would eventually attend American universities and aspire, as did every other immigrant group, to use their parents' work in the fields and factories as a springboard to a better life.

In 1929, a group of Nisei college graduates in California and Washington State founded the Japanese American Citizens League "in an effort to unify the Nisei and to help the second generation assimilate to white ideology." Some of the group's founders had been forced to attend segregated schools as children and were convinced that only "the complete immersion of Japanese Americans into the white community" would allow Nisei "to rise above any misconceptions or suspicions that white Americans may have had."[4] They promoted Nisei as a "cultural bridge between East and West," all the while encouraging native-born Japanese Americans to dress like Americans, eat like Americans, sing and dance like Americans, and even pray like Americans. In order to set an example, to be model Americans, "American citizens of Japanese ancestry," some advocated Nisei renouncing dual citizenship to "American only."

But as the American dream grew among the Nisei, race hatred by whites grew right along with it. They were convinced that the Japanese living in the United States, even those native-born, held a primary allegiance to Japan and constituted a threat not just to workers in the United States, but also to the nation's security.

The situation was complicated by enormous political and social changes in Japan itself. The 1920s and 1930s were decades of turmoil and change in Japan, both of which would cast shadows over both Asia and a broad span of the Pacific.

Emperor Meiji had died in 1912, and was succeeded by his son Yoshihito, called Emperor Taisho. From the early days of his reign, however, Taisho was in poor health, and in 1921 his son, Hirohito, was appointed prince regent. He inherited a nation beset by problems, including financial stagnation that was causing growing discontent: "The Japanese economy of the 1920s suffered from a retrenchment after the boom of World War I. For most of the decade, the real economy remained dull, with low economic growth, mild deflation, and an unsettled financial system."[5] Economic stagnation was exacerbated by two stock market crashes, bankers who made a spate of bad loans, and a population that was becoming a good more urban, literate, and middle class and therefore more dependent on sound financial decisions in the government and the private sector. A growing labor movement and increased political activity among the nation's vast population of tenant farmers applied continuous pressure on the government to provide solutions.

Although the Meiji constitution had created a bicameral legislature, the Diet, in 1889, neither house represented the vast majority of Japanese. The upper house was appointed and the voting for the lower house was restricted to male property owners who had paid a certain minimum in taxes. Although election to the lower house became somewhat more democratic during World War I, a restive population considered the expansion unacceptably puny. In the years following the war, a coalition of reformers, labor activists, intellectuals, and tenant farmers forced the government to adopt universal manhood suffrage in 1925, to take effect in 1928. Taisho died in 1926, but Hirohito, to be called Emperor Showa, would not be officially installed for two years, coinciding with the opening of the vote. Left-wing parties celebrated universal suffrage, but conservatives and militarists focused on the coronation of the new emperor as a continuation of tradition.

Although in theory expansion of the vote gave liberal and progressive political groups the opportunity for an increased voice in the nation's affairs, the left never coalesced around a single group or program, but rather remained splintered and fractious, thus making it a good deal easier for conservatives and traditionalists to remain in power. Conservatives took particular aim at Japan's recently formed Communist Party, whose platform demanded an end to tenant farming, abolition of the monarchy, recognition of the Soviet Union, and withdrawal of Japanese troops from the Asian mainland. When conservatives initiated mass arrests of avowed communists in 1923, Daisuke Nanba, a radical student from a prominent family, launched a failed assassination attempt on Hirohito. Nanba was executed shortly thereafter, shouting, "Long live the Japanese Communist Party," which did little to further the cause of the Japanese left.

In response, in 1925, the Diet passed the first "Peace Preservation Law," which was aimed specifically at the Communists, but whose sweep would take in members of a number of left-wing parties. The law stipulated, "Anyone who organizes a group for the purpose of changing the national polity or of denying the private property system, or anyone who knowingly participates in said group, shall be sentenced to penal servitude or imprisonment not exceeding ten years. An offense not actually carried out shall also be subject to punishment."[6] In 1928, in the wake of mass arrests of communists, the penalty for violating the law was raised from ten years in prison to death.

The formal installation of Hirohito, also in 1928, launched a new thrust to traditionalism and extreme nationalism by the right wing. They favored a "Showa Restoration," which "glorified the emperor and traditional Japanese virtues to the exclusion of Western influences, which were perceived as greedy, individualistic, bourgeois, and assertive. The ideals of the Japanese family-state and self-sacrifice in service of the nation were given a missionary interpretation and were thought by their ultranationalist proponents to be applicable to the modern world."[7]

As the government of Japan lurched about, the military began to increasingly encroach on civilian rule. Militarism was merely an extension of nationalism, which in turn were natural extensions of the samurai culture that had never lost influence on both domestic and foreign policy after the Meiji Restoration. Victory over Russia, the successful annexation of Korea, being on the winning side in World War I, and a strong military, commercial, and diplomatic presence in China further emboldened the nationalists, even during periods of economic distress.

Japan saw itself as a world power, and national pride demanded that other nations treat it as one.

At the 1919 Versailles peace conference, although more than two dozen nations attended, Japan had been seated along with the "four powers," the United States, Great Britain, France, and Italy. Its delegation arrived with two key goals. It wanted recognition of title over the German colonial possessions in China that Japan had occupied during the fighting. In addition, perhaps more importantly, Japan demanded recognition as an equal with the nations sitting with them at the conference table. Crucial to this demand was "racial equality," which Japan formally requested be included in the charter of the proposed League of Nations.

The proposal stated, "The equality of nations being a basic principle of the League of Nations, the High Contracting Parties agree to accord as soon as possible to all alien nationals of states, members of the League, equal and just treatment in every respect making no distinction, either in law or in fact, on account of their race or nationality."[8] Although a majority of the nations present favored the proposal, some nations with racial issues of their own, such as Australia, objected. As a means to kill the request, and at the risk of infuriating Japan, Woodrow Wilson persuaded the other attendees that a unanimous voted was required. Japan did not get its equality clause, and Wilson drove a rift into American–Japanese relations that would only deepen over time.

Japan fared only slightly better in 1921, when the world's great naval powers attended a nine-nation conference aimed on limiting the arms race and the clash of imperial ambitions in the Pacific. Three treaties eventually resulted from this conference, the first and most important limiting warship tonnage of the world's five largest navies. The United States and Britain were allowed 500,000 tons each, Japan 300,000 tons, and France and Italy each 175,000 tons. The United States and Great Britain argued that they needed larger tonnage ceilings because they were forced to maintain a presence in both the Atlantic and the Pacific. Japan grudgingly agreed because, in the throes of near depression, it could not afford to undertake a significant expansion. Still, militarists in Japan took the lower number allowed to them as a slight. As a further strain on relations, Japanese nationalists viewed the tightening, and eventually the elimination, of immigration to the United States on racial grounds as an unforgivable insult.

Subsequent treaties added certain specifications to close some loopholes in the first treaty and reasserted an open-door policy in post-revolutionary China, which was in good part to deter Japanese ambitions on the mainland. From the United States perspective, these agreements were a success. As noted by the Department of State, "Together, the treaties signed at the Washington Conference served to uphold the status quo in the Pacific: they recognized existing interests and did not make fundamental changes to them. At the same time, the United States secured agreements that reinforced its existing policy in the Pacific, including the Open Door in China and the protection of the Philippines, while limiting the scope of Japanese imperial expansion as much as possible."[9]

"As much as possible" would turn out to be "not nearly enough." In 1931, to gain access to the iron and coal it lacked at home, Japan ignored the Kellogg–Briand Pact, which outlawed war, it had signed three years earlier and overran the Chinese province of Manchuria in a matter of days, installing a puppet government.[10] In two days, the Japanese army had occupied the Manchurian capital, Mukden, and taken control of the railway lines that might be used to bring Chinese reinforcements to its overmatched garrison. Japan claimed that an explosion at a railroad siding owned by the Japanese had been set by Chinese nationalists and that it was merely acting in self-defense. Chinese authorities insisted the explosion had been set off by the Japanese themselves and that the takeover had been planned for months. Japan issued angry denials, but the Chinese version was most likely true.[11]

The Chinese had not been blameless. The previous July, a Japanese army officer Shintaro Nakamura had been arrested on spying charges while making maps in Manchuria, which the local Chinese general claimed were to be used during a Japanese invasion. Nakamura, who claimed to have had Chinese permission to survey the area, and three traveling companions were executed by a firing squad the following day.[12] Whether the spying charges were true or not, that the Japanese were increasing their presence in Manchuria at the expense of Chinese sovereignty was unquestioned.

Although Western powers attempted to diffuse the Manchurian situation, both with direct diplomacy and through the League of Nations, the Japanese continued to do precisely what they pleased. When the situation stabilized, any remaining doubt that Japan was a world military power with extreme imperialist ambitions had been dispelled. For white supremacists on the West Coast, who remained convinced that Japanese immigrants and their Nisei children were potential or actual agents of the Japanese government, fear of a fifth column preparing for an invasion of the United States became rampant.

To the consternation of racial purists on both sides of the Pacific, however, some prominent cultural groups in Japan and the United States were growing closer, with mutual fascination, and one of the primary vehicles was what was fast becoming the Japanese national game—baseball.

Although American baseball players had visited Japan in the 1880s and 1890s, the first genuine tour came in 1910, when the team from the University of Chicago visited Waseda University in Tokyo. One of the American organizers was famed football coach Amos Alonzo Stagg. The visit was an enormous success—the Waseda team copied Chicago's maroon and white uniforms—culturally and on the field. One Japanese newspaper headlined, "Chicago Wins First International Game; Midway Team Defeats Waseda in Opening Match; Friendly and Clean Contest; Superior Batting of the American Players Spells Downfall for the Local Boys."[13]

Chicago sent another team in 1915, by which time almost every Japanese university was fielding a team, and then again in 1920 and 1925, when baseball had grown into a national rage. In 1931, just months after Japan had evoked worldwide condemnation by attacking Manchuria, a group of wealthy Japanese businessmen who had been organizing an eight-team professional league invited a team of major leaguers featuring future Hall of Famers Lou Gehrig, Al Simmons, Lefty Grove, and Mickey Cochrane to barnstorm against Japanese teams.

Small major league tours had taken place in the 1920s, but the 1931 tour attracted enormous attention both among the Japanese public and government officials. Foreign Minister Count Yasuya Uchida, and the vice minister of foreign affairs, Mamoru Shigemitsu, two architects of the Manchuria incursion, hosted the American organizers, Herb Hunter and Lefty O'Doul, at dinners, and government officials would court the American visitors in the hopes of furthering good relations with the United States government.

The only thing missing from the 1931 tour was Babe Ruth, the most famous baseball player in the world, as much of an idol in Japan as he was in the United States. That would be remedied three years later when an even more prestigious team, replete with future Hall of Famers, headlined by the Bambino, docked in Tokyo on November 1. Also on the team was a backup catcher named Moe Berg. Berg, a graduate of Princeton and Columbia Law School, became well known after World War II for having been a spy with the OSS. He took many photographs while in Japan, some of which may or may not have been used to plan bombing raids during the war.

The 1934 tour had been sponsored by John Shibe, owner of the Philadelphia A's and Matsutaro Shoriki, owner of the *Yomiuri Shinbum*, Japan's most popular newspaper. After the team's arrival, upward of 500,000 people lined the streets to welcome the Americans to Tokyo. "When we walked off the train at the Tokyo station," recalled New York Yankee Hall of Fame pitcher Lefty Gomez, "the Japanese spectators awaiting Babe's arrival rushed forward almost crushing him. Babe had to push his way through the crowds as they were running by, tearing at his clothes for souvenirs. The fans were desperate to have a memento of something that Babe was wearing. They pulled at his jacket, his pants, his hat, and the crowds and their passion about Babe never let up for one second wherever he went."[14]

From a baseball standpoint, there was little suspense. Although the Americans were playing the "All-Nippon team," the Japanese lost all eighteen games on the schedule by a combined score of 189–39. Still, on November 20, a seventeen-year-old pitcher named Eiji Sawamura lost 1–0, the only run scoring on a Gehrig seventh-inning home run. Sawamura struck out nine, including Ruth, Gehrig, Charlie Gehringer, and Jimmy Foxx.[15]

The Americans were treated like visiting royalty. Joe Cascarella, one of the pitchers, recalled, "Emperor Hirohito was the 'Son of Heaven,' a god, and mere mortals like us were not supposed to cast an eye on him. Most Japanese had never heard or seen him. And yet, here are the ballplayers and their wives in his presence in a magnificent reception hall, exchanging pleasantries through an interpreter. Protocol demanded that we be respectful and stand facing the Emperor and there was a lot of bowing. Suddenly, we heard Moe Berg conversing with Hirohito in Japanese, and the Emperor was hanging on his every word. I don't know what Moe said, but the Emperor's face broke into a smile."[16]

When the major leaguers left Japan, they did so as national idols, at least to large numbers of ordinary Japanese. But not everyone was pleased that the Americans were so beloved. Less than two months after the team departed, a young ultranationalist army officer leapt from the shadows and attempted to behead Shoriki with a sword as he was leaving his home. But Shoriki, although almost fifty years old, was also one of Japan's foremost judo masters. He moved quickly enough to take only a glancing blow. He spent fifty days in the hospital but recovered and lived until 1969.

The following year, baseball diplomacy saw a bigger milestone when, at Lefty O'Doul's invitation, a team of "all stars" from Japan's first professional baseball team toured the United States and competed against minor league clubs from California to Ohio. Americans, who had read accounts of the 1934 tour, could not wait to see if players from across the Pacific could hold their own in the American "national game." Although the Japanese did not win any games, they showed surprising skill, "deftly turning double plays and bowing to umpires in small cities like Pocatello, Idaho, and Madison, Wisconsin. Writers and diplomats alike spoke of shared values [and] raised profound questions about the nature of Japanese people and society."[17]

For Japanese Americans, both trends bore on their treatment through the 1930s. Many, particularly those away from the West Coast, who still thought of the Chinese as a "foreign" race were forced to admit that the Japanese in the United States might be different. They worked hard at being "American," always trying to integrate themselves into the wider—and whiter—population without forcing themselves on those who thought them pariahs. But 70 percent of Japanese Americans lived in California, and even among their supporters there lurked a suspicion that some, perhaps even many, in the Japanese community harbored a secret loyalty to Japan that would present a grave risk to American national security if war ever came.

In July 1937, that prospect became a good deal more likely. Once again claiming to be acting in self-defense, Japanese troops attacked Chinese forces in northern China. There was bloody fighting near Beijing (then called Peiping), and Chinese leader Chiang Kai-Shek ordered 50,000 troops to prevent the region from suffering the same fate as Manchuria six years earlier. The Japanese were soon sending 10,000 soldiers a day through the Great Wall to attack Beijing, while Chiang, in the capital, Nanking, had to decide whether to try to protect the city from encirclement and annihilation.

Although the Chinese communists called a temporary truce with Chiang's forces, the Japanese proved themselves superior in both commitment and training, and within weeks had overwhelmed the Chinese and pushed south, occupying more and more of China's east coast. The anti-Japanese press, aware that mistreatment of the Chinese would not arouse American indignation, took every opportunity to put an American slant on the events. On July 21, for example, the *Examiner* reported that two American women, one the daughter of a naval officer, had been "kicked and beaten" by Japanese soldiers.[18]

In December, however, it became no longer necessary to contrive sensationalism. When the Japanese army reached Nanking, it resulted in "one of the most tragic military debacles in the history of modern warfare. In attempting to defend Nanking, the Chinese allowed themselves to be surrounded and systematically slaughtered."[19] But it was civilians in Nanking who became the victims of unspeakable atrocities. As many as a quarter million were butchered and thousands of women raped, many mutilated afterward. Looting stripped the city bare of food, medicine, and the personal possessions of the hapless occupants, including many refugees who had arrived with almost nothing. Although reporters were warned not pass along details of the carnage, some word got out.

"The mass executions of war prisoners added to the horrors the Japanese brought to Nanking," the *New York Times* reported. "After killing the Chinese soldiers who threw down their arms and surrendered, the Japanese combed the city for men in civilian garb who were suspected of being soldiers. In one building in the refugee zone, 400 men were seized. They were marched off, tied in batches of fifty, between lines of riflemen and machine gunners, to the execution ground . . . Nanking's streets were littered with the dead. Sometimes bodies had to be moved before automobiles could pass."

The barbarism of the Japanese military eventually received wide coverage in the American press, but on the West Coast much of the attention was initially focused on the sinking by Japanese bombers of a gunboat, the USS *Panay*, which was ferrying American evacuees out of Nanking in the days before the Japanese invasion, and attacks on three Standard Oil tankers in the same convoy. Initial reports had sixty-two dead or missing on what the *Examiner* proclaimed was "a mission of mercy."[20] There were many more wounded, including the *Panay*'s captain, who suffered a broken femur.

Japanese authorities immediately issued an apology, claiming the pilots had not seen American markings on the *Panay*, thinking the ship Chinese, although large United States flags were plainly visible on both the gunboat and its lifeboats, which were filmed by a Movietone newsreel cameraman who was one of the *Panay*'s passengers. Lifeboats ferried the survivors and the wounded to shore, where they were forced to trek overland to get help. An Italian journalist died on the way.

Over the next days, the crisis escalated, with Japan offering reparations and President Roosevelt demanding an official apology and a statement of regret from the emperor. After revelations that the Japanese airplanes had strafed the *Panay* before dropping its bombs, and then shot at the lifeboats trying to reach the shore, the head of the Japanese naval air forces was dismissed from his post.

The incident then became steeped in confusion. The Japanese backtracked and denied machine-gunning the boat either before it was hit by bombs or as it was sinking, but the newsreel footage showed bullet holes. The possible death toll was revised upward and then reduced. The apology from Hirohito was never forthcoming—an admiral was assigned the task—nor did the Japanese ever admit firing on survivors, even though many witnesses insisted they had. Finally, the following April, the Japanese government paid $2 million in reparations and the incident was closed.

Inevitably, the behavior of the Japanese military and government officials was seized on by anti-Japanese forces in the West. On December 17, the same day the Japanese military began its campaign of terror in Nanking, the Labor Council in San Francisco demanded a total boycott of Japanese-made goods and Japanese-owned businesses in the city.

The ruthlessness of Japanese expansionism was seen as a crisis in Washington, DC, especially since Japan seemed focused on sea power: "In 1934, Japan renounced its obligations under the Washington Naval Treaty to limit the size of its navy. By 1940, the Japanese fleet had grown to 375 ships, with an emphasis on aircraft carriers." As a result, American military and political officials could not help but be cognizant that Japanese ambitions might threaten Hawaii and even the West Coast. Avoiding a military buildup in the 1930s, Congress and President Roosevelt made certain that the navy would be prepared to meet the Japanese threat: "By 1940, the United States had a fleet of 478 naval combatants, including fifteen battleships and six air-craft carriers. In addition, in the 1930s, the United States forward deployed much of its Pacific fleet from California to Hawaii to dissuade Japan from further expansion. Japanese officials interpreted the growth and shift of U.S. sea power as a threat to its own sea control, trade, national well-being, and strategy."[21] It was, ironically, this redeployment to Hawaii, although

Pearl Harbor was thought to be "impregnable," that made the fleet vulnerable to attack.

Once more, even though there was no evidence that the Japanese men and women who had immigrated to the United States and struggled to make better lives for themselves and the their children were any less loyal to their adopted country than immigrants from Great Britain or France or Sweden or even Germany, racial stereotypes made them vulnerable to government repression in a way that European immigrants were not: "As U.S.–Japan relations worsened in the early 1930s, the American government became increasingly suspicious of its large concentration of Japanese residents. Most Japanese, whether immigrants or native born, were regarded as potentially subversive; and by 1932, the entire community was under surveillance by the intelligence agencies."[22]

Fear of Japanese intelligence-gathering turned out to be justified, but the source would turn out to be far different than white supremacists on the West Coast were convinced it would be.

17 | Loyalty

From early in the 1930s, with President Roosevelt's approval, the FBI and the Office of Naval Intelligence (ONI) began to formulate lists of potential Japanese agents living in the western United States. Those efforts increased as Japanese aggression in Asia did, and were ramped up still further after the sinking of the *Panay* and the massacre in Nanking. By 1940, the list had grown to almost 5,000 names from California alone. The methodology under which the lists were compiled, however, was questionable: "Members of Japanese businesses and cultural organizations, including Shinto and Buddhist priests, were classified as potential spies or saboteurs."[1] Constantly prodded by Hearst, McClatchy, the Native Sons, and labor groups, many government leaders in Washington, DC, became convinced that the Japanese in the United States were secretly taking orders from anti-American leaders in Japan, and were preparing to attack as soon as they received word to do so.

Martin Dies, a congressman from Texas who wanted to be a senator, helped stoke the fires. In 1940, Dies, chairman of the House Committee on Un-American Activities, initiated an investigation of possible subversion on the West Coast, making sure to keep both his "findings" and his name in the newspapers. In July 1941, Dies proclaimed, "It is now time for a showdown on Japanese spy activities in this country." In language that would later be copied by Joseph McCarthy, Dies told reporters he had proof that "thousands of Japanese on the west coast are under the direct domination of Japan and [are] cooperating fully with their mother country in fifth column spy and traitor activities." Although Japanese fisherman were the main focus because of their ability to surveil and potentially sabotage naval vessels, "accusations were also made against Japanese language schools, Buddhist and Shinto organizations, Japanese cultural associations, and Japan's consular corps," charges for which Dies had not a shred of evidence. The committee's report "concluded that 'all Japanese' shared an 'absolute reverence for Japan' and that 'no Japanese can ever be loyal to any other nation other than Japan.' In addition, it claimed that even native-born second-generation Japanese 'cannot become thoroughly Americanized.'"[2]

To blunt this perceived threat, ONI assigned three of its best operatives to seek out potential sources of espionage among the Japanese. The focus of counterespionage shifted south, to San Diego, site of a major naval base and "one of, if not the most important, active centers for counterintelligence operations against the Japanese." Once again, fishermen came under particular scrutiny, but the entire community of Issei and Nisei were put under heavy surveillance.

It did not take very long for the ONI men to discover that their suspicions of heavy Japanese intelligence activity were correct, and that disloyal Americans were feeding sensitive information to Japanese spies. Those Americans, however, turned out in every case to be white.

In the most famous case, a former yeoman in the U.S. Navy, twenty-six-year-old Henry Thomas Thompson, was arrested in 1935 because a cashier's check for $300 he had cashed was found to have been debited against the account of a Japanese exchange student at Stanford University, Toshio Miyazaki, in the United States to study languages.[3] Miyazaki, who in photographs was nattily dressed in a tie, pullover, and sport jacket, was in fact a lieutenant commander in the Japanese navy. Thompson, a former sailor, who had been dismissed from the navy for insubordination, would don his uniform to gain access to naval bases where he would gather as much information as he could and pass it back to the Japanese. None of this seems to have been done with a great deal of subterfuge—not many spies are willing to be paid by check—but it took months for the three ONI agents to arrest Thompson and issue a warrant for Miyazaki. The warrant was never served because Miyazaki got wind of the investigation and quickly left the United States, probably by crossing into Mexico, before he could be arrested.

Only in 1936 was a grand jury empaneled "in heavily-cloaked secrecy" because of "delicate considerations," but from the first day, its existence was widely reported in California newspapers. Thompson, held in lieu of $20,000 bond, was initially charged only for illegally wearing a naval uniform, but after a former roommate was brought from Texas to testify as a material witness, Thompson decided to offer to cooperate.[4] His lawyer told investigators that Thompson was innocent but would name naval officers who "proposed to Thompson that he sell naval plans to an Oriental."[5]

The government charged, however, that Thompson operated in San Diego and Los Angeles and was reported to have "exhibited curiosity as to naval movements." On one occasion, "papers were stolen from several battleships prior to departure of the fleet in the Spring maneuvers of 1934 giving information as to ship movements 90 days in advance." Thompson also stole data on gunnery, engineering, and especially on the specifications of aircraft.[6]

Intelligence officers were uncertain how large the "spy ring" was. At one point they sought a "beautiful Japanese woman" alleged to have been Thompson's companion, who turned out to be a married waitress who may or may not have been involved with Thompson romantically. (Her husband was removed from the courtroom for causing a disturbance.) There were rumors of an "Agent K," another naval officer, but his identity remained unknown. In the end, only Thompson and the absent Miyazaki were charged. Thompson pled not guilty, but, after the bank records, a letter Thompson had written to Miayzaki, and the roommate's testimony were introduced into evidence, he was convicted in Los Angeles by a jury that needed only ten minutes to reach their verdict.

Before he was to be sentenced, however, Thompson offered to name the "top men" in a spy ring he claimed was a good deal larger than the government was aware of. He faced a sentence of twenty years—if he had been convicted in wartime it would have been the death penalty—but prosecutors agreed to reduce the sentence if Thompson's revelations proved accurate. Although Thompson's information, or even whether or not he imparted any, was never made public, he received only a fifteen-year sentence. Miyazaki went to on command destroyers and eventually became the commander of two aircraft carriers, serving in that role until the war ended in 1945.

Almost to the day Thompson received his sentence, another sensational spy case broke, this one in Washington, DC, not California. A former naval lieutenant commander and Annapolis graduate, John Farnsworth, was arrested and charged with accepting money from two naval attaches at the Japanese embassy, Yoshiuki Itamiya and Okira Yamaki, to obtain top secret material. Farnsworth, like Thompson, had been dishonorably discharged from the navy, and used his previous contacts and old uniform to gain access to top secret information. After Farnsworth had come under suspicion and his Japanese handler stopped paying him, he attempted to interest a well-known right-wing journalist in his story, perhaps in the hopes of passing himself off as a double agent. The journalist tipped off ONI and Farnsworth was arrested. He first agreed to plead guilty, but then contested the charges, at one point claiming impaired judgment because of an airplane accident while he was serving, which was found to be fabricated. He eventually went to trial and in 1937 was sentenced to four to twelve years in prison. Once again, the sentence was short because the crime had occurred in what was technically peacetime.

As relations between the United States and Japan continued to deteriorate, the Japanese beefed up their intelligence networks. In June 1941, once more using the guise of language students, two Japanese naval officers were arrested in Los Angeles and charged with trying to obtain classified material from the navy. From there, ONI uncovered a large, well-organized spy ring, run by one of the arrestees, Itaru Tachibana, a naval commander, and which included, among others, Charlie Chaplin's former valet. A good bit of the evidence against the spies, and lists of potential (but not actual) agents, was obtained when an agent of ONI, Kenneth Ringle, borrowed a safecracker from San Quentin prison and staged a break-in at the Japanese consulate in Los Angeles. Although the FBI used the proceeds of the burglary to draw up lists of Japanese to be arrested in case of war, once again most of the actual intelligence gathering had been done by Americans recruited and paid by the Japanese.

Although part of the reason was that white Americans would generally have more access to the sort of information the Japanese military sought, another was that few Japanese Americans were able to be enlisted to betray their adopted country. On the contrary, there was extensive evidence that not only were Japanese Americans almost universally loyal to the United States, but that authorities in Japan thought them traitors because they had abandoned Japan. On May 9, 1941, "in a cable that American authorities intercepted, Consul Nakauchi Kenji of the Los Angeles consulate reported to Tokyo that through Japanese 'whom we can't trust completely,' efforts were being made to utilize Caucasians and Blacks to obtain intelligence."[7]

That not a single Japanese American, Issei or Nisei, was found to have been even peripherally involved any anti-American activities, indeed even that many expressed revulsion, did not mitigate the conviction among most of whites in the United States that, if war came, many if not most of the more 100,000 of them were awaiting a signal from Japan to attack. But many Americans who lived close to the Japanese and interacted with them every day were just as certain that they were every bit as loyal as any white American.

When war did come, these forces initially came into play, before bigotry and fear overwhelmed tolerance and common sense. And so began one of the most shameful episodes in United States history.

18 | Fear and Fiction

At 7:55 AM on December 7, 1941, the Japan began its attack on American forces at Pearl Harbor. They used more than 300 torpedo planes, bombers, dive-bombers, and fighters launched from four aircraft carriers. Their attack fleet also included more than fifty additional warships, from battleships to midget submarines to oilers. In one hour and fifteen minutes, 2,335 U.S. military personnel and 68 civilians were dead—almost half of the civilians were Japanese fishermen; more than 1,000 people were wounded. Nineteen ships, including eight battleships, were either destroyed or heavily damaged. Only because three aircraft carriers were out to sea was some of the Pacific Fleet salvaged.

December 7, 1941, is one of the pivotal dates in United States history. The Pearl Harbor attack not only propelled the nation into a war most Americans had been desperate to avoid, but also told them that even two oceans could not insulate them from world events. The United States changed overnight from a country that could learn of carnage around the world with complacency to one that would harness its immense resources in a fight that had suddenly become personal.

Response to shock tends to be either immobilizing or hyperactive; in the United States it was surely the latter. Almost from the moment the last Japanese plane was returning to an aircraft carrier, American military, civilian, and government agencies were on a war footing. As President Franklin Roosevelt was asking Congress for a declaration of war, battle plans were redrawn, reservists were called up, factories ordered converted to war production, newspaper reporting was restricted, blackouts were imposed—and Japanese Americans on the West Coast were arrested.

For the anti-Japanese whites, Pearl Harbor had justified the warnings they had tried to impart to the country about Japanese treachery for decades. That it was a sneak attack fit perfectly into the caricature. For those who had defended Japanese Americans, insisting they were as loyal as any other American, the task became infinitely more difficult, if not impossible.

Having been caught so woefully unprepared at Pearl Harbor, the government had no intention of waiting for the acts of disloyalty and

The Philadelphia Inquirer
PUBLIC LEDGER
An Independent Newspaper for All the People
LATEST WAR EXTRA
CIRCULATION: November Average: Daily 415,750, Sunday 1,226,235
TUESDAY MORNING, DECEMBER 9, 1941
Second Largest 3c Morning Circulation in America
THREE CENTS
JAP WAR PLANES OVER CALIFORNIA

One of the many post–December 7 newspaper articles that was totally fabricated.

even sabotage they had been convinced by western racists were imminent. The FBI and ONI had extensive lists of potential Japanese agents, and mass arrests began almost immediately: "In the hours following the attack, the FBI arrested over 1,200 Japanese immigrant (Issei) men: businessmen, Buddhist priests, Japanese language teachers, and other community leaders."[1] In almost every case, the person arrested had been placed on the list for activities as banal as corresponding with family members in Japan—perhaps the letters were in code, authorities thought—or observing traditional rituals—proved their loyalty was to Japan: "More than 5,500 Issei men were eventually picked up and held as potential threats to national security. Most of these men were taken first to Immigration and Naturalization Service (INS) detention stations and then to Department of Justice (DOJ) internment camps to undergo hearings. Officially, these internment cases were given individual legal review, but in practice, the majority of Issei were imprisoned without evidence that they posed any threat to national security. Internees were not allowed legal representation."[2] The purported spies and fifth columnists were held incommunicado, and the FBI prohibited the publication of their names, in many cases preventing family members from having any idea what had happened to their fathers, husbands, or brothers.

The potential innocence of those arrested was not of interest to West Coast newspapers. On December 8, on page 1, the *Los Angeles Times* reported a "great man hunt" underway for three hundred "subversives": "During the afternoon and night, close to 200 suspicious Japanese were rounded up by police, deputy sheriffs, and special officers working under the direction on FBI agents." In San Francisco, traditional hub of anti-Japanese activity, the reports were no less lurid. Hearst's *Examiner* on December 8, in a page 1 column, "S. F. Rounds Up Japs," reported that FBI agents and police "ranged through San Francisco's Japanese section, taking into custody undisclosed numbers of 'suspicious aliens,' considered as potential saboteurs." The following day, the *Examiner* reported on a purported raid on the city by Japanese warplanes. "Air Alarm Held Real," the banner headline read. It was not.

The government's attack on domestic Japanese included strangling them financially: "All Japanese branch banks were immediately closed and taken over by the state bank superintendent or the Alien Property Custodian who called in all outstanding loans. In addition, approximately $27.5 million of business enterprises and real estate owned by Japanese aliens was taken over by the Alien Property Custodian. Finally, the Treasury froze the dollar deposits of both citizens and aliens who had been dealing with Japan before the war, releasing only small monthly payments to the account holders. Cumulatively, these measures affected not only most Issei and people in the import-export business but a very large proportion of the Japanese American community."[3]

Fear of Japanese subversion swept the nation. Immediately following the attack, executives from United Airlines, American Airlines, and TWA announced it would prohibit travel by "any person who is a Japanese national or who is suspected of being a Japanese national," which meant anyone who looked Japanese. Although some German Americans and Italian Americans were also taken into custody, the vast majority of purported subversives were Japanese.

Anti-Japanese sentiment was reinforced when Secretary of the Navy Frank Knox went to Hawaii on December 9, 1941, to find out what had gone so tragically wrong. Rather than place the blame on lax security and gross errors in judgment by American military personnel—that would come later—Knox instead chose a convenient target. On December 15, back in California, he told the reporters, "I think the most effective Fifth Column work of the entire war was done in Hawaii with the possible exception of Norway." As a congressional study observed decades later, "This laid major blame for the Pearl Harbor defeat at the door of the ethnic Japanese in the United States. Knox's statement was not only unfounded: it ignored the fact that Japanese Americans in large numbers had immediately come to the defense of the islands at the time of the attack."[4]

From the first, Japanese American societies and individual Japanese tried to demonstrate their devotion to the United States. With forbearance the government did not deserve, by and large they did not protest the arrests but rather proclaimed their loyalty to the United States. Saburo Kido, president of the Japanese American Citizens League (JACL), sent a telegram to President Roosevelt: "In this solemn hour we pledge our fullest cooperation to you, Mr. President, and to our country . . . now that Japan has instituted this attack upon our land, we are ready and prepared to expend every effort to repel this invasion together with our fellow Americans."[5] At its convention in January 1942, the JACL would vote to require an oath be taken by each member, then signed, and notarized: "I, ______, do solemnly swear that I will support and defend the Constitution of the United States against all enemies, foreign and domestic; that I will bear true faith and allegiance to the same; that I hereby renounce any other allegiances which I may have knowingly or unknowingly held in the past; and that I take this obligation freely without any mental reservation or purpose of evasion. So help me God."

None of these expressions of patriotism were sufficient to deter Hearst, McClatchy, and their fellow race-baiters, but even the *Examiner* was forced to note, albeit in one line at the very bottom of an inside page, that some young native-born Japanese, grudgingly acknowledged as citizens, were serving in the military. In fact, according to military intelligence, 5,000 Nisei had enlisted.

What also went unreported was that just weeks before the attack, a report commissioned by Roosevelt himself concluded few Japanese in United States were any threat to internal security, and a second more authoritative report would be produced soon after the attack that concluded the same thing. If anything, these accounts, both of which were disseminated to FDR and senior officials at the War Department, indicated that Japanese Americans, especially Nisei, could be a significant resource in the fight against the Japanese Empire.

The first of these was produced in autumn 1941 by a wealthy Chicago businessman, Curtis Munson, who had been recruited by journalist and Roosevelt intimate John Franklin Carter. Munson was one of a small cadre of private Roosevelt "spies," sent out to supplement official reports when the president suspected he might not be getting the whole story. Munson traveled both to the West Coast and Hawaii, posing as a government official.

Munson, though technically an amateur, had previously done work for FDR in the Caribbean, and was known for thorough, well-sourced reports. After spending almost a month speaking with local FBI agents, naval intelligence officers, local Japanese, and whites who lived and worked in their proximity, Munson concluded that in each of the three Naval Districts on the West Coast, "there are about 250 to 300 suspects under surveillance. It is easy to get on the suspect list, merely a speech in favor of Japan at some banquet, being sufficient to land one there. The Intelligence Services are generous with the title of suspect and are taking no chances. Privately, they believe that only 50 or 60 in each district can be classed as really dangerous."[6] This out of a population of more than 100,000.

Munson sent additional reports to Carter between December and February, including a long report on Hawaii, most of which "found their way to Roosevelt's desk." His assessment of the threat level on the West Coast did not change: "After Pearl Harbor, where Japan received no aid from fifth column activity or sabotage, Munson pointedly noted that '[a]n attack is the proof of the pudding,' and remained firmly persuaded that the number of people on the West Coast who could reasonably be suspected of a menacing degree of loyalty to the enemy was small—and not demonstrably greater among the ethnic Japanese than other racial groups."

In Munson's report was also a statement from a British intelligence agent, echoed by other professionals, which gave "savage irony" to the internment program: "It must be kept in mind when considering the Security to be derived from the mass evacuation of all Japanese, that the Japanese in all probability employed many more whites than Japanese for carrying out their work and this 'white' danger is not eliminated by the evacuation of the Japanese."[7]

Munson also differentiated Japanese immigrants, barred from citizenship, from those born in the United States. Of the Issei, he noted that they are "considerably weakened in their loyalty to Japan by the fact that they have chosen to make this their home and have brought up their children here. They expect to die here." The Nisei were considered "universally estimated from 90 to 98 percent loyal to the United

States if the Japanese-educated element of the Kibei [American-born children who spent considerable time in Japan] is excluded. The Nisei are pathetically eager to show this loyalty. They are not Japanese in culture. They are foreigners to Japan." The Kibei "are considered the most dangerous element," and he also noted "that many of those who visited Japan subsequent to their early American education come back with added loyalty to the United States. In fact, it is a saying that all a Nisei needs is a trip to Japan to make a loyal American out of him."[8]

The second report was prepared after Pearl Harbor by Kenneth Ringle, the naval intelligence officer who masterminded the consulate burglary that broke the Tachibana ring. Ringle was likely the American military's foremost authority on Japan and the Japanese. He spoke the language fluently, had spent eight years in Japan as a student of Japanese culture, a year as a naval intelligence officer in Hawaii, and two more in the same job in Los Angeles. He was asked to study the potential for subversion and sabotage and make recommendations. By his own account, he "has over the last several years developed a very great interest in the problem of the Japanese in America, particularly with regard to the future position of the United States citizen of Japanese ancestry, and has sought contact with certain of their leaders."[9]

From the strong relationships he had developed among the Nisei and law enforcement and intelligence agents, Ringle would conclude that no more than 300 Japanese on the West Coast were even potentially disloyal—which matched Munson's estimate—and that these could be identified relatively easily. He suggested boards of inquiry to determine which among them were genuine threats.

Other of Ringle's findings also mirrored Munson's: "The Japanese Consular staff, leaders of the Central Japanese Association, and others who are known to have been sympathetic to the Japanese cause do not themselves trust the Nisei. . . . A very great many of the Nisei have taken legal steps through the Japanese Consulate and the Government of Japan to officially divest themselves of Japanese citizenship (dual citizenship), even though by so doing they become legally dead in the eye of the Japanese law, and are no longer eligible to inherit any property which they or their family may have held in Japan."

"In short," Ringle concluded, "the entire 'Japanese Problem' has been magnified out of its true proportion, largely because of the physical characteristics of the people; that it is no more serious that the problems of the German, Italian, and Communistic portions of the United States population, and, finally that it should be handled on the basis of the individual, regardless of citizenship, and not on a racial basis."

Roosevelt and other officials in Washington chose not to make either of these reports public, perhaps because sentiment against the Japanese was running so high that defending them would have had political costs. In addition, the president would have to contend with the wild rumors that were flying about that the Japanese were planning an imminent attack on the West Coast—or that they had already attacked. Even the staid *New York Times* reported on December 9 that Japanese planes had been sighted over San Francisco.

But not everyone joined in the hysterics. Newspapers in both San Francisco and Los Angeles, albeit not the most widely read ones, preached calm and cautioned readers not to judge Americans by how they appeared but rather by how they behaved. Schoolteachers instructed students not to shun or abandon their Japanese friends and classmates, and many tried to reassure their Japanese schoolmates that their loyalty was not in question. California governor Culbert Olson proclaimed, "Californians have kept their heads. . . . The American tradition of fair play has been observed. All the organs of public influence and information—press, pulpit, school, welfare agencies, radio and cinema—have discouraged mob violence and have pleaded for tolerance and justice for all law-abiding residents of whatever race."[10] For the first weeks, there were many voices in the West that insisted most Japanese residents were loyal Americans who wanted nothing more than to aid their nation in time of war.

But moderation was soon swept away by a combination of fact, fiction, rumor, and just plain bad luck. The fact was that the Japanese military was sweeping across the Pacific, overwhelming overmatched foes with a combination of relentless attack and hideous brutality. They took Wake Island and Guam almost immediately and Hong Kong weeks later. After the surrender, Japanese soldiers massacred British, Canadian, and Indian soldiers across the colony, including several doctors and medical personal and at least one woman. There were reports of other women, including nurses, who were raped.

The Japanese also attacked the Philippines, where, despite initial reports from General MacArthur that the situation was "in hand," they soon achieved enormous, and disheartening, success against the U.S.

military. By mid-February 1942, they would conquer the "impregnable" British stronghold in Singapore and threaten Australia—and Hawaii.

Japanese submarines attacked American shipping so close to the West Coast that on December 23, "while scores of California beach residents looked on through the dim light of dawn, a Jap submarine sent the big Union Oil tanker *Montebello* to the bottom, with a combination of torpedo and shell fire which rocked the coast."[11] Residents also witnessed other tankers limping back to port after surviving attacks by other submarines. In some cases, ships that were due into port never appeared. That the western United States was under risk of bombing or even invasion, and Hawaii even more so, could not be denied. And if either of those eventualities came to pass, would treachery within the nation's borders make a weakened nation even more vulnerable?

The fiction was that a campaign of sabotage was already underway. Japanese farmers were said to have embarked on a campaign to poison the food and water supplies, and that Japanese fishermen were actually naval officers, waiting for a signal to attack American warships as they lay at anchor. As far away as Alabama on December 8, the Montgomery Alabama *Journal* ran an article, "How Jap Could Easily Poison City's Water Supply," complete with a picture of a "patriotic American" perched on a roof posing as a Japanese saboteur.[12] There were vivid descriptions of nonexistent bombings or attacks on military installations. The scope of the reports, not one of which proved true, was astonishing, even just by their volume alone. It seemed to leaders in Washington, DC, 3,000 miles away, to be at least somewhat reflective of the actual situation.

The bad luck was that the officer in charge of the Western Command, General John DeWitt, a talentless bureaucrat who had served in the army for more than forty years without ever commanding a combat unit, believed just about every outrageous report or rumor that came across his desk. DeWitt was an ignorant, narrow-minded bigot who was convinced he needed to save the nation from loathsome foreigners who were bent on destroying it. "A Jap is a Jap," he regularly remarked. And he would tell a subordinate, "There isn't such a thing as a loyal Japanese, and it is just impossible to determine their loyalty by investigation—it just can't be done."[13]

DeWitt was personally responsible for a good bit of rumor-mongering that destroyed any chance of Japanese Americans avoiding an hysterical response from American officials. He was also responsible for injecting hysteria into the civilian population. On December 8, DeWitt emphatically confirmed a preliminary report that two squadrons of Japanese airplanes were driven off by air defenses just outside of Oakland—the alert lasted only nine minutes—and also confirmed that American airplanes turned back an imminent attack on San Francisco Bay. Neither report was found to contain a scintilla of truth, but, without bothering to wait for actual confirmation, DeWitt claimed that there was no doubt the planes had been launched from an aircraft carrier just off the California coast.[14]

The following day, when it became clear that the reports were untrue, DeWitt "angrily denied the air raid alarms were hoaxes," and warned "death and destruction are likely to come to this city at any moment." He added, "People of San Francisco do not seem to appreciate that we are at war in every sense." (A phrase that would come to have a deeper meaning in the weeks to come.) "These planes were over our community for a definite period. They were enemy planes. Why bombs were not dropped I do not know. It might have been better if some bombs had dropped to awaken this city."[15] DeWitt caused further consternation by ordering blackouts, suspending the opening of Santa Anita racetrack, and ordering the Rose Parade in Pasadena be canceled.

The bad luck was compounded because DeWitt's second-in-command was General Joseph W. "Vinegar Joe" Stilwell, who was highly intelligent, totally competent, and convinced that the rumors to which DeWitt gave so much credence were utter nonsense. In his diary, he referred to DeWitt as a jackass. Had the order of command been reversed, history might have been far different. As it was, Stilwell soon left for Washington to help plan an invasion of North Africa, and DeWitt was left to peddle his conspiracy theories to senior military and political officials, including President Roosevelt. The only way to secure the West Coast, DeWitt told anyone who would listen, was to clear the Japanese out.

Into this increasingly incendiary brew leapt California's ambitious attorney general and future governor, Earl Warren. Although he would come to deeply regret his actions, Warren became perhaps the most influential civilian voice in support of DeWitt's initiative.

Earl Warren was born in March 1891 on "Dingy Turner Street" in Los Angeles, the son of a Norwegian immigrant father, who changed his name from Varren, and a Swedish immigrant mother. His father, a railroad repairman, lost his job when Earl was three years old and the family moved to a small town near Bakersfield. His father worked nights repairing railroad cars, and young Earl held a variety of afterschool jobs to help the family pay their bills, including delivering ice, working in a bakery, and driving a grocery wagon.[16]

Warren's father was determined that his son go to college and saved enough for Warren to enroll at Berkeley. Once Warren left the "arid landscape," the dust, and the 100-degree heat of Bakersfield, he resolved to never go back. "The idea of returning there," he said, "seemed to me like giving up my freedom."[17]

Although he remained at Berkeley for six years, first as an undergraduate, then as a law student, he was largely indifferent to academics, but was attracted to "a community of lively, stimulating people rather than a community of scholars." Warren had only the most limited personal connection with any Chinese or Japanese living in the area and "associated the Chinese community in San Francisco largely with opium dens, and he remembered the Chinese in Sumner as cheap laborers who 'kept themselves completely isolated from the community.'"[18]

Warren soon found himself drawn to Progressivism, with its anticorruption, antimonopoly, anti-entrenched-wealth message. He was especially admiring of the former Republican governor and by then California Senator Hiram Johnson, Teddy Roosevelt's running mate in 1912. But Johnson, even more than most Progressives, loathed the Chinese and Japanese presence in California—he was as responsible as anyone for the 1913 Alien Land Law—and Warren, who soon became Johnson's protégé, adopted those sentiments as well.

After working at a law firm in Oakland for two years, Warren enlisted in the army when the United States entered World War I. He was initially assigned to Camp Lewis in Washington State, the same installation at which Bhagat Singh Thind would serve, but Warren had likely been reassigned to Virginia before Thind arrived. Like Thind, however, Warren was discharged in December 1918. He returned to Oakland and edged toward a career in politics. Warren first served as clerk of the California Assembly Judiciary Committee, then, in 1920, was hired as deputy district attorney of Alameda County. In 1925, he was appointed to fill a vacancy as Alameda County's district attorney, won close election to keep the job the following year, even though he rejected political contributions, and then was reelected in landslide victories in 1930 and 1934.

During his tenure, he acquired a reputation for incorruptibility—an uncommon trait in Bay Area politics—fairness, and reverence for the rule of law. But Warren was not easy to work for: "He demanded absolute loyalty from subordinates. He favored activism in office, but he selected the issues on which he would be active rather than reacting to outside pressures. As district attorney, he launched vigorous prosecutions of bail-bond brokers, confidence men, and corrupt law enforcement officials."[19] Warren was especially tenacious in enforcing Prohibition, not an especially popular stance in an area that was one the main ports of call for rumrunners coming from both north and south.

Although he did not take a personal hand in the anti-Japanese activities championed by James Phelan and Ulysses Webb, his membership in Native Sons of the Golden West, the American Legion, and the Loyal Order of Moose left little doubt of his sentiments: "Warren was true to [the Progressive] vision of assisting the disadvantaged and the outsider. Like many nativist California Progressives, however, he believed that governmental largesse should be bestowed selectively not universally, so as to promote an ideal vision of California that excluded 'undesirable' persons, ideologies and cultures."[20]

In 1938, Warren, by then one of the most admired politicians in California, ran for state attorney general to replace Ulysses Webb, who was retiring. He had become a staunch Republican and chairman of the state party, but nonetheless won the Democratic and Progressive primaries and so was elected largely without opposition.

Once in office, Warren exhibited the same bifurcated view of the law as when he had been district attorney. On the one hand, he was personally honest and ran a disciplined, well-organized office, whose function was primarily to protect the well-being of California's citizenry. Warren fought corruption, "shut down dog tracks, which were illegal in California, began raids on gambling ships located off the coasts of Santa Monica and Long Beach, and fought the attempted intrusions of organized crime into California."[21]

As the prospect of war in Europe increased, he organized law enforcement agencies in a program of civil defense, but his focus initially was Europe. "Do not be deceived," he said in the spring of 1941, "that [the totalitarian powers] are not attempting to exercise fifth column activities . . . in this country. They would like nothing better than to create the same situation here that they developed in France, Denmark and Holland."[22] That changed after Pearl Harbor, when Warren's commitment to national defense, political ambition, and racism fused together to form a weapon directed at innocent Americans of Japanese descent.

In the weeks after the attack, Attorney General Warren focused mainly on defense issues, such as supporting a statewide air raid alarm system and standardizing rules for blackouts. He also opposed Governor Olson's declaration of a state of emergency because it would, in Warren's opinion, allow Olson to "rule by decree."[23] Although Olson scoffed at the notion that he sought dictatorial powers, it is perhaps an indication that Warren was already considering challenging Olson for governor's chair.

Two weeks after Pearl Harbor, Warren began to turn his focus to Japanese Americans. Testifying before the state senate's finance committee, Warren announced his support for a large appropriation sought by General DeWitt to aid in domestic security. "California is in grave danger of sabotage," he warned the committee. "There has been no war declared by the axis powers that has not been followed by a wave of sabotage."[24] To protect against those activities, DeWitt had established ninety-nine "forbidden zones," and two "restricted zones." As a result, thousands of noncitizens from axis nations—German, Italian, and Japanese—were forced to relocate, among them Giuseppe DiMaggio, a fisherman from Sicily who had lived in the United States for forty years without bothering to become a citizen, and whose son Joe had won the 1941 American League MVP award after hitting safely in fifty-six straight games.

For the remainder of 1941 and into 1942, Warren remained immersed in civil defense. Of particular focus was ensuring California cities and towns had adequate firefighting capability in case of the expected bombing raids. Ironically, Warren was also instrumental in setting up a committee to "help protect the civil liberties and rights of California residents in war time," and was named its chairman. The committee "was appointed to demonstrate America can maintain democratic civil liberties while outproducing and outfighting totalitarian nations . . . preserving our basic freedoms while we face the fanatics of tyranny abroad."[25] Although the rhetoric was lofty, Warren and his fellow committee members had no interest in preserving the civil liberties of Japanese Americans, but rather focused on ensuring enlistees had their jobs protected and that men in uniform could purchase alcohol.

In mid-January, Warren clashed with Governor Olson as to the best way to protect California's oil fields from "Axis sabotage." Olson, Warren insisted, by assigning the security to local law enforcement, had left the facilities vulnerable. Warren proposed closing the areas around them to vehicular traffic, restricting access, and installing specially hired guards. Still, however, Warren spoke of the country's enemies in general and did not focus specifically on the Japanese.

That would soon change.

19 | An Illusion of Disloyalty

In the wake of Defense Secretary Knox's report blaming the Pearl Harbor disaster largely on spies and traitors of Japanese descent, President Roosevelt appointed Supreme Court justice Owen Roberts to head a five-man commission of admirals and generals to determine what were the real reasons for Japan's ability to succeed with such a devastating attack. It is unclear whether Roosevelt found Knox's failure to condemn military leaders too convenient or, as was his habit, he wanted multiple takes on an important subject.

Roberts and his colleagues conducted a far more thorough examination than had Knox: "The Commission examined 127 witnesses and received a large number of documents. All members of the Military and Naval Establishments, and civil officers and citizens who were thought to have knowledge of facts pertinent to the inquiry, were summoned and examined under oath. All persons in the island of Oahu, who believed they had knowledge of such facts, were publicly requested to appear, and a number responded to the invitation and gave evidence."[1]

Their findings were submitted on January 23, 1942, and could not have been more in opposition to what Knox had put forward. The commissioners placed responsibility for the failure to adequately defend the base squarely on the admiral in charge of the Pacific Fleet, Husband Kimmel, and the army general in charge of the land forces, Walter Short. The report acknowledged that some failures of communication from Washington had contributed to the lax security, but it cited some unforgivable lapses—which it termed "dereliction of duty"—by the two commanders who had been made all too aware of the imminent threat of sneak attack by the Japanese. Kimmel and Short had failed to coordinate the island's defenses, for example, and there were no regular air patrols to detect the presence of an enemy at sea, nor were submarine nets in place at the mouth of the harbor to prevent attack from underwater. Although both Kimmel and Short protested that they were scapegoated and had been given inadequate information as to how imminent was the potential for attack, each man would retire from the military within weeks of the report's release.

The bulk of Roberts's report dealt with military preparedness and the failure to detect the presence of the Japanese navy, but a small portion was devoted to the Japanese in Hawaii. One paragraph in particular would be seized on by anti-Japanese whites: "There were, prior to December 7, 1941, Japanese spies on the island of Oahu. Some were Japanese consular agents and others were persons having no open relations with the Japanese foreign service. These spies collected and, through various channels transmitted, information to the Japanese Empire respecting the military and naval establishments and dispositions on the island."

Roberts added, "It was believed that the center of Japanese espionage in Hawaii was the Japanese consulate at Honolulu. It has been discovered that the Japanese consul sent to and received from Tokyo in his own and other names many messages on commercial radio circuits."[2] Less often mentioned was that it was the practice of Japanese spies among the diplomatic corps to recruit disaffected white men to do the actual spying, so that could well have been to whom Roberts was referring. In fact, Roberts had detected no spying or anti-American activity at all within Hawaii's Japanese American population, although the FBI had conducted a thorough investigation to unearth that very activity.

The condemnation of Kimmel and Short was front-page news across the United States, but the brief passage about Japanese spying received disproportionate attention on the West Coast, distorted to condemn those that Roberts's investigators had found blameless. As a result, "the Roberts report stirred the anxious imagination of the public. Soon, no tale of treachery was too outrageous for public consumption." One rumor that made the rounds was "that the night prior to the attack, Japanese Hawaiian sugar cane workers had cut the cane into arrow patterns which pointed the Japanese pilots toward Pearl Harbor."[3]

Earl Warren did not wait for the report to be officially made public before proposing action against the Japanese in California. One of the most persistent rumors, even though there was absolutely no hard evidence to support it, was that the Japanese on the West Coast would launch attacks and acts of sabotage from their homes and farms. On January 23, the day the report was delivered, Warren prompted a "check on alien land holdings in the state, with especial reference to the legality of Japanese occupation of farm areas." If any of the small "truck gardens" in the San Joaquin and Sacramento valleys were found to be violation of the alien land laws, Warren intended to initiate legal proceedings to have them seized by the state.

As Assistant Attorney General Warren Olney recounted, "We gave immediate attention to this and concluded that the enforcement of the Alien Land Law might produce the desired result in at least some instances. The law provided that if agricultural land came into the ownership of an alien ineligible for American citizenship, the land would be forfeited and would escheat to the state. Inquiry convinced us that some of the agricultural land near some of the important strategic installations was, in fact, owned by Japanese aliens ineligible for citizenship and, hence, was subject to escheat proceedings and the ouster of those in present possession."[4]

Warren insisted everyone's civil rights would be protected: "We believe that in the view of the proximity of a lot of these ownerships to essential war industries and even to military establishments, it becomes essential for us to survey the situation and see if the law is being violated."[5] He called a meeting for February 2 of sheriffs and district attorneys in the targeted areas. Warren's "original intention had been to invite only the district attorneys and sheriffs of those few counties where we thought it was likely that there was a provable case. But at the suggestion of the army and navy and other federal authorities, he expanded the list of invitees to include the district attorneys and sheriffs from all counties where the federal government felt there was a security problem."[6]

Warren was already considering mass evacuation as a means to prevent Japanese espionage and sabotage. Just days after the Roberts Commission report, Warren discussed the feasibility of removing all Japanese from what he considered "sensitive military areas," which, as the February 2 meeting demonstrated, turned out to be virtually the entire state. He also met personally with General DeWitt, who seemed to be in favor of removing every Japanese resident from the West Coast, citizen or not. In the midst of this turmoil, the California Republican Committee revealed that Warren was the party's leading candidate to run for governor in 1942 in every section of the state.[7]

Sentiment to remove the Japanese was growing. On January 27, 1942, for example, the Los Angeles County Board of Supervisors petitioned the federal government to remove 13,000 Japanese. Their petition was filled with misrepresentations or outright lies: "The hazard of these Japanese aliens . . . [most were citizens] . . . near vital defense points . . . [most lived in farm country] . . . is evidence by the fact that 80 per cent of Japanese residents here retain their native Buddhist and Shinto religions . . . [at least half were Christian]." At the same time, the

American Legion asked that 93,000 Japanese, "alien and native born alike, be interned for the duration of the war."[8] Los Angeles also reported that police officers of Japanese descent had been fired.

Warren's anti-Japanese pronouncements became increasingly arch. He warned of hundreds of Japanese secret societies throughout California that could bring about another Pearl Harbor if they were not stamped out, and insisted that "the Japanese situation as it exists in this state today may well be the Achilles heel of the entire civil defense effort."[9]

By the February 2 meeting, Warren's rhetoric had lost all traces of fair-mindedness. He told the law enforcement officials, "The Japanese as an entire race of people, men, women, and children alike—especially United States citizens of Japanese ancestry—are poised to take disloyal action against the United States at any moment, to move to commit acts of sabotage, espionage, and disloyalty upon some mysterious signal to be issued to them by the Japanese enemy."[10] The nearly one hundred sheriffs and district attorneys present enthusiastically agreed. They voted unanimously to ask United States Attorney General Francis Biddle to immediately remove all alien Japanese—by which they meant all Japanese—"from all territories in the state of California within 200 miles of the Pacific Coast for the duration of the war."[11]

In advance of that, law enforcement agencies were determined to strike preemptively: "We became much concerned about these patterns of Japanese land occupancy. It seemed impossible that they could be the result of coincidence alone. This ringing or blanketing by Japanese of strategic points throughout the state, we believed, must have had some plan and direction behind it."[12]

And so, under Warren's direction, an official in each county was assigned to locate and map all Japanese-occupied land and compare it with "important installations" in the vicinity.

The assistant attorney general described the process:

> We secured a set of maps of each county on a scale large enough to make it possible to indicate with respect to each parcel whether it was or was not owned or occupied by Japanese. The maps were on a uniform scale and it usually took three or four sheets to cover a single county. The maps for each county were sent to the district attorney and sheriff and they, in conference with the local agricultural agents, marked each parcel of agricultural land which was occupied or owned by Japanese, and with this information the

maps were then returned to the attorney general's office. Of course, the maps could not show who was a citizen and who was not or where the occupants loyalties lay.[13]

Warren "executed this mission with the precision of a military operation." Each parcel that was "owned, controlled or occupied by persons of the Japanese race, whether citizens or not [was] marked on the maps in red. He also asked each county official to designate 'important installations' so that proximity of Japanese Californians could be easily compared."[14]

Although originally the "intention in gathering this information was to use it in deciding where and against whom escheat proceedings should be filed for Alien Land Law violation," the program "was expanded into one of general enforcement of the Alien Land Law, with the resulting escheat of large land areas without regard to whether they were or were not near military or other important installations."[15]

When the survey was complete, Warren and his associates found that it had revealed a pattern, "which none of us had ever suspected. The maps disclosed that from Point Reyes south, virtually every feasible landing beach, airfield, powerhouse, oilfield, water reservoir or pumping plant, radio station, and other points of strategic military importance had several and usually a considerable number of Japanese-occupied properties in their immediate vicinity. The same was true with respect to military camps and other defense installations."[16]

From there, Warren's team concluded that the Japanese in California were ideally located to undertake a massive campaign of sabotage. In their zeal to detect a threat, however, they had undertaken the task with fatally flawed methodology. Using the broadest possible definition of an "important installation" rendered it nearly impossible for any resident of the state not to live in proximity to one or more of them: "Officials in Warren's office 'worked by rule of thumb' and 'without any definition' of a 'military installation' and 'without any defined limitation' of 'proximity.'"[17] In addition, Warren had included only Japanese living in rural areas and so vastly overstated the percentage of the population living near these "sensitive" locations. The surveyors made no attempt to discover if the rural Japanese had chosen to live where they had because soil and climate conditions were favorable for growing. And they had worked backward—they did not research how long the Japanese farmers and their families had lived on the land in question and whether it predated the arrival of these "important installations." "For example, the alarm expressed over Japanese residing near airports obscured the fact that the issei had made their homes in these now-sensitive locations long before airports existed."[18] Convinced, however, that he had uncovered a nefarious conspiracy, Warren forwarded his caricature to the army.

Although Roosevelt for a time had remained uncertain, pressure from General DeWitt and the seemingly incontrovertible evidence gathered in California convinced him that large-scale relocation was necessary. On February 19, 1942, the president signed Executive Order 9066, which authorized and directed "the Secretary of War, and the Military Commanders whom he may from time to time designate, whenever he or any designated Commander deems such action necessary or desirable, to prescribe military areas in such places and of such extent as he or the appropriate Military Commander may determine, from which any or all persons may be excluded, and with respect to which, the right of any person to enter, remain in, or leave shall be subject to whatever restrictions the Secretary of War or the appropriate Military Commander may impose in his discretion."[19]

The "Military Commander" was, of course, John DeWitt, and FDR's grant of open-ended authority meant that DeWitt would have virtually dictatorial powers, which for the first time would include the authority to remove American citizens without trial or hearing in the absence of martial law. No burden of proof need be met, nor would there be oversight established either in Congress or the military hierarchy. And although technically those of Italian or German extraction were also subject to draconian provisions not seen since the Civil War, there was little question about at whom the order was aimed. And although General DeWitt could hardly be described as objective, DeWitt's chief adjutant, a young, bright, ambitious, and extremely bigoted "serial liar" named Karl Bendetsen would exacerbate the already cataclysmic prospects for Japanese Americans.

Bendetsen had been born "Bendetson" to a prominent Orthodox Jewish family but would change the spelling after he was assigned to DeWitt to make it seem less Jewish. His parents "had emigrated from Lithuania in 1869, settling first in Elmira, New York, then moving west to the Seattle area. But in 1929, he denied all that, claiming to be a Christian to get into a Stanford fraternity, Theta Delta Chi, which barred Jews from membership. As the years went by, he created a new biography under the name Bendetsen, saying he was from a Danish logging family and that a fictional great-grandfather "had come from Denmark to America."[20]

Bendetsen was both smarter and more ruthless than his boss, and DeWitt came to unquestioningly trust him. As Bendetson, he had visited Hawaii in the fall of 1941, where, according to his recollection, he had spoken with Admiral Kimmel and General Short, both of whom complained that they had not been allowed to take adequate security measures because of interference from Washington. Though this allegation was later proven false, Bendetsen had a habit of injecting himself into the center of matters in which his involvement had been peripheral. He also claimed to have drafted the language of Executive Order 9066, which he did not, but his insistence that every Japanese American was a direct threat to national security contributed to the decision to issue the order.

As soon as Bendetson arrived in California, he began to press for a full and forcible evacuation. DeWitt's original plan was to evacuate only resident aliens from all three axis nations. "However General DeWitt may have felt during December about the treatment of enemy aliens," an official history later noted, "he was then firmly opposed to any evacuation of citizens."[21] In late December 1941, in response to a request from Los Angeles Chamber of Commerce to evacuate all Japanese Americans living in the city, DeWitt replied:

> If we go ahead and arrest the 93,000 Japanese, native born and foreign born, we are going to have an awful job on our hands and are very liable to alienate the loyal Japanese from disloyal. . . . I'm very doubtful that it would be a commonsense procedure to try and intern or to intern 117,000 Japanese in this theater . . . those people should be watched by the police and people of the community in which they live and have been living for years . . . and then inform the FBI or the military authorities of any suspicious action so we could take necessary steps to handle it . . . rather than try to intern all those people, men, women and children, and hold them under military control and under guard. I don't think it's a sensible thing to do. . . . An American citizen, after all, is an American citizen. And while they all may not be loyal, I think we can weed the disloyal out of the loyal and lock them up if necessary.[22]

But after Bendetsen wrote a planning paper recommending the designation of military areas "from which all persons who do not have express permission to enter or remain [would be] excluded as a measure of military necessity," the malleable DeWitt decided to adopt a more severe view.[23] He sent a set of recommendations to Secretary of War Henry Stimson, although Bendetsen likely wrote the draft, which said, "It, therefore, follows that along the vital Pacific Coastal Frontier over 112,000 potential enemies, of Japanese extraction, are at large today. There are indications that these are organized and ready for concerted action at a favorable opportunity. The very fact that no sabotage has taken place to date is a disturbing and confirming indication that such action will be taken."[24]

Despite the hard-line sentiment from Western Command, the wording of Executive Order 9066 did not mandate the deportation of Japanese Americans, but merely gave General DeWitt the authority to do so. There remained widespread opposition to the idea, both in the civilian population and among military leaders. To get a firsthand picture, the House of Representatives Select Committee Investigating National Defense Migration traveled to San Francisco for special hearings, which took place only two days after the executive order had been issued. It was at those hearings, on February 21, that Earl Warren brought his damning, spurious evidence of Japanese American perfidy to the national stage.

Armed with a copious array of exhibits, Warren opened his statements by referring to his maps, which showed "a disturbing situation . . . along the coast from Marin County to the Mexican border virtually every important strategic location and installation has one or more Japanese in its immediate vicinity. The same situation exists in those counties of the Sacramento and San Joaquin Valleys that have any considerable Japanese population, and in San Bernardino, Riverside, and Imperial Counties."

He was happy to go into specifics: "The sheriff of one coastal county has reported to me that in his county Japanese farmers are working within a grenade throw of coast-defense guns; and the sheriff of another that it is necessary to pass through the yards of three Japanese farmers to reach certain coast-defense installations located in his county." Although Warren granted that "the presence of many of these persons in their present locations is mere coincidence," he added that "it would seem equally beyond doubt that the presence of others is not coincidence."

Warren used Santa Barbara County to illustrate his point:

> In the northern end of that county is Camp Cook where, I am informed, the only armored division on the Pacific coast will be located. The only practical entrance to Camp Cook is on the secondary road through the town of Lompoc. The maps show this entrance is flanked with Japanese property, and it is impossible to move a single man or a piece of equipment in or out of Camp Cook without having it pass under the scrutiny of numerous Japanese. I have been informed that the destruction of the bridges along the road to Camp Cook would effectually bottle up that establishment for an indefinite time, exit to the south being impossible because of extremely high mountains and to the north because of a number of washes with vertical banks 50 to 60 feet deep. There are numerous Japanese close to these bridges.[25]

Adding to the threat, Warren told the committee members, was the degree to which the Japanese were organized through a web of interlocking societies and organizations, up to 2,700 of them, most with roots in Japan, which controlled the actions and behavior of individual Japanese in the United States. This was nonsense, but Warren had come armed with lists and examples, most taken out of context, which nonetheless depicted the very sort of racist distortion that his predecessors had fomented in the decades before. Japanese Americans, Warren concluded, were "ideally situated with reference to points of strategic importance, to carry into execution a tremendous program of sabotage on a mass scale should any considerable number of them be inclined to do so." He added that Roosevelt's executive order was "most wise" and "points the way to a real solution of our problem," because the lack of a single incident of sabotage meant that Japanese traitors, including American citizens, had "lulled us into a false sense of security."[26] Warren, as had DeWitt, had absurdly interpreted a lack of sabotage in the present as confirmation of sabotage in the future, which would have earned each of them failing grades in the most basic course in formal logic.

The congressmen, however, were so suitably impressed that none of them thought to question Warren's methodology or inquire as to whether his presentation had been contrived to suit his conclusions.

That Warren was so widely praised for his testimony and thorough and seemingly comprehensive findings is no surprise, given that his presentation fit perfectly with the preconceptions that most Americans had developed about the Japanese. But there were other reasons as well. As one white farmer put it, "We're charged with wanting to get rid of the Japs for selfish reasons. We do. It's a question of whether the white man lives on the Pacific Coast or the brown men. They came into this valley to work, and they stayed to take over. If all the Japs were removed tomorrow, we'd never miss them in two weeks because the white farmers can take over and produce everything the Jap grows. And we do not want them back when the war ends, either."[27]

In fact, the process had already begun. Thousands of Japanese Americans, most of them Issei, were already in custody. Many of those had seen their homes ransacked, their possessions manhandled or destroyed, their businesses ruined, and, in some cases, their land or farms sold for virtually nothing to eager speculators.

After the Tolan Committee hearings, it was only a matter of time until tens of thousands more joined them.

20 | No Island Paradise

For the Japanese population in Hawaii, the post–Pearl Harbor period held two important distinctions to the situation on the mainland. First, of course, the threat of attack had turned into an actual attack and, sitting approximately 2,500 miles from the mainland, the islands were a good deal more vulnerable to invasion than was the West Coast. The prospect of such an attack was all too real: "Admiral Isoroku Yamamoto, the architect of the Pearl Harbor attack, planned to annihilate American aircraft carriers at the Battle of Midway and then seize the Hawaiian Islands and use their civilian population of over 460,000 as a bargaining chip to secure a quick negotiated peace."[1] The Battle of Midway turned out to have a far different result. After a crushing defeat for the Japanese navy in June 1942, Yamamoto's gambit was shelved forever.

Second, more than one-third of the islands' 450,000 occupants were of Japanese extraction, and of the approximately 158,000 ethnic Japanese, more than 120,000 were natural-born United States citizens. Hauling them all off to internment camps would cripple the economy and create chaos in the routine functions of government and civil society. With a massive increase in military personnel expected, the need for Japanese civilian workers would become more, not less, acute.

Still, drastic action was needed. Before the sun had set on December 7, Hawaii had been put under martial law. Territorial governor Joseph Poindexter suspended habeas corpus and transferred judicial authority to General Short, who became "military governor," responsible for all civil activities across Hawaii. Constitutional protections for anyone of Japanese descent, citizen or alien, were suspended: "Acknowledging that the 'imminence of attack by the enemy and the possibility of invasion make necessary a stricter control of your actions than would be necessary or proper at other times,' [Short] warned that those who disobeyed his ordinances 'will be severely punished by military tribunals or will be held in custody until such time as the civil courts are able to function.'"[2]

Short had cautioned against the Japanese population for years. He "felt the most imminent danger to the army was the danger of sabotage, because of the known presence of large numbers of alien Japanese in

Honolulu. Ironically, among the measures he took to act against sabotage was bunching the planes on the various fields on the Island close together so that they might be carefully guarded against possible subversive action by Japanese agents. This action, of course, made the planes an easy target for the Japanese bombers on December 7."[3]

Supervision of Hawaii's judiciary was assigned to the chief legal officer on the islands, Colonel Thomas Green, who would also be in charge of regulating the activities of ethnic Japanese. Green issued more than 250 general orders that "regulated virtually every aspect of civilian conduct," including empaneling military-run courts to adjudicate violations of law.[4] In a move that left him none too popular with the white population, Green also closed every saloon and suspended the sale of intoxicating liquor.

Since the 1930s, the FBI and ONI had been compiling lists of those they considered the most dangerous members of Hawaii's Japanese population, people, almost all men, who would be arrested the moment hostilities broke out between the two nations. In a memo to J. Edgar Hoover written on December 4, 1941, the FBI agent in charge wrote, "Those aliens who have been listed for custodial detention comprise the alien leadership in Hawaii in every branch of alien activity, namely: businessmen, consular agents, Japanese language school teachers and principals, Buddhist and Shinto priests, and others of no particular affiliation who by reason of their extreme nationalistic sentiments would be a danger to our security as well as others who have seen Japanese military service."[5]

Still, unlike on the mainland, where no attempt to differentiate those (few) Japanese who might constitute a threat from those (many) who did not, economic and civic necessity required a more surgical approach. In addition to those on the FBI list, first to be examined would be Kibei, native-born American citizens who had been sent to Japan, either to live with family or for all or some of their education. Although Attorney General Warren had testified that such a practice was widespread, the number of Kibei in Hawaii was actually quite small, only about 3,000 throughout the territory.

Beginning on the afternoon of December 7, even before war had been declared, FBI agents began rounding up those on the lists. Although the memo had specified "aliens," some citizens were taken away too, and then often held incommunicado: "In many cases, the head of the family simply disappeared, and several weeks passed before his family learned he had been interned; in other cases, children were left unattended when both parents were interned. The sweep teams searched homes and business properties; they regarded the possession of Japanese flags, patriotic literature, swords or other Japanese treasures, or even board games in the Japanese language as ample evidence to detain the owners."[6]

More than 2,000 arrests were made in the initial sweep and, although an additional 10,000 individuals identified as potential subversives would be examined by the FBI or ONI, most of those later incarcerated were in this first group. Many who were not arrested or even under the vaguest suspicion lost their jobs saw their businesses boycotted, or had bank loans or mortgages called in.

Ten days after the Pearl Harbor attack, Walter Short was relieved of command and replaced by General Delos Emmons, whose views of both the Japanese and island security were far more enlightened. On December 21, Emmons broadcast a radio address in which he praised the populace for its resolve in the face of unprecedented trial: "Hawaii has always been an American outpost of friendliness and good will and now has calmly accepted its responsibility as an outpost of war." In a demand for tolerance, Emmons added, "In accepting these responsibilities it is important that Hawaii prove that her traditional confidence in her cosmopolitan population has not been misplaced." Addressing the workers who were fired, he told employers, "I wish to emphasize the fact that if the courage of the people of these islands is to be maintained and morale of the entire population sustained, we cannot afford to unnecessarily and indiscriminately keep a number of loyal workers from useful employment."[7]

Emmons also assured Hawaiians that any threat of subversive activity was being actively investigated and that a number of potential fifth columnists had been detained. But, he cautioned, "These people are not prisoners of war and will not be treated as such." In this Emmons was being disingenuous, as he was when he asserted, "There is no intention or desire on the part of the federal authorities to operate mass concentration camps. No person, be he citizen or alien, need worry provided he is not connected with subversive elements."

That turned out not at all to be true—almost 2,000 Japanese were eventually sent to the mainland for internment, and a smaller number would be interned on the islands. Still, the vast majority were allowed to remain in their homes.

But that does not mean they were well treated. Hawaii remained under martial law, with legal guarantees suspended until 1944. Japanese were not allowed to travel more than ten miles from their homes, or to change jobs or residences, without approval from the army. Soldiers often conducted random searches without warrants of the homes of Japanese citizens, looking for anything that might signal disloyalty.

Curfews and blackouts were strictly enforced: "At the Puna Hongwanji temple, American soldiers shot their rifles at a flashing light in the tower after one insisted it was a spy sending coded light signals to the Japanese in violation of the blackout regulations. Explaining that the tower was a columbarium where the deceased members' ashes were kept, a lay Buddhist member of the temple led the soldiers up the stairs, where they found a large mirror, reflecting the moonlight."[8]

Japanese were forbidden to own boats, and so fishermen could not work. Others were barred from certain jobs, and Japanese were not allowed to teach school. Many Nisei were required to wear black badges issued by the army, on which the word "Restricted" was printed. Anyone wearing such a badge could not work in areas designated as "sensitive" by the military. All activities considered "un-American" were targeted, including religion. "The Office of the Military Governor's official policy was to 'discourage Japanese religious activities other than Christian,'" and Buddhists were "encouraged" to attend Christian churches.[9] Thus, even free, Japanese Americans were never allowed to forget they were considered enemies of their country.

Evaluating Emmons's role is difficult. Many innocent Japanese Americans were indeed displaced, while the remainder suffered gross violations of their constitutional rights. But there is also the view that although "Emmons gave lip service to the need for an evacuation, he really staged a shrewdly calculated deliberate delaying action, raising one obstacle after another to any mass evacuation scheme. This required no small degree of moral courage. . . . The path he followed carried no small risk of having his career blighted or ended by obstructing Washington's plan. But he held to his course of preventing mass evacuation."[10]

21 | Infamy

In mid-January 1942, Governor Olson and Attorney General Warren, likely opponents in the 1942 California gubernatorial election, competed in pandering to what they perceived to be public opinion and advocated full evacuation of the Japanese population, but sentiment against the Japanese did not really turn until publication of the Roberts Commission report: "Editorial opinion had run about five to one favoring fair treatment of the Japanese prior to the Roberts Commission report. After its publication, editorials dramatically pivoted to six to one against."[1] Even a cursory reading of Roberts's findings would have actually absolved Japanese Americans and identified probable anti-American activities as emanating almost exclusively from consular personnel and other Japanese officials in Hawaii. But the drumbeat of treachery was by then sufficient to prime Americans on the West Coast to embrace almost any conspiracy theory.

The arrival of Karl Bendetsen in early February eliminated any chance that Japanese Americans would be treated with even a scintilla of justice. Before Bendetsen appeared on the scene, DeWitt, as he often did, had vacillated between demanding full displacement, because "a Jap is a Jap," and considering such an enormous task a crazy idea. Major General Allen W. Gullion, the army's provost marshal, responsible for security, had been advocating displacing every person of Japanese ancestry to concentration camps since Pearl Harbor and had grown frustrated with DeWitt's lack of resolve.[2] Gullion chose Bendetson, then only a captain, whose work in Washington on Gullion's staff had revealed the right combination of brains, ambition, and amorality to get the job done. As a reward for keeping DeWitt pointed in the right direction, Bendetsen would be promoted an astounding three times in February 1942, ending the month as a full colonel.

Bendetsen turned out to be precisely the right man for an odious job. On February 4, he put his plan into motion with a memo to Assistant Secretary of War John McCloy, "Alien Enemies on the West Coast." The content was pure fabrication, a pursuit in which Bendetsen excelled. "A substantial majority of the Nisei bear allegiance to Japan, are well controlled and disciplined by the enemy, and at the proper time will engage in organized espionage, particularly should a raid along the West Coast be attempted by the Japanese."[3]

No action was taken at the time because many in Washington, including Attorney General Francis Biddle and FBI director J. Edgar Hoover, along with many senior military personnel, such as Delos Emmons, thought the threat massively overblown, and that if any individual Japanese Americans were security risks, they could be dealt with using normal police procedures.

With Bendetsen urging him, DeWitt contacted Secretary of War Henry Stimson to make the case for mass deportation under aegis of the army. On February 14, he wrote to Stimson insisting that "the Japanese race is an enemy race," and that Japanese Americans, even those born in the United States, will "turn against this nation when the final test of loyalty comes."[4]

Although FDR remained skeptical, the threat—more precisely, the illusion of threat—had become too immediate to ignore. The decision to issue Executive Order 9066 seemed justified when the Tolan Committee hearings provided irrefutable scientific evidence that the Japanese presence in the West would prove catastrophic. Warren's charts, lists, testaments, and testimony demanded immediate action, and one week later DeWitt and Bendetsen took it.

On March 2, under the authority of the executive order "to prescribe military areas in such places and of such extent as he or the appropriate Military Commander may determine, from which any or all persons may be excluded," DeWitt created Military Areas 1 and 2. Area 1, considered the more sensitive, took in the western halves of Washington and Oregon, the western half of California north of Los Angeles, all of southern California and southern Arizona. The rest of these states made up Military Area 2, that is, the remainder of Washington, Oregon, California, and Arizona.

The original plan was that anyone of Japanese descent, citizen or not, would be forbidden from Area 1, but they were free to voluntarily relocate, including to Area 2. Anyone leaving Area 1 voluntarily, which initially included German and Italian aliens, but not citizens, need only submit a form with their new address to the post office. Area 2 would be monitored, but there would be no evacuations. One week later, the army acquired land in Owens valley, an arid, desolate, sparsely populated area east of the Sierra Nevada Mountains, freezing in winter and broiling in summer, which would eventually become the Manzanar internment camp.

The Japanese were made aware an evacuation order was coming. The day before DeWitt published the proclamation, Mike Masaoka, of the Japanese American Citizens' League, told reporters, "We are preparing our people to move out. We want them to go without bitterness, without rancor, and with the feeling that this can be their contribution to defense of the United States. Naturally, our people would leave instantly on orders from the Army, but we hope to leave, you might say, before the Army sees fit to kick us out."[5] Not everyone in the Japanese American community was happy to be so malleable, and Masaoka would remain a controversial figure for his acquiescence, but there was widespread feeling that nothing should be done that implied a lack of patriotism.

On March 16, four more zones were added, covering Idaho, Nevada, Montana, and Utah, but these were subject to "restrictions" rather than evacuation. The main purpose of the new designations, however, was to provide sites for relocation camps when the need arose. The military designation became necessary when a number of state governors objected to locating internment camps within their borders. The March 16 proclamation also included an extensive list of installations and infrastructure, such as railroad tunnels, that were specifically off limits. Two days later, President Roosevelt signed another executive order, which created the War Relocation Authority and named General Eisenhower's brother Milton as director. Two days after that, Santa Anita racetrack was acquired to serve as a temporary detention center.

It had become clear to DeWitt, likely at Bendetsen's urging, that voluntary resettlement would not accomplish the goal. Most Japanese in Area 1 had no place else to go and were reluctant to leave their homes, possessions, and employment behind to travel inland to an uncertain future. DeWitt had been empowered to enact curfews and institute other security measures, which he had, and some Japanese Americans had already been removed from military areas considered highly sensitive, but no one in the government or military, except perhaps Gullion or Bendetsen, wanted American troops or local police to be seen forcibly dragging tens of thousands of people from their homes and herding them on to buses or trucks. It did not seem astute public relations for a nation that had denounced fascism.

Instead, at the behest of DeWitt and Secretary of War Stimson, on March 21, Congress passed Public Law 503, which mandated a year in prison and a $5,000 fine for "whoever shall enter, remain in, leave, or commit any act in any military area or military zone prescribed . . . contrary to the restrictions applicable to any such area or zone or contrary to the order of the Secretary of War or military commander."[6] Six days later, DeWitt issued his fourth proclamation, prohibiting voluntary relocation of Japanese civilians from military areas. In a way, this was the most cynical, since the excuse of "military necessity" that DeWitt, Bendetsen, and the others had been advancing would not be at all served by preventing Japanese Americans of their own volition from leaving areas considered vulnerable. It was this order that reduced every person of Japanese ancestry, regardless of age, sex, or previous behavior, to an enemy of the United States. From here, there was no doubt that the worst fears of 80,000 United States citizens and 40,000 Issei were to be realized.

No facilities existed to house 100,000 deportees, so the Army Corps of Engineers set to converting racetracks and athletic stadiums to temporary holding facilities while crude housing, "tar paper-covered barracks of simple frame construction without plumbing or cooking facilities of any kind," was thrown up by private contractors in more than a dozen locations, mostly in barren, isolated sections of the West.[7] It would be more than a year before the authorities thought to provide some bare insulation in the crude huts to ward off frigid winter temperatures.

Eventually, a vast concentration camp machinery was created, containing assembly centers, relocation centers, detention facilities, and isolation facilities, some run by the War Relocation Authority, some by the Department of Justice, some by the Federal Bureau of Prisons, some by the army, and some by the Immigration and Naturalization Service. Most were in the West, but of the relocation centers, which housed most of the internees, one had been built in Arkansas. Responsibility for identifying those to be deported, getting them to debarkation centers, and then transporting them to their grim destinations fell to the military, as did the job of providing security once the internees had arrived at the barbed-wire-enclosed camps. One of relocation centers, at Tule Lake in northeast California, was designated for Japanese Americans deemed security risks or "problems," which often meant those who had the temerity to protest being treated in a manner that violated, among other constitutional provisions, Fourteenth Amendment guarantees of

Japanese families having their possessions loaded on a bus leaving Manzanar for relocation, 1942. Photograph by Ansel Adams. Courtesy of Library of Congress Prints and Photographs Division.

due process and equal protection of the law. Most of the camps were patched together in spring and summer of 1942, but some were not completed until fall, although that was after the Japanese carrier fleet was decimated at Midway in early June, effectively ending any threat of invasion.

When the time came to report to debarkation stations, most Japanese Americans acquiesced and came to the appointed areas with only the scant possessions they could carry, some of which would be lost or destroyed by soldiers who considered them enemy prisoners of war. They were herded onto buses or railroad cars and taken to parts of the nation in which few white people thought fit to live. Most would remain there for three years.

The conditions in the camps were appalling. American citizens accused of no crimes had been deported to "spare, prison-like compounds situated on sunbaked deserts or bare Ozark hillsides, dotted with watchtowers and surrounded by barbed wire. The sites of the camps—Topaz in Utah, Minidoka in Idaho, Gila River and Poston in Arizona, Heart Mountain in Wyoming, Amache in Colorado, Rohwer and Jerome in Arkansas, and Tule Lake and Manzanar in California—had been chosen for their remoteness, and for most internees they must have seemed as alien as the surface of the moon. Life in the camps had a military flavor; internees slept in barracks or small compartments with no running water, took their meals in vast mess halls, and went about most of their daily business in public."[8]

In some cases, Japanese families were forced to live in what had been stalls for horses. Toilet facilities were inadequate and sometimes nonexistent. Food shortages were common, made worse by camp workers skimming such items as sugar and selling them on the black market. Medical facilities were primitive and medical supplies sparse.

With the resolve that had allowed them to make lives for themselves in a country in which they were largely despised, most Japanese in the camps tried desperately to create some semblance of normal life, especially for children. They set up schools, athletic activities, published camp newspapers—strictly censored by the army—and had even a police force and jails. The more the internees tried to make life seem normal, however, the more it was clear that it was not.

Military authorities encouraged "Americanization programs" for tens of thousands of people who were already American, and in a final insult required internees to sign loyalty oaths. "Japanese Americans who cooperated with the program were rewarded while those who resisted were isolated and labeled as 'troublemakers,'" and were sent to Tule Lake.[9] The physical conditions at Tule Lake were not substantially worse than at many of the other camps, but those assigned were considered little more than prisoners of war and were constantly harassed and denied even minimal civil liberties. That it was only the exercise of constitutionally guaranteed civil liberties that got an internee transferred to Tule Lake seemed lost on the War Department, Congress, and the White House.

What was remarkable was that unspeakable treatment did not cause the internees to turn against the country that had treated them so shabbily. Instead, many Japanese shamed the nation with their patriotism. In 1943, the War Department finally decided that native-born Americans of Japanese descent were perhaps not enemy aliens and were eligible

Members of the 442nd Regimental Combat Team salute the American flag, 1944. Many were enlisted from internment camps. Courtesy of Library of Congress Prints and Photographs Division.

to participate in the war effort. Not in the Pacific, of course—Japanese Americans could not be trusted *that* much. But the army asked for volunteers for a unit to be assigned to Europe. Almost immediately thousands of young men from either Hawaii or the mainland answered the call, many while being held in internment camps. Later in March 1943, 2,686 volunteers from Hawaii and 1,500 from the U.S. mainland went to Camp Shelby, Mississippi, to begin training.

The 442nd Regimental Combat Team, composed of these volunteers, was sent to Italy and fought with astonishing bravery, with more than 800 killed and hundreds more wounded. Eventually, more than 13,000 Nisei would serve in the most decorated unit for its size in the entire U.S. Army: "They won seven Distinguished Unit Citations, including one awarded personally by President Harry Truman who said, on July 15, 1946, 'You fought the enemy abroad and prejudice at home and you won.' In addition, after an exhaustive survey of individual awards from WWII, twenty more Medals of Honor were awarded, bringing the total to twenty-one. Over 4,000 Purple Hearts, 29 Distinguished Service Crosses, 588 Silver Stars, and more than 4,000 Bronze Stars were awarded to the men of the 442nd RCT for action during WWII."[10] One of those Medal of Honor winners was a twenty-year-old from Hawaii, Daniel Inouye, who lost an arm fighting in Italy, and so had to give up his dream of becoming a surgeon. Instead, he went on to be elected to the U.S. Senate, where he served for almost fifty years.

The brilliant record of those in combat did little to change the attitudes of military and civilian leaders spending the war years in the United States. The families of members of the 442nd learned of the heroism of their sons from behind barbed wire.

22 | Four Who Refused

Almost all Japanese were willing to endure both indignity and hardship to prove their patriotism, but some refused. Among them were four who would eventually force the Supreme Court to rule on whether Congress and the president had violated the Constitution by imprisoning without trial American citizens who had never been accused of even the most trivial prewar misdemeanor. Two would intentionally violate the dictates of Executive Order 9066 specifically to force such a court decision, the third would sue to regain employment, and the fourth would stay behind simply to remain with his girlfriend.

Just hours after General DeWitt's curfew order for Japanese took effect at 6 PM on March 28, 1942, Minoru Yasui approached a police officer in Portland, Oregon, and asked to be arrested. When the police officer refused, Yasui marched into the police station and demanded to be arrested there. The officer on duty did so. A lawyer and member of the Oregon bar, Yasui intended to test in court the constitutionality of a curfew that did not treat all citizens equally, the first challenge to DeWitt's dictatorial authority.

Yasui was born in Hood River, Oregon, in October 1916 to immigrant parents, the second of seven children. He was raised as a Methodist and attended public schools, although he also attended Japanese language school for three summers without gaining proficiency. His father, Masuo, was a success within the immigrant community. He owned an apple orchard and was part owner of 1,000 acres of land, which required him to have extensive, and largely cordial, dealings with his white counterparts. Masuo Yasui was a member of the Rotary Club and the Apple Growers Association and was friendly with the local bank president, who was his neighbor.

Min Yasui enrolled at the University of Oregon at seventeen, joined ROTC, and at age twenty-one was commissioned as a lieutenant in the Army Reserves. The same year, he entered law school and graduated two years later at age twenty-three. Unable to find enough work as a lawyer to support himself, Yasui accepted a job as an attaché at the Japanese consulate in Chicago, registering with the State Department as a foreign agent.

The day after Pearl Harbor, Yasui received a telegram from his father, Masuo: "Now that this country is at war and needs you, and since you are trained as an officer, I as your father urge to enlist immediately."[1]

Yasui immediately resigned from his consular job. As a reserve lieutenant, he had been ordered to report to Fort Vancouver, but the railroad refused to sell a train ticket to a "Jap." It was only after Yasui met with a Union Pacific lawyer, showed him the orders from the army, and lectured him on the Fourteenth Amendment that he was able to travel to Oregon.[2]

When he arrived at Fort Vancouver, he was put in charge of a platoon. The next day, however, the army declared him unacceptable for service and he was ordered off the base. Yasui, stubborn by his own admission, tried eight more times to enlist and was refused each time. A few days after that, his father was arrested and sent to an internment camp in Missoula, Montana.[3]

Yasui, determined to do what he could to help others in the Japanese community, opened a law practice in Hood River to help with their legal needs, the only attorney of Japanese heritage in Oregon. At one point, he traveled to Missoula to represent his father in the hearing that would determine whether Masuo Yasui was a threat, but he was not allowed to participate in the hearing: "I was permitted to sit in as a member of the family. The hearing was a complete farce. They produced some very childish maps of the Panama Canal, and they were saying, 'Do you know what these are?' Dad looked at them and said, 'They look like maps of the Panama Canal.' 'How did you get them,' he was asked. 'Well, my kids drew these maps in school.' They were illustrations of how the locks worked. The questioner said, 'This shows how you were really trying to disguise a nefarious plot to blow up the Panama Canal.' Dad said, 'Of course not.' 'Prove that you didn't have such an intention.'"[4]

Min Yasui said later, "Why a businessman and agriculturist with an impeccable reputation, living in a far-off rural town like Hood River—two hundred miles from the ocean and possibly three thousand miles from the Panama Canal—should have to prove that he had no intent to blow up the Panama Canal seemed to me then, and seems to me now, to be the height of absurdity."[5]

Absurd though it may have been, Masuo Yasui was classified as "disloyal" and was not released until 1945.

Min Yasui returned to Portland just in time to learn of Executive Order 9066, and he immediately sought to launch a test case: "We were going to find a Nisei who'd served in the Army and had an honorable discharge, with two or three little kids." When that did not work out and Yasui learned of the curfew to be instituted at 6 PM on March 28, he decided to be the test case himself. "No military authority," he said, "has the right to subject any United States citizen to any requirement that does not equally apply to all other U.S. citizens."[6]

He had his secretary call the police and report a Japanese man on the streets after curfew. The police ignored the call while Yasui walked along the Portland streets for hour after hour. Finally, at 11 PM, he approached a police officer and asked to be arrested. The officer told him to run along home before he got in trouble. He was forced to try a police station, where the officer on the desk obliged, and Min Yasui spent his first of many weekends on jail. The local newspaper ran a headline story, "Jap Spy Arrested."[7]

Gordon Kiyoshi Hirabayashi was born in Seattle, Washington, in April 1918, to Issei parents who operated "a fruit and vegetable store, more a roadside stand," in a farming village twenty miles south of the city.[8] His parents had been raised as Buddhists, but both had converted to Christianity before they left Japan in 1907. The sect they joined "had beliefs and values very like the Quakers," and they passed those convictions on to their children.

After high school, Hirabayashi enrolled at the University of Washington. In the summer of 1940, he attended a YMCA leadership conference at Columbia University in New York, which cemented his opposition to war. When he returned home, Hirabayashi joined the Quakers and registered as a conscientious objector.

"I remember that December 7, 1941 was a quiet Sunday morning in Seattle," Hirabayashi recalled. "We had just finished Meeting for Worship at the Friends Meeting. . . . One of our members broke the news. Japan has attacked Pearl Harbor in Hawaii! We are at war! It was unreal. . . . My immediate worry was what would happen to my parents and their generation . . . war with Japan instantly transformed them in 'enemy aliens.'"[9]

The potential impact of the attack on his own life did not immediately sink in: "I was a pretty naïve country hick; my most serious problem was trying to earn enough to continue school." When the curfew took effect on March 28, Hirabayashi realized the next move would be to begin evacuating those of Japanese ancestry from the West Coast. Still at the university, Hirabayashi obeyed the curfew for six weeks, rushing back to his dormitory from the library or coffee shop at 7:55 PM. Then, one time, he stopped and thought, "Why the hell am I running back and nobody else is?" Like Min Yasui, Hirabayashi would have considered a curfew for everyone reasonable, but this was different, "so obviously a violation of what the Constitution stood for, what citizenship meant."[10]

Hirabayashi decided to ignore the curfew and continued to move about freely as a law-abiding citizen. Assuming he would not be able to remain in school, he had not registered for the spring term, but he remained on campus where no one bothered him. He worked with the American Friends Service Committee, which was aiding Japanese families in which the father had already been interned. To reunite the families, he sometimes drove a mother, her children, and their belongings to the fairgrounds Puyallup where those awaiting relocation were held.

When the mandatory evacuation order was issued in May, Hirabayashi decided to resist, and refused to register. On May 16, accompanied by a lawyer and fellow Quaker, he walked into the FBI office, shook hands with the agent in charge, handed the agent a four-page explanation of his reasons, and waited to be arrested. The FBI agent attempted to talk him out of it, even drove him to a registration office to give Hirabayashi one last chance to change his mind. At that point, Hirabayashi had not thought of a test case. He was simply determined to insist that his constitutional rights as a United States citizen were upheld.

Mitsuye Endo, the only woman among the four resistors, was the daughter of grocery store clerk and a housewife and grew up with three siblings in a section of Sacramento dominated by Japanese families: "My father came to the United States in 1916, went back to marry, and then came back again in 1918 and never returned to Japan after that."[11] Mitsuye Endo went to secretarial school after high school in Sacramento and was then hired for a clerical job by the California Department of Motor Vehicles. Her employment included a background check, which revealed she was Methodist, she had a brother in the army—drafted in mid-1941—did not speak or read Japanese, had never been to Japan, and was totally loyal to the United States.

In the weeks after Pearl Harbor, Endo and other civil servants of Japanese origin heard rumors that they were all to be fired from their jobs. In January 1942, they were given lengthy questionnaires to complete to determine what if any sympathy they had for Japan. In the meantime, pressure to dismiss all state workers of Japanese background was growing, and few politicians were willing to take a stand against what they saw as popular sentiment.

After Executive Order 9066, the employees "were 'advised' to stay home from work although they were not formally dismissed." On April 2, all were suspended, and eleven days later each received a "statement of charges," in which they were accused of "failure of good behavior, fraud in securing employment, incompetency, inefficiency, and acts incompatible with and inimical to the public service." The charges were rife with absurd accusations, including that each employee was "violently opposed to a Democratic form of government."[12] In the face of these indictments, all were fired.

James Purcell, the lawyer who had been hired to assist the state workers, was preparing motions when the orders came through for all of Japanese ancestry to report to assembly centers for relocation. Mitsuye Endo reported to the Tanforan center, which, like Santa Anita, had previously been a racetrack. Here also, entire families were forced to live in what had been stalls for horses, some with the manure not fully swept out. Watchtowers had been erected and the guards manned machine guns. Soon afterward, she was transferred with her parents to Tule Lake.

Purcell examined the backgrounds of about one hundred of the fired employees looking for the right plaintiff and narrowed it to just a few: "While we were there, a representative of the attorney came into camp and wanted to select three or four of us and they started off with me because they thought I had the best background. They felt I represented a symbolic 'loyal' American."[13] Purcell recalled that Endo's résumé seemed "perfect," but the two would never meet. On July 12, he filed a petition of habeas corpus "asking the court to require Milton Eisenhower, as director of the War Relocation Authority and as the person responsible for her detention, to show cause why Mitsuye Endo should not be released from internment."[14]

The judge sat on the petition and would for almost a year. The authorities were well aware that Purcell would appeal an adverse ruling, which evidently made them uneasy. Endo was a demure, attractive, twenty-two-year-old woman with a spotless record, the very type of person who might just arouse sympathy in the press. An official from the

WRA offered to release her from internment if she agreed to remain out of the restricted zone. She could live and work wherever else she liked, but the entire state of California would be off limits. Her lawsuit, of course, would be dropped.

Endo refused. She told Purcell to press on with the case.

The fourth resister was both the least likely and destined to be the most famous.

Fred Toyosaburo Korematsu was born in Oakland, California, on January 30, 1919, to parents who ran a plant nursery. After graduating from high school, he worked as a shipyard welder until, like Mitsuye Endo, he lost his job after Pearl Harbor. When the order for relocation came, his parents and three brothers reported to Tanforan, but Fred Korematsu ignored it. His reasons were in no way political. He was in love with Ida Boitano, an Italian American, and, according to Korematsu, they had intended to travel to the Midwest and be married.

After Executive Order 9066, aware that he could be arrested at any time, Korematsu visited the offices of Bennett Masten, a plastic surgeon, and told the doctor he was married to an American woman and wanted to change his appearance to avoid harassment. Masten cautioned Korematsu that although he could make some minor adjustments, he could not make him look "American." But Korematsu insisted, and in early April, for $100, Masten completed some minor procedures on Korematsu's nose and eyelids. Calling himself "Cyde Sarah," Korematsu went about his business, confident he would not be recognized as Japanese.

But he was, and on May 30, 1942, three weeks after the mandatory evacuation date, Fred Korematsu was arrested in San Leandro, California. Although he initially claimed to be of Spanish/Hawaiian descent and refused to reveal his true identity, the documents he produced were obvious fakes and his story soon collapsed. Once he realized he was caught, Korematsu became cooperative and recounted his entire story to FBI agents. Ida Boitano confirmed that the couple had once planned to elope, but she had since realized that the idea was foolish and regretted ever being involved with Korematsu.

While awaiting trial for violating Public Law 503, he was visited in jail by an attorney with the San Francisco branch of the American Civil Liberties Union. The California ACLU was looking for someone for whom it could file suit to test the constitutionality of Executive Order 9066. Korematsu would have seemed an unlikely choice to accept the risks of being a plaintiff in a test case. Others who had been arrested for avoiding displacement had declined and chosen to plead guilty. But Korematsu turned out to be committed and stubborn, with a determination to fight injustice that made him perfect to become the named plaintiff in one of the most important equal rights cases in United States history. Later, he would say, "I didn't feel guilty because I didn't do anything wrong. . . . Every day in school, we said the pledge of the flag, 'with liberty and justice for all,' and I believed all that. I was an American citizen, and I had as many rights as anyone else."[15]

The California ACLU would also file for Min Yasui and Gordon Hirabayashi, but neither or their cases would attain the notoriety of the man who violated an unfair law to be with his girlfriend.

From the first, the treatment of the four resistors bore little resemblance to the judicial process that most Americans believed was based on fairness and justice. Min Yasui was let out on bail, but in May but was arrested once more and sent to the North Portland Livestock Pavilion, which had been converted none too carefully into a holding station. He remained literally penned up in stifling quarters with minimal light or ventilation all summer. In September, he and the other internees were piled into railroad cars and shipped to Idaho, where they were loaded into U.S. Army trucks for a long, bumpy ride to the Minidoka Relocation Camp: "We saw again the barbed wire fences, the watchtowers, guardhouses, the MP detachments . . . block after block of black, tar-paper barracks, about 120 feet long and about 20 feet wide."[16]

The conditions were ghastly, but for Yasui they were about to get worse. In November, he was returned to Portland where he was convicted by a federal judge and sentenced to a year in prison and a $5,000 fine, the maximum under the law. The judge's reasoning was as flawed and prejudicial as had been common when one of the parties was a United States citizen of Japanese ancestry. After he announced his intention to appeal, Yasui was held in solitary confinement in the county jail for nine months, denied exercise periods, and for three months showers and a haircut.

Gordon Hirabayashi spent five months in jail, held without bail, and then went to trial in front of Judge Lloyd Black, who had described the

Japanese as "unbelievably treacherous and wholly ruthless." After Black dismissed the constitutional challenge as a "technical interpretation of the Fifth Amendment," the trial lasted only one day, including ten minutes for jury deliberation. Hirabayashi was sentenced to ninety days in addition to time served, which should have allowed him to be assigned to a work camp, but no one could figure out what the arrangements should be, so Hirabayashi remained in a cell while his conviction was appealed.

After four months, he and Judge Black had "become sort of like old friends in terms of his knowledge of me," and so the judge, whose attitudes had softened, assigned Hirabayashi to work as a field officer in a new American Friends Service Committee office in Spokane, which was outside the restricted zone. All Hirabayashi need do was give his word not to return to the restricted zone, which he did.[17]

Mitsuye Endo was the most anonymous of the four resistors but would become perhaps the most important. In July, Purcell filed for a writ of habeas corpus, claiming Endo was "being held against her will by General DeWitt."[18] Her petition was denied, and Purcell appealed.

As the appeal was working its way through the legal system, Endo was transferred from Tule Lake to the Topaz Relocation Center in Utah, set, as were the other camps, in a barren stretch outside the town of Delta. Although the conditions at Topaz were marginally better, the transfer actually extended Endo's incarceration. Purcell had filed Endo's appeal with the court in San Francisco, which no longer had jurisdiction, and so the process had to begin anew. At Topaz, a government lawyer tried once more to bribe her into abandoning her appeal. "You're clearly a person who has been loyal to the United States all the time," he told her. "You've never said or done anything to raise the slightest question. The FBI report gives you complete clearance. All you need do is ask for the right to leave the center and you can go. Any leave we grant you will expressly exclude return to the restricted area, but we'll help you relocate anywhere else in the United States."[19] As she had before, she refused.

In the end, Endo would never appear in court. Her case went from *Endo v. Eisenhower* to *Ex parte Endo*. She shunned publicity during the case and afterward.

Korematsu was briefly released on bail, then rearrested and taken to Tanforan. The ACLU filed motions on his behalf, but he refused bond a second time, preferring San Francisco County Jail to a converted horse stall. In September, Earl Warren, by then the Republican candidate for governor and overwhelming favorite to win, filed a brief supporting DeWitt's authority to order evacuations, even though martial law had not been declared on the Pacific Coast.[20] The following day, the judge rejected the ACLU motions and upheld both FDR's authority to issue Executive Order 9066 and General DeWitt's authority to issue evacuation orders to enforce it. At his one-day trial the following week, Korematsu was convicted of violating the evacuation order. Although the judge admitted that Korematsu had "no evil intentions," he sentenced him to five years' probation, but hoped that a "higher court would rule on the case."[21]

The judge set bail at $2,500 pending the appeal, which the ACLU announced its intention to post. A military policeman in the courtroom immediately grabbed him. "I was supposed to be free to go, but the MP got all excited," Korematsu said later. "He wasn't going to let me on the street, and he pulled a gun on me and said he was not going to let me go." After some confusion, Korematsu was led out under armed guard and returned to Tanforan, after which he was sent back to Topaz.[22]

The ACLU filed its appeal in circuit court in December, while Korematsu languished at Topaz. The appeal read: "that aliens here from neutral countries should enjoy greater rights than those unfortunate people (Americans of Japanese ancestry) is unwarranted; that Japanese nationals (those born in Japan) should enjoy rights equal to theirs indefensible; that alien enemies, nationals of Nazi Germany and Fascist Italy, should possess greater rights, privileges, immunities, and liberties in America than those native-born citizens is a disgraceful travesty of justice."[23]

23 | A Caricature of Justice

In all four appeals, there were no shortage of technical questions of law, such as whether the military could take responsibility for judicial or quasi-judicial functions in the absence of a declaration of martial law or while civilian courts were active, or the constitutional extent of "war powers." But jurisprudence was almost certainly beside the point. In the end, the courts of appeals and then the Supreme Court would be forced to decide whether to overrule the president and Congress in time of war. The task should not have been difficult. Edward Ennis, the director of the Justice Department's Alien Enemy Control Unit, informed the solicitor general that the Hirabayashi and Masui cases were weak and should be dismissed. The government plowed ahead.

The government's arguments, like the laws from which they sprung, were indeed deeply flawed. As one government lawyer pointed out, the orders in effect left John DeWitt and Karl Bendetsen—who by this time was well known—free on their own to decide the guilt or innocence of 80,000 U.S. citizens.

The court of appeals heard three of the cases, all but *Ex parte Endo*, on February 19, 1943, the one-year anniversary of Executive Order 9066.[1] Lawyers for both sides argued the merits of their cases, the government largely relying on "military necessity" as a justification for its behavior, while the lawyers for the resistors continued to insist that military necessity or not, the government's actions were prompted only by ethnicity and not by genuine national security concerns. They did not, however, have access to the Ringle report, which may well have buttressed their arguments, because the government had suppressed its distribution.

None of this turned out to matter a great deal. Rather than issue a ruling on any of the cases, in March 1943, the court on technical grounds referred the case to the Supreme Court. The justices on the high bench could have returned the cases to circuit court but, in April, chose instead to accept them. Oral arguments were scheduled for May 10, leaving little time for either side to prepare.

Government lawyers were in a bind. If the justification for the extraordinary action of displacing 80,000 U.S. citizens without trial was the presence of an extraordinary threat, there would seem to be some need to demonstrate that the threat actually existed. But there had been no acts of sabotage, no indictments for espionage, no evidence of fifth column activity at all. In addition, not a single Japanese American had admitted that loyalty to Japan outstripped his or her loyalty to the United States, or even in fact that there existed any loyalty to Japan at all. Quite the reverse. DeWitt had made no attempt to discern whether the Niseis'—and Isseis' for that matter—professed loyalty to the United States was untrue. He had just assumed it was.

But the Supreme Court was in a bind too. If the Court ruled against the government, immense resources would have to be diverted from the war effort to return more than 100,000 people to their homes, to say nothing of the police presence that would have been required to prevent them from attacks by vengeful whites. And so, the Court did what the Court often does when a no-win case is put before them.

They dodged it.

They returned the only case in which ruling on the validity of the evacuation order was unavoidable, *Korematsu*, to circuit court, and then confined their rulings in *Hirabayashi* and *Yasui* to the legality of the curfew, a much less explosive question with little practical implication. The only issue, then, was "whether, acting in cooperation, Congress and the Executive have constitutional authority to impose the curfew . . . and whether the order itself was an appropriate means of carrying out the Executive Order for the 'protection against espionage and against sabotage.'"[2]

On June 21, by a unanimous vote, the Court ruled that the curfew was reasonable and upheld both convictions.

The principal ruling was in *Hirabayashi*. Although the technical question was whether allowing DeWitt to make up the rules as he went along was an unconstitutional delegation of congressional authority, the real issue was simply whether the government was allowed, in wartime, to discriminate against a specific class of citizens simply because they decided, without evidence, that those citizens constituted a threat.

Chief Justice Harlan Fiske Stone authored the main opinion. Stone, who had been dean of Columbia Law School and member of a Wall Street law firm, in earlier years had been a passionate defender of free speech. Most significantly, however, Stone was the author of the famous "Footnote Four," in *United States v. Carolene Products* (1938), "arguably the most important footnote in U.S. constitutional law," which "presages a shift in the Supreme Court from predominately protecting property rights to protecting other individual rights, such as those found in the First Amendment."[3] In his note, Stone pointed out that even though legislation aimed at economic regulation should enjoy a presumption of constitutionality, "there may be narrower scope for operation of the presumption of constitutionality when legislation appears on its face to be within a specific prohibition of the Constitution, such as those of the first ten amendments, which are deemed equally specific when held to be embraced within the Fourteenth."[4] In those cases, "more exacting judicial scrutiny" was required.

But more exacting judicial scrutiny would not help Gordon Hirabayashi. In fact, Stone accepted the military necessity argument entirely and pressed in conference to make the decision unanimous. The power to wage war, he wrote "extends to every matter and activity so related to war as substantially to affect its conduct and progress. The power is not restricted to the winning of victories in the field and the repulse of enemy forces. It embraces every phase of the national defense, including the protection of war materials and the members of the armed forces from injury and from the dangers which attend the rise, prosecution and progress of war."[5]

To do so, he concluded that, because Japanese Americans had been largely shunned by whites, which "tended to increase their isolation, and in many instances their attachments to Japan and its institutions," the government was within its rights to deem them a threat, even those who were American citizens. In other words, Japanese Americans were allowed to be discriminated against because they had previously been discriminated against.

And so, making scant distinction between Japanese naval officers and Japanese Americans, and buying into the racist screeds of Phelan, Webb, Hearst, McClatchy, and Earl Warren, "we conclude that it was within the constitutional power of Congress and the executive arm of the Government to prescribe this curfew order for the period under consideration and that its promulgation by the military commander involved no unlawful delegation of legislative power."

Three justices wrote separate opinions, including Frank Murphy, who wrote a concurrent opinion that for a while sounded very much like a dissent. (He had originally written a scathing dissent but had been talked out of publishing it "for the good of the country"):

> Today is the first time, so far as I am aware, that we have sustained a substantial restriction of the personal liberty of citizens of the United States

> based upon the accident of race or ancestry. Under the curfew order here challenged no less than 70,000 American citizens have been placed under a special ban and deprived of their liberty because of their particular racial inheritance. In this sense it bears a melancholy resemblance to the treatment accorded to members of the Jewish race in Germany and in other parts of Europe. The result is the creation in this country of two classes of citizens for the purposes of a critical and perilous hour—to sanction discrimination between groups of United States citizens on the basis of ancestry. In my opinion this goes to the very brink of constitutional power.

Murphy, a noted liberal, had been appointed by Franklin Roosevelt after a long and varied career in public life, which included establishing a civil liberties division in the Justice Department when he was Roosevelt's attorney general. But here, Murphy too was willing to give in to racist propaganda: "In view, however, of the critical military situation which prevailed on the Pacific Coast area in the spring of 1942, and the urgent necessity of taking prompt and effective action to secure defense installations and military operations against the risk of sabotage and espionage, the military authorities should not be required to conform to standards of regulatory action appropriate to normal times. Because of the damage wrought by the Japanese at Pearl Harbor and the availability of new weapons and new techniques with greater capacity for speed and deception in offensive operations, the immediate possibility of an attempt at invasion somewhere along the Pacific Coast had to be reckoned with."

The *Yasui* opinion was brief, differing only as to whether Min Yasui had forfeited his citizenship by opposing the government's actions, which had already been rendered moot. His conviction, as a citizen, was also sustained.

But the Court's rulings, as Justice Owen Roberts would later put it, applied only to "a case of keeping people off the streets at night," not to the broader question of whether forced displacement was permissible under the Constitution.[6] That would wait for Fred Korematsu.

After his Supreme Court appeal was denied, Gordon Hirabayashi's odyssey became surreal. He still had ninety days to serve, which qualified him to do so at a work camp, but the nearest work camp was in Tucson, Arizona. The FBI agent in charge agreed to let Hirabayashi go there—

unaccompanied—from Spokane, if he paid his own way. The agent even wrote a letter in case Hirabayashi ran into problems on the way. But Hirabayashi was unwilling to spend money to transport himself to a prison sentence, so he hitchhiked 1,600 miles, stopping off in Idaho on the way to visit his parents, who had been transferred there from Tule Lake, and then saw friends in Salt Lake City.

Two weeks later, when he arrived at Tucson, the U.S. marshal in charge of the camp had no paperwork and told Hirabayashi to return to Spokane. Hirabayashi told him to look again and the paperwork was found, but only after the marshal had allowed Hirabayashi to see a film in an air-conditioned movie theater. Hirabayashi completed his sentence, was given a bus ticket to return to Spokane, and spent the rest of war working for the Friends Committee, aiding Japanese families.

Min Yasui remained in solitary confinement awaiting sentencing for almost two months after the Supreme Court's decision. Like Hirabayashi, he would face a legal establishment whose attitudes had changed. The war in the Pacific, still raging, had turned decisively the United States' way, and there seemed little doubt of the ultimate outcome. The West Coast was secure, free of sabotage, and the army felt safe enough with the loyalty of Japanese Americans that it had recruited Nisei men to form the 442nd Regimental Combat Team.

In late July or early August 1943, Yasui's lawyer told him that the judge considered time served sufficient to complete his sentence and in addition waived the $5,000 fine. A U.S. marshal drove him to Idaho and the Minidoka camp: "I came out of Multnomah County Jail pale and pasty-faced, and a bit bloated and flabby, having been confined to a space of less than forty-eight square feet for nine months . . . it's almost as if my life had been suspended for nine months."[7]

When Yasui arrived at Minidoka, he volunteered for the army infantry but was rejected.

24 | The Courage to Do What's Right

The Supreme Court had returned *Korematsu* to circuit court, and in December 1943 the circuit court unanimously kicked it right back. Whether the Supreme Court was stalling for time or naïvely hoped the circuit court would relieve it of a disagreeable responsibility is not clear, but that the case would ultimately be decided in Washington, DC, was inevitable. *Endo* was also certain to end up on the high court docket.

When the petitions to the Court arrived in spring or fall of 1944, they were heard under vastly altered political and military conditions than when the cases had originally been heard. The Japanese had continued to be pushed back toward their home islands. Australia was no longer under threat, and retaking the Philippines seemed on the horizon. In Europe, the Allies were moving through Italy and an invasion of France from across the English Channel was only a matter of time. In addition, although the vast majority of interned Japanese Americans remained behind barbed wire, more and more were being released to work, and sometimes relocated, outside the restricted zone. Delos Emmons had replaced John DeWitt as head of Western Command, and "military necessity" seemed an outdated justification for continuing internment. In fact, Secretary of War Stimson had stated that very thing in a cabinet meeting in May 1944. Still, even after Emmons proposed beginning a large-scale return of internees to the restricted zone in the summer, FDR, with his election to a fourth term only months away, decided it would be unwise "to do anything drastic or sudden."[1]

However the practicalities of undoing mass displacement were finally determined, they would not effect whether the nation was willing to face up to the responsibility for initiating the policy in the first place, or whether it had done so legally. It is easy to see why the justices of the Supreme Court were in no hurry to be the ones making that determination. Declaring the policy illegal would not only amount to an unprecedented rebuke of a wartime president and Congress but also would create equally unprecedented civil liability for tens of thousands falsely imprisoned and tens of millions in monetary losses. Upholding a policy that was increasingly seen as born of racial prejudice was hardly a more palatable alternative. Although the Court stalled and deferred *Korematsu* and *Endo* until the fall term, on October 11 and 12, 1944, the justices could no longer avoid being forced into that very choice when *Korematsu v. United States* and *Ex parte Endo* were argued before them.

Neither Fred Korematsu nor Mitsuye Endo were in the courtroom to hear the proceedings. In March, Korematsu had been released from Topaz, but not from custody, to work as a welder in Detroit. Endo remained incarcerated, and she had refused to accept any relocation other than to return to her home.

Once again, although the arguments seemed to be on the fine points of the law or whether "military necessity" technically existed or whether Congress needed to sign off on Executive Order 9066 or specifically what laws and orders Korematsu had violated or whether Endo had cause to be fired or whether General DeWitt had acted in good faith, these cases were about a larger and more fundamental question of justice in the United States, and it is hard to believe a single person in the courtroom did not know it.

One telling line of argument came from James Purcell, representing Endo. One of the most controversial aspects of the displacements was that the innocent were swept along with (possibly) guilty. The government had taken the position that the threat was so immediate that there was simply no time to separate the loyal from the disloyal. (They ignored pronouncements such as DeWitt's that "there were no loyal Japs.") But Endo *had* been separated—her background check by the state of California had judged her totally loyal. Purcell insisted that once that had occurred, the government had forfeited the right to subject her to any action that would restrict her liberty or violate her constitutional rights.

By the time the justices retired to discuss the cases, more than one-quarter of those who had been interned had been released to live and work outside the restricted zone. There had not been a single occasion in which even one of them had displayed a scintilla of disloyalty. Among those paroled was Min Yasui. Denied the opportunity to serve in the military, Yasui had traveled to Chicago to work not as a lawyer but as a laborer in an ice plant.

The decisions were rendered on December 13, 1944. Once again, Chief Justice Stone had attempted to attain unanimity, especially in *Korematsu*. This time he failed. Although the decision, as in the previous cases, was for the government, three justices issued stinging dissents.

Rather than write the majority opinion himself, Stone delegated the task to Associate Justice Hugo Black. A native Alabaman, Black had been appointed by FDR in 1937 because the president wanted an "evangelical New Dealer" to replace retired Justice Willis Van Devanter, a personal nemesis. Black was a bit of an enigma—a strict constructionist who believed the Fourteenth Amendment guarantees bound states and also the federal government, and a Ku Klux Klan member until age forty who had made his reputation in 1911 representing a Black woman prisoner who had been forced into slave labor. Black would serve on the Court until his death in 1971, and become known as one of the Court's leading civil libertarians.

He would not be so in *Korematsu*, however, and Black and his fellow justices were well aware the case was about a good deal more than one person's violation of an order. "We are being asked to pass at this time upon the whole subsequent detention program in both assembly and relocation centers," he wrote.

As the Court had in almost every racially discriminatory ruling, Black began with a lofty statement of principles, in this case borrowing from Stone's *Carolene Products* footnote: "All legal restrictions which curtail the civil rights of a single racial group are immediately suspect. That is not to say that all such restrictions are unconstitutional. It is to say that courts must subject them to the most rigid scrutiny. Pressing public necessity may sometimes justify the existence of such restrictions; racial antagonism never can." Moreover, "exclusion from the area in which one's home is located is a far greater deprivation than constant confinement to the home from 8 PM to 6 AM. Nothing short of apprehension by the proper military authorities of the gravest imminent danger to the public safety can constitutionally justify either."[2]

From there, Black proceeded to postulate pressing public necessity where none existed and deny the racial antagonism that was there for all to see: "In this case, the petitioner challenges the assumptions upon which we rested our conclusions in the *Hirabayashi* case. He also urges that, by May 1942, when Order No. 34 was promulgated, all danger of Japanese invasion of the West Coast had disappeared. After careful consideration of these contentions, we are compelled to reject them. . . . Like curfew, exclusion of those of Japanese origin was deemed necessary because of the presence of an unascertained number of disloyal members of the group. . . . It was because we could not reject the finding of the military authorities [in *Hirabayashi*] that it was impossible to bring about an immediate segregation of the disloyal from the loyal that we sustained the validity of the curfew order as applying to the whole group."

Black felt the need to append an apologia that was both hypocritical and insulting: "We are not unmindful of the hardships imposed by [the order] upon a large group of American citizens. But hardships are part of war, and war is an aggregation of hardships. All citizens alike, both in and out of uniform, feel the impact of war in greater or lesser measure. Citizenship has its responsibilities, as well as its privileges, and, in time of war, the burden is always heavier. Compulsory exclusion of large groups of citizens from their homes, except under circumstances of direst emergency and peril, is inconsistent with our basic governmental institutions. But when, under conditions of modern warfare, our shores are threatened by hostile forces, the power to protect must be commensurate with the threatened danger."

In his final paragraph, Black wrote, incredibly, "To cast this case into outlines of racial prejudice, without reference to the real military dangers which were presented, merely confuses the issue."

Does it indeed . . .

Justices Roberts, Jackson, and Murphy dissented, and they did so with undisguised bitterness, in part clearly of regret for not opposing Stone in *Hirabayashi.*

Robert Jackson, who would later serve as the lead prosecutor at the Nuremberg war crimes trial, made it clear that racial prejudice did not confuse the issue at all: "A citizen's presence in the locality, however, was made a crime only if his parents were of Japanese birth. Had Korematsu been one of four—the others being, say, a German alien enemy, an Italian alien enemy, and a citizen of American-born ancestors, convicted of treason but out on parole—only Korematsu's presence would have violated the order. The difference between their innocence and his crime would result, not from anything he did, said, or thought, different than they, but only in that he was born of different racial stock."

The damage went beyond Korematsu himself or even Japanese Americans. Jackson insisted that in upholding the conviction, "the Court for all time has validated the principle of racial discrimination in criminal procedure and of transplanting American citizens. The principle then lies about like a loaded weapon, ready for the hand of any authority that can bring forward a plausible claim of an urgent need. Every repetition imbeds that principle more deeply in our law and thinking and expands it to new purposes."

Justice Roberts, who wrote the report that, unwitting as it may have been, was instrumental in supporting the extreme measures that followed, declared that this was a "case of convicting a citizen as a punishment for not submitting to imprisonment in a concentration camp, based on his ancestry, and solely because of his ancestry, without evidence or inquiry concerning his loyalty and good disposition towards the United States. If this be a correct statement of the facts disclosed by this record, and facts of which we take judicial notice, I need hardly labor the conclusion that Constitutional rights have been violated."

Unable to avoid a dash of sarcasm, Roberts concluded, "It is a new doctrine of constitutional law that one indicted for disobedience to an unconstitutional statute may not defend on the ground of the invalidity of the statute, but must obey it though he knows it is no law, and, after he has suffered the disgrace of conviction and lost his liberty by sentence, then, and not before, seek, from within prison walls, to test the validity of the law."

But the most vicious attack on the majority came from Frank Murphy, who had been talked out of dissenting in *Hirabayashi.* Mincing no words, he characterized the decision as falling "into the ugly abyss of racism . . . no reasonable relation to an 'immediate, imminent, and impending' public danger is evident to support this racial restriction, which is one of the most sweeping and complete deprivations of constitutional rights in the history of this nation in the absence of martial law." Murphy went to the heart of DeWitt's "a Jap is a Jap" pronouncement: "No adequate reason is given for the failure to treat these Japanese Americans on an individual basis by holding investigations and hearings to separate the loyal from the disloyal, as was done in the case of persons of German and Italian ancestry."

Murphy concluded, "I dissent, therefore, from this legalization of racism. Racial discrimination in any form and in any degree has no justifiable part whatever in our democratic way of life. It is unattractive in any setting, but it is utterly revolting among a free people who have embraced the principles set forth in the Constitution of the United States."

Would that others had agreed with him.

Ex parte Endo was decided just afterward and, using James Purcell's distinction, allowed the justices who had upheld Korematsu's conviction to find a bit of cover. Mitsuye Endo was to be freed. The decision was unanimous, and the majority opinion was written by another Roosevelt appointee and future champion of civil liberties, William O. Douglas. Although the decision was the reverse of that in *Korematsu*, Douglas, as had Black, tried to keep the question narrow and duck the central issue. Also as in *Korematsu*, Frank Murphy and Owen Roberts did not let him get away with it.

After an extensive recapitulation of the orders, proclamations, and rules under which Japanese Americans were confined and in some cases released outside the restricted zone, Douglas pronounced, "We are of the view that Mitsuye Endo should be given her liberty." He was careful to add, however, "In reaching that conclusion, we do not come to the underlying constitutional issues which have been argued." The reason for the release, as Purcell had argued, was that "whatever power the War Relocation Authority may have to detain other classes of citizens, it has no authority to subject citizens who are concededly loyal to its leave procedure."[3] To justify that distinction, which had never been made in the past, Douglas resorted to a good deal of smoke-and-mirrors legal distinctions, such as that Endo was not being held by the military but rather by the civilian-run WRA, or the difference between executive and legislative authority. Conspicuous by its absence was any mention that the entire basis of *Endo*, as it had been in three previous cases, was the very sort of racial discrimination that the Fifth Amendment had been enacted to outlaw.

Justice Murphy filled that gap: "I join in the opinion of the Court, but I am of the view that detention in Relocation Centers of persons of Japanese ancestry regardless of loyalty is not only unauthorized by Congress or the Executive, but is another example of the unconstitutional resort to racism inherent in the entire evacuation program."

Although released, Endo continued to be barred from the restricted zone, which Murphy found repugnant: "If, as I believe, the military orders excluding her from California were invalid at the time they were issued, they are increasingly objectionable at this late date, when the threat of invasion of the Pacific Coast and the fears of sabotage and espionage have greatly diminished. For the Government to suggest under these circumstances that the presence of Japanese blood in a loyal American citizen might be enough to warrant her exclusion from a place where she would otherwise have a right to go is a position I cannot sanction."

Owen Roberts also zeroed in on the continued restriction of Endo's movements: "The court is squarely faced with a serious constitutional question—whether the relator's detention violated the guarantees of the Bill of Rights of the federal Constitution, and especially the guarantee of due process of law. There can be but one answer to that question. An admittedly loyal citizen has been deprived of her liberty for a period of years. Under the Constitution, she should be free to come and go as she pleases. Instead, her liberty of motion and other innocent activities have been prohibited and conditioned. She should be discharged."

Roberts and Murphy aside, the Court took refuge in the false distinction between the *Endo* case and the other three. *Endo* was different, Douglas wrote, because she had been investigated and proven loyal, which did not address how more than 100,000 Japanese Americans had been demonstrated to be even potentially disloyal. But he dodged the most important question: "In reaching that conclusion . . . we do not come to the underlying constitutional issues which have been argued." In the face of a government that had merely, against all evidence, assumed disloyalty, he added, "Whatever power the War Relocation Authority may have to detain other classes of citizens, it has no authority to subject citizens who are concededly loyal to its leave procedure."

Douglas also neglected to mention that many other former government and private employees had successfully undergone background checks and had been incarcerated anyway, Min Yasui, an army reservist, being a prominent example. Without contorting the law, it is difficult to see how the fundamental circumstances of *Endo* and *Korematsu* were at all different.

Perhaps by ruling for Endo and against Korematsu, Chief Justice Stone and the majority merely sought an exit strategy from what had become an increasingly disagreeable predicament. By December 1944, that Japan would lose the war seemed certain, and officials in Washington were growing just a bit squeamish about their treatment of the Japanese. John DeWitt had been transferred to command the Army War College, another job for which he was unsuited. (He was promoted to full general by an act of Congress in 1954.) An increasing number of detainees had already been released, some even allowed to return to their homes in the (now much less) restricted zone. Although the *Endo* ruling was narrow, many other internees were suddenly judged as "concededly loyal" and released.

Within months, the camps were closed.

25 | Shame

By the time World War II in the Pacific ended on September 2, 1945, almost all of those that the Supreme Court had deemed legally imprisoned had been freed to return to the West Coast and attempt to piece together their broken lives. A few would find that their homes and property had been protected by sympathetic white residents, but for most, it meant virtually starting over, as if they were once again immigrants entering a foreign country. Records of their ownership of homes, property, and businesses had been largely destroyed, so most were unable to press claims for compensation.

Gordon Hirabayashi eventually earned a PhD in sociology at the University of Washington and taught both in the Middle East and Canada. For five years, he was chair of the Sociology Department at the University of Alberta. In 1987, the Ninth Circuit Court of Appeals set aside his conviction. There is a kiosk named for him in the Coronado National Forest, near the site of the prison in which he was held. Hirabayashi died on January 2, 2012, at age ninety-three, and that May, President Obama posthumously awarded him the Presidential Medal of Freedom, the country's highest civilian honor award.

After Min Yasui was released, "he took the Colorado bar exam in 1945 and had the highest scores of all the candidates. However, he was denied admission to the state's bar because of his wartime criminal record. He appealed to the state supreme court and won that case; he was admitted to the Colorado bar in January of 1946."[1]

Yasui opened a law practice in Denver and spent the rest of his life fighting discrimination and injustice. He represented other Japanese Americans, often without fee, but "also fought discrimination beyond the Japanese community. He was a founding member of the Urban League of Denver, an African American organization, in 1946, and helped found the Latin American Research and Service Agency (an Hispanic civil rights organization) and Denver Native Americans United."[2]

Unlike Hirabayashi's, Yasui's conviction was not set aside in his lifetime. His appeal was pending when he died in 1986, and only afterward was his record cleared. He too was awarded the Presidential Medal of Freedom posthumously by President Obama.

Fred Korematsu moved on from Salt Lake City to Detroit where he worked as a draftsman before returning to California. His conviction, which had prevented him from getting a good job, was set aside in in 1983. Like Min Yasui, Korematsu became a crusader against discrimination in all forms. After 9/11, he filed an amicus curiae brief with the Supreme Court in support of those detained at Guantanamo Bay. In 1999, Korematsu was the only resistor to be awarded the Medal of Freedom while still alive. He died six years later at age eighty-six.

Mitsuye Endo was released shortly after the ruling in her favor and in 1946 married Kenneth Tsutsumi, whom she had met in the camps. They moved to Chicago, where they lived in a neighborhood favored by other Japanese families, and there raised their three children. Endo lived such an unassuming life that her daughter was in her twenties before she learned of her mother's role in ending internment.

Earl Warren was elected governor of California and then, in 1953, was named by President Eisenhower to be Chief Justice of the Supreme Court. One of the first cases he heard was *Brown v. Board of Education*, which sought to declare segregation in public schools unconstitutional. For Warren, it was a chance at redemption. As he wrote later, he "deeply regretted the removal order and my own testimony advocating it, because it was not in keeping with our American concept of freedom and the rights of citizens. . . . Whenever I thought of the innocent little children who were torn from home, school friends, and congenial surroundings, I was conscience-stricken. . . . It was wrong to react so impulsively, without positive evidence of disloyalty."[3]

The new chief justice navigated his way through many obstacles and obtained a 9–0 decision that proclaimed school segregation was wrong. But it was too late for more than 100,000 innocent men, women, children for whom Warren had decreed that segregation was right.

The scars, inflicted by some and borne by many, would last generations. Eventually, the government would make feeble attempts to right the terrible wrong. In 1948, President Truman signed the Japanese American Evacuation Claims Act, which set aside $25 million to settle claims made by interned Japanese for property lost or damaged after they were deported. Eventually, 23,689 claims were filed totaling $131,949,176. The program required extensive documentation for each claim and the speed with which claims were processed through the government bureaucracy was glacial, not especially helpful for people who returned home to find themselves left with nothing. Eventually, approximately $38 million was disbursed, with the final claim was not settled until 1965.

In 1952, a new immigration law finally guaranteed the right of Japanese and Chinese immigrants to become naturalized citizens. In 1988, reparations of $20,000 per person were granted to surviving Japanese internees.

But the Supreme Court would not officially admit its error until Chief Justice John Roberts, in *Trump v. Hawaii*, ruled that the government had the right to prevent Muslims from entering the United States. "Korematsu was gravely wrong the day it was decided [and] has been overruled in the court of history," he wrote in a decision transparently targeting members of another largely powerless group at which the government had taken aim.

Overruled in the court of history? Hardly. None of the four resistors would have applauded.

Like all incidents of officially sanctioned bigotry, neither the *Korematsu* decision nor the appalling violations of basic rights wrought of internment were created in a vacuum. Both were inevitable by-products of a nation that had spent a century either perpetuating or acquiescing in slander and bigotry. Harold Fiske Stone, Earl Warren, John DeWitt, and Karl Bendetsen were no more responsible for the injustices perpetrated in the 1940s than were Horace Page, Ulysses Webb, James Phelan, Samuel Gompers, V. S. McClatchy, and William Randolph Hearst. Bigotry cannot be turned on and off like a water faucet. True democracy requires a constant commitment to not only safeguard the rights of those who cannot safeguard them themselves, but also not to tolerate those who would oppress the weak either through ignorance or for personal gain. Those who stand by and allow evil to be perpetrated when they are capable of doing something to stop it are as culpable as those who perpetrate it themselves.

The story of the racism and oppression foisted on Americans of Asian ancestry for almost a century by individuals, government officials, and justices of the Supreme Court is, sadly, one that resonates today. "White supremacy," the banner under which these injustices were perpetrated, not only to those of Asian heritage, but also to Black, brown, and Native Americans, has been revived, not simply as an outlook hidden in the shadows, but as one that many are willing, even proud, to proclaim publicly.

Alexander Hamilton's insistence in *Federalist*, no. 78, that the judiciary would be the “people’s” branch of government, there to protect the weak against injustices that might be foisted by the legislative or the executive, has been cited countless times by scholars on both the left and the right as a profound statement of American democratic principles.

For Asian Americans, however, as with other groups not white enough, democracy failed.

Notes

HSB *Honolulu Star Bulletin*
NYT *New York Times*
SFCa *San Francisco Call*
SFCh *San Francisco Chronicle*
SFE *San Francisco Examiner*

Prologue: Bigotry Triumphant

1. Oliver Wendell Holmes wrote for an 8–1 majority, which included famed progressive Louis Brandeis noting memorably, "Three generations of imbeciles are enough."

2. Casey C. Sullivan, "13 Worst Supreme Court Decisions of All Time," FindLaw, October 14, 2015, https://blogs.findlaw.com/supreme_court/2015/10/13-worst-supreme-court-decisions-of-all-time.html.

3. Baron Shimpei Gotō, "The Anti-Japanese Question in California," *Annals of the American Academy of Political and Social Science* 93 (January 1921): 104.

4. James D. Phelan, "Why California Objects to the Japanese Invasion," *Annals*, 17.

5. John S. Chambers, "The Japanese Invasion," *Annals*, 24–25.

6. Kristofer Allerfeldt, "Race and Restriction: Anti-Asian Immigration Pressures in the Pacific North-west of America during the Progressive Era, 1885–1924," *History* 88 (January 2003): 54.

7. Jenna Johnson, "Trump Calls for 'Total and Complete Shutdown of Muslims Entering the United States,'" *Washington Post*, December 7, 2015, https://www.washingtonpost.com/news/post-politics/wp/2015/12/07/donald-trump-calls-for-total-and-complete-shutdown-of-muslims-entering-the-united-states/.

8. 585 U.S.___ (2018).

9. Anil Kahlan, "*Trump v. Hawaii* and Chief Justice Roberts's 'Korematsu Overruled' Parlor Trick," American Constitution Society, June 29, 2018, https://www.acslaw.org/expertforum/trump-v-hawaii-and-chief-justice-robertss-korematsu-overruled-parlor-trick/.

Chapter 1. Free and White

1. The Articles of Confederation were not ratified until March 1781.

2. *Annals of the Congress of the United States*, House of Representatives, 1st Cong., 2nd Sess., 1149.

3. *Annals of the Congress of the United States,* 1150.

4. 1 Statutes at Large 103.

5. William Maclay, *The Journal of William Maclay,* ed. Kenneth R. Bowling and Helen E. Veit (Baltimore: Johns Hopkins University Press, 1988), 208.

6. John Emerson, an army doctor who had brought Scott north, had died and left his entire estate to his wife, Irene, who decided that the Scotts were included in her inheritance.

7. 60 U.S. 393.

8. *Philadelphia North American,* October 14, 1864, 6.

Chapter 2. White, Black . . . and Gold

1. Lawrence Douglas Taylor Hansen, "The Chinese Six Companies of San Francisco and the Smuggling of Chinese Immigrants across the U.S.-Mexico Border, 1882–1930," *Journal of the Southwest* 48 (Spring 2006): 38.

2. Previous pacts, such as the Treaty of Tianjin in 1858, gave the United States and some European powers access to Chinese ports, allowed Christian missionaries to operate freely, and legalized the import of opium, giving the Chinese nothing in return, except the promise not to overrun their country.

3. *Congressional Globe,* 40th Cong., 3rd Sess., Part 2, 1034.

4. *Congressional Globe,* 40th Cong., 3rd Sess., Part 2, 1036.

5. *Congressional Globe,* 41st Cong., 2nd Sess., Part 1, 756.

6. 16 Statutes at Large 254.

7. *San Francisco Examiner* [*SFE*], May 8, 1878, 3. Henceforth cited at *SFE.*

8. C. C. Williams, *Congressional Career of the Hon. H. F. Page, Representative of the Second District of California and Re-nominated for a Fifth Term* (San Francisco: Francis, Valentine & Co., 1880), 3.

9. Williams, *Congressional Career of the Hon. H. F. Page,* 10.

10. The term "coolie" was centuries old, but of uncertain derivation. By the nineteenth century, however, it had evolved into a racial slur applied to Asian, especially Chinese, common laborers.

11. George Anthony Peffer, "Forbidden Families: Emigration Experiences of Chinese Women under the Page Law, 1875–1882," *Journal of American Ethnic History* 6 (Fall 1986): 28.

12. Proxy marriages, common in China, and polygamy would not be recognized in the United States. Still, even for traditional marriages conducted in China, it would fall to an immigration officer to decide legality.

13. Appendix to the *Congressional Record,* 43rd Cong., 2nd Sess., Vol. 3, 44.

14. Joshua S. Yang, "The Anti-Chinese Cubic Air Ordinance," *American Journal of Public Health* (March 2009), https://www.ncbi.nlm.nih.gov/pmc/articles/PMC2661442/.

15. Yang, "Anti-Chinese."

16. National Archives, http://recordsofrights.org/events/125/pigtail-ordinance.

17. Hansen, "The Chinese Six Companies of San Francisco," 38.

18. Paul Kens, *Justice Stephen Field: Shaping Liberty from the Gold Rush to the Gilded Age* (Lawrence: University Press of Kansas, 1997), 205.

19. Kens, *Justice Stephen Field*, 212.

20. *Ah Kow v. Nunan*, 12 F. Cas. at 253, 256–257.

21. *SFE*, July 8, 1879, 2.

22. *Ah Kow v. Nunan*, 12 F. Cas. at 253.

23. *New Orleans Democrat*, May 23, 1878, 4.

24. *New York Herald*, November 28, 1878, 5.

25. Bethany R. Berger, "Birthright Citizenship on Trial: *Elk v. Wilkins* and *United States v. Wong Kim Ark*," *Cardozo Law Review* 37 (April 2016): 1220.

26. Louis Menand, "Morton, Agassiz, and the Origins of Scientific Racism in the United States," *Journal of Blacks in Higher Education* (Winter 2001–2002): 110.

27. Of Blacks, he would say, "The brain of the Negro is that of the imperfect brain of a seven month's infant in the womb of a White."

28. Richard Hofstadter, *Social Darwinism in American Thought* (New York: George Braziller, 1959), 17.

29. *New York Times* [*NYT*], March 28, 1860, 3. Henceforth cited at *NYT*.

30. "Design theory," its opposite, posited that species were initiated fully formed. Most, though not all design theorists, assumed that the initiation was done by God.

31. Francis Bowen, "Latest Form of the Development Theory," *Memoirs of the American Academy of Arts and Sciences*, n.s., 8, no. 1 (1861): 106–107.

32. Darwin's second great work, *The Descent of Man, and Selection in Relation to Sex*, would put the final nail in the polygenist coffin. *Descent*, of course, in ascribing man's origins to other primates was to arouse even more controversy than *Origin of Species* and supply no shortage of fodder to those who preached racial stratification.

33. In Darwin's actual system, of course, chance and coincidence played quite a vital role, but race theorists chose to overlook this part of the construct.

34. Hofstadter, *Social Darwinism*, 36.

35. Spencer's theory was actually closer to Lamarck than Darwin. At the end of the eighteenth century, Jean-Baptiste Lamarck, a French biologist, proposed that nonphysical alterations to an organism acquired during its life span from, say, hard work or intense study, would then be passed to its offspring. Lamarck had a devoted following until Darwinism overwhelmed his hypothesis and Lamarckism was dismissed as pseudoscience. Ironically, with the recent rise of epigenetics, which asserts that the manner in which genes function, or "express," can be both altered environmentally and passed on to subsequent generations, Lamarck has made something of a comeback.

36. Herbert Spencer, "Progress: Its Law and Causes," *Westminster Review* 67 (April 1857): 446.

37. Spencer, "Progress," 447.

38. Hofstadter, *Social Darwinism*, 39.

39. Herbert Spencer, *Essays on Education and Kindred Subjects* (Dutton 1861, 1911), 164.

40. 5 Sawyer 155; 6 *Central Law Journal* 387 (1878).

Chapter 3. Enter the Japanese

1. Nobutaka Ike, "Western Influences on the Meiji Restoration," *Pacific Historical Review*, 17 (February 1948): 2.

2. Eijiro Honjo, "From the Tokugawa Period to the Meiji Restoration," *Kyoto University Economic Review* 7 (1932): 32.

3. Jeffrey A. Keith, "Civilization, Race, and the Japan Expedition's Cultural Diplomacy, 1853–1854," *Diplomatic History* 3 (April 2011): 179.

4. Keith, "Civilization, Race," 181.

5. Sujin Eom, "The Specter of Modernity: Open Ports and the Making of Chinatowns in Japan and South Korea," *Traditional Dwellings and Settlements Review* 24 (2013): 42.

6. Honjo, "From the Tokugawa period," 46.

7. Hideichi Horie, "Revolution and Reform in Meiji Restoration," *Kyoto University Economic Review* 22 (1952): 28.

8. Patrick Parr, "American President Ulysses S. Grant Talks Peace in Meiji Era Japan,"
https://japantoday.com/category/features/lifestyle/american-president-ulysses-s-grant-talks-peace-in-meiji-era-japan.

9. Horie, "Revolution and Reform," 33.

10. The proper mark between the final two letters is an "okina," which appears as an upside-down apostrophe, but the official spelling was changed to eliminate it when Hawaii became a state in 1959. "Hawaiian" was never marked. This book will use the post-1959 spelling.

11. Gannemono, http://www.discovernikkei.org/en/journal/2018/8/30/gannenmono/.

12. Gannemono, http://www.discovernikkei.org/en/journal/2018/8/30/gannenmono/.

13. Northeast Museum Services Center, *Archeology & Museum Blog*, https://nmscarcheologylab.wordpress.com/2014/03/18/a-tale-of-two-nations-victorian-america-and-the-japan-craze/.

14. The Philadelphia Centennial, https://www.wrightsjapan1905.org/timeline/philadelphia-centennial-exhibition/.

15. H. D. Miller, "An Eccentric Culinary History," https://eccentricculinary.com/the-great-sushi-craze-of-1905-part-1/.

16. Parr, "American President Ulysses S. Grant."

17. Known as the Satsuma Rebellion, the uprising was led by disaffected samurai Takamori Saigo, who died during the rebellion's final major battle. The entire episode was romanticized in the film *The Last Samurai*, starring Tom Cruise.

18. Parr, "American President Ulysses S. Grant."

19. "Jenn M.," "A Tale of Two Nations: Victorian America and the Japan Craze," *Archeology & Museum Blog*.

20. Williams, *Congressional Career of the Hon. H. F. Page*, 3.

21. For the most complete and incisive exploration of Chinese exclusion, see Beth Lew-Williams, *The Chinese Must Go: Violence, Exclusion, and the Making of the Alien in America* (Cambridge, MA: Harvard University Press, 2018).

22. "Restrictions on Immigration; Private-Contract Immigration; Free Immigration," Nisei Veterans Legacy, https://www.nvlchawaii.org/restrictions-immigration-private-contract-immigration-free-immigration.

23. "Hawaii: Life in a Plantation Society," Library of Congress, https://www.loc.gov/classroom-materials/immigration/japanese/hawaii-life-in-a-plantation-society/.

24. Roger Daniels, *The Politics of Prejudice: The Anti-Japanese Movement in California and the Struggle for Japanese Exclusion* (Berkeley: University of California Press, 1977), 1.

25. Japan had also signed a similar but less comprehensive treaty with Great Britain, but that would not take effect until 1899.

26. *NYT*, November 25, 1894, 5.

27. *San Francisco Morning Call*, May 4, 1892, 8.

28. *San Francisco Morning Call*, May 6, 1892, 6.

29. Emily Anderson, "Immigration," Densho Encyclopedia, http://encyclopedia.densho.org/Immigration.

30. Paul Finkleman, "Coping with a New 'Yellow Peril': Japanese Immigration, the Gentleman's Agreement, and the Coming of World War II," *West Virginia Law Review* 117, no. 3 (2015): 1426–1427.

31. Devon Carbado, "Yellow by Law," *California Law Review* 97 (June 2009): 641.

Chapter 4. Birthright

1. For a thorough treatment of the question of the conflicting philosophies of citizenship, see Carol Nackenoff and Julie Novkov, *American by Birth: Wong Kim Ark and the Battle for Citizenship* (Lawrence: University Press of Kansas, 2021), chap. 1.

2. Senator Edger Cowan of Pennsylvania, in which state there were virtually no Chinese, raised the specter of "Mongolians" overrunning California, but the risk of Chinese gaining citizenship was never a focus of the debates.

3. Although Wong Kim Ark's birth year is generally given as 1873, the only document that contains that date is his habeas corpus petition. Most other documents, including his immigration form, list the year as 1871, which given the later timeline is more likely.

4. Wong's travels are detailed in Berger, "Birthright Citizenship on Trial."

5. *San Luis Obispo Tribune*, October 1, 1895, 1.

6. *Sacramento Daily Union*, January 4, 1896, 3.

7. *Chicago Law Journal*, January 1896, 7, 150

8. *Sacramento Daily Union*, December 28, 1895, 11.

9. *Sacramento Daily Union*, December 30, 1895, 6.

10. The Geary Act and the subsequent McCreary amendment in 1893 required all Chinese immigrant laborers to carry domestic passports with proof of residence and identity, lack of which could result in one year of hard labor followed by deportation. The identification requirements were upheld by the Supreme Court in 1893, but the imprisonment and deportation provisions were struck down three years later. Still, the law remained largely moot since most Chinese laborers refused to register and the government was unwilling to commit the necessary resources to undertake mass deportations. See Gabriel Chin and Daniel Tu, "Comprehensive Immigration Reform in the Jim Crow Era: Chinese Exclusion and the McCreary Act of 1893," *Asian American Law Journal* 23, no.1 (2019): 40–42.

11. *Sacramento Daily Union*, January 4, 1896, 5.

12. *Honolulu Evening Bulletin*, January 24, 1896, 1.

13. *Honolulu Evening Bulletin*, January 24, 1896, 1.

14. *SFCh*, March 29, 1896, 19.

15. *SFCh*, March 29, 1896, 19.

16. 169 U.S. 649.

17. *Santa Cruz Evening Sentinel*, August 1, 1898, 4.

18. See Dara Linddara, "Birthright Citizenship, Explained," Vox, October 30, 2018, https://www.vox.com/2018/7/23/17595754/birthright-citizenship-trump-14th-amendment-executive-order. Some Supreme Court justices, notably Clarence Thomas, have indicated a willingness, even a desire, to overturn certain precedents, so the Court's eventual reaction to a challenge to birthright citizen is not at all clear.

Chapter 5. Yellow Peril

1. Mrs. Fremont Older, *San Francisco: The Magic City* (New York: Longmans, Green, 1961), 187.

2. Older, *San Francisco*, 78.

3. *SFCa*, November 7, 1896, 9.

4. Roger Daniels, *The Politics of Prejudice: The Anti-Japanese Movement in California and the Struggle for Japanese Exclusion* (Berkeley: University of California Press, 1977), 47.

5. *San Francisco Call* owner Charles Shortridge was both less visible and less vocal but the Call was hardly a voice of tolerance.

6. *SFE*, March 7, 1900, 4.

7. *SFE*, March 8, 1900, 3.

8. *SFCa*, May 8, 1900, 12.

9. *SFE*, May 8, 1900, 7.

10. *SFE*, May 8, 1900, 7.

11. *SFCa*, May 8,1900, 12.

12. *San Jose Mercury News*, May 9, 1900, 4.

13. Kiichi Kanzaki, "Is the Japanese Menace in America a Reality?," *Annals of the American Academy of Political and Social Science* 93 (January 1921): 88–97.

14. Japanese immigration was more than halved the following year, dropping from more than 12,000 to just less than 5,000.

Chapter 6. Workers of the West Unite

1. *SFC,* April 20, 1891, 7.
2. *Stockton Evening Mail,* July 22, 1901, 1.
3. Thomas Walker Page, "The San Francisco Labor Movement in 1901," *Political Science Quarterly* 17 (December 1902): 668.
4. *SFE,* July 22, 1901, 1.
5. *SFE,* July 21, 1901, 2.
6. *SFC,* July 24, 1901, 9.
7. *SFC,* July 24, 1901, 9.
8. *SFE,* July 25, 1901, 3.
9. *SFE,* July 26, 1901, 3.
10. Page, "The San Francisco Labor Movement in 1901," 679.
11. Page, 682.
12. *SFC,* July 14, 1901, 15.
13. *SFE,* September 6, 1901, 10.
14. Jules Tygiel, " . . . Where Unionism Holds Undisputed Sway: A Reappraisal of San Francisco's Union Labor Party," *California History* 62 (Fall 1983): 203.
15. Page, "The San Francisco Labor Movement in 1901," 683.
16. *SFCa,* September 28, 1901, 12.
17. Page, "The San Francisco Labor Movement in 1901," 684.
18. *SFE,* October 10, 1901, 6.
19. *SFE,* October 16, 1901, 1, 8.
20. *SFCa,* November 6, 1901, 1.
21. George Kennan, "The Fight for Reform in San Francisco," *McClure's,* September 1907, 547. Kennan was a world-famous explorer who had written of his travels in such books as *Tent Life in Siberia: Adventures among the Koraks and Other Tribes in Kamtchatka and Northern Asia.* He was a cousin of diplomat George Kennan.
22. Beull, "The Development of the Anti-Japanese Agitation in the United States," 612.
23. Beull, 612.
24. Buell, 609.

Chapter 7. Tremors

1. *Call=Chronicle=Examiner,* April 19, 1906, 1.
2. The Richter scale was not developed until the 1930s, so the estimate was formulated later and only a guess.
3. Earthquake in Chinatown, https://artsandculture.google.com/exhibit

/earthquake-the-chinatown-story-chinese-historical-society-of-america/gQrsWsc?hl=en.

4. NPR, https://www.npr.org/templates/story/story.php?storyId=5337215.

5. Earthquake in Chinatown.

6. *SFE*, April 25, 1906, 4.

7. *SFCa*, April 28, 1906, 2.

8. *Oakland Tribune*, May 10, 1906, 6.

9. Anna Naruta, "Relocation," Chinese Historical Society of America, https://www.chsa.org/wp-content/uploads/2013/04/Relocation.pdf.

10. Naruta, "Relocation."

11. *SFCa*, May 3, 1906, 4.

12. Raymond W. Rast, "The Cultural Politics of Tourism in San Francisco's Chinatown, 1882–1917," *Pacific Historical Review* 76, no. 1 (2007): 53–54.

13. George Kennan, "The Fight for Reform in San Francisco," *McClure's Magazine*, September 1907, 554.

14. *Spokane Press*, October 10, 1906, 4.

15. *San Francisco Examiner*, September 16, 1906, 1.

16. Kiyo Sue Inui, "The Gentlemen's Agreement: How It Has Functioned," *Annals of the American Academy of Political and Social Science* 122 (November 1925): 189.

Chapter 8. Gentlemen . . . and Ladies

1. Raymond L. Buell, "The Development of the Anti-Japanese Agitation in the United States," *Political Science Quarterly* 37, no. 4 (1922): 623.

2. Buell, "Development of the Anti-Japanese Agitation," 623.

3. Buell, 624.

4. A surprise attack on an adversary's main naval base would be used again, but the war's outcome would be far different.

5. *SFE*, September 8, 1905, 20.

6. Japanese population in 1900 was 1,781, which grew to 4,518 in 1910, but there was a large-scale influx of Japanese women after 1907; see https://www.sfgenealogy.org/sf/history/hgpop.htm.

7. *SFCa*, October 18, 1906, 9.

8. Masuda Hajimu, "Rumors of War: Immigration Disputes and the Social Construction of American–Japanese Relations, 1905–1913," *Diplomatic History* 33 (January 2009): 11.

9. Photo of decoded telegram from Wright, docs.google.com/viewerng/viewer?url=https://diva.sfsu.edu/bundles/preview/352014?token%3DLoZkALVIjH.

10. David Brudnoy, "Race and the San Francisco School Board Incident: Contemporary Evaluations," *California Historical Quarterly* 50 (September 1971): 297.

11. Buell, "Development of the Anti-Japanese Agitation," 624.

12. Photo of Letter from Roosevelt to Metcalf, https://diva.sfsu.edu/collections/ga1907/bundles/215932.

13. *Boston Globe*, December 2, 1906, 4.
14. *SFE*, December 20, 1906, 1.
15. Densho Encyclopedia, https://encyclopedia.densho.org/San_Francisco_school_segregation/.
16. *SFCa*, December 11, 1906, 7.
17. *SFE*, December 19, 1906, 1.
18. *SFE*, October 23, 1906, 1
19. *SFCa*, October 26, 1906, 1
20. *SFCa*, October 26, 1906, 1.
21. *SFE*, October 26, 1906, 2.
22. Buell, "Development of the Anti-Japanese Agitation," 612.
23. Photo of letter from White to TR, https://diva.sfsu.edu/collections/ga1907/bundles/216052.
24. *SFCa*, February 4, 1907, 1.
25. *SFCa*, February 8, 1907, 1.
26. *NYT*, February 9, 1907, 8.
27. *NYT*, February 19, 1907, 4.
28. 34 Stat. 898.
29. Roger Daniels, *The Politics of Prejudice: The Anti-Japanese Movement in California and the Struggle for Japanese Exclusion* (Berkeley: University of California Press, 1977), 44.
30. Yuji Ichioka, "Amerika Nadeshiko: Japanese Immigrant Women in the United States, 1900–1924," *Pacific Historical Review* 49 (May 1980): 341.
31. Male Chinese and Japanese immigrants had no choice but to seek brides of their own race. Beginning in 1860, western states passed laws forbidding interracial marriage. Chinese were sometimes referred to as "Mongolians," which cut a broader swath through nonwhite populations and included the Japanese, but those states that had specifically targeted the Chinese soon expanded the definition. By the time the Gentlemen's Agreement went into effect, racial intermarriage was forbidden throughout the West except, curiously, in Washington State. See Deneesh Sohoni, "Unsuitable Suitors: Anti-Miscegenation Laws, Naturalization Laws, and the Construction of Asian Identities," *Law & Society Review* 41, no. 3 (2007): 587–618; and Hrishi Karthikeyan and Gabriel Chin, "Preserving Racial Identity: Population Patterns and the Application of Anti-Miscegenation Statutes to Asian Americans, 1910–1950," *Asian Law Journal* 9, no. 1 (2002): 1–39.
32. Ichioka, "Amerika Nadeshiko," 347.
33. Ichioka, 354.
34. Ichioka, 355.

Chapter 9. This Land Is (Not) Your Land

1. Herbert P. Le Pore, "Prelude to Prejudice: Hiram Johnson, Woodrow Wilson, and the California Alien Land Law Controversy of 1913," *Southern California Quarterly* 61, no. 1 (1979): 100.

2. Roger Daniels, *The Politics of Prejudice: The Anti-Japanese Movement in California and the Struggle for Japanese Exclusion* (Berkeley: University of California Press, 1977), 47.

3. Daniels, *Politics of Prejudice*, 46.

4. Masuda Hajimu, "Rumors of War: Immigration Disputes and the Social Construction of American-Japanese Relations, 1905–1913," *Diplomatic History* 33 (January 2009): 18.

5. *SFCa*, December 8, 1909, 1.

6. Le Pore, "Prelude to Prejudice," 99–100.

7. 57 Statutes at Large 1504.

8. *SFCa*, February 22, 1908, 3.

9. Le Pore, "Prelude to Prejudice," 100.

10. Daniels, *The Politics of Prejudice*, 55.

11. Thomas Bailey, "California, Japan, and the Alien Land Legislation of 1913," *Pacific Historical Review* 1, no. 1 (1932): 38.

12. Masakazu Iwata, "The Japanese Immigrants in California Agriculture," *Agricultural History* 36 (January 1962): 29.

13. James D. Startt, *Woodrow Wilson and the Press: Prelude to the Presidency* (New York: Palgrave Macmillan, 2004), 157.

14. Woodrow Wilson, *A History of the American People* (New York: Harper and Brothers, 1903), 5:213–214.

15. Daniels, *The Politics of Prejudice*, 55.

16. *The American Journal of International Law*, 5, no. 2. Supplement: Official Documents (April 1911): 107–108.

17. *Porterfield v. Webb*, 263 U.S. 225 (1923).

18. *SFE*, March 20, 1913, 1; Le Pore, "Prelude to Prejudice," 105.

19. Le Pore, "Prelude to Prejudice," 108.

20. Franklin Hichborn, *Story of the Session of the California Legislature of 1913* (San Francisco: Press of the James H. Barry Company, 1913), 262.

21. Edwin E. Ferguson, "The California Alien Land Law and the Fourteenth Amendment, *California Law Review* 35, no. 1 (1947): 68.

22. Ferguson, "California Alien Land Law," 43.

23. Charles Wallace Collins, "Will the California Alien Land Law Stand the Test of the Fourteenth Amendment?," *Yale Law Journal* 23, no. 4 (1913–1914): 333.

24. Collins, "Will the California Alien Land Law Stand the Test of the Fourteenth Amendment?," 338.

25. "The California Alien Land Law," *The Lawyer and Banker and Bench and Bar Review* 6, no. 3 (1913): 253.

26. 207 F. 115 No. 992 May 3, 1913.

Chapter 10. A Home of One's Own (Children)

1. Keith Aoki, "No Right to Own? The Early Twentieth-Century 'Alien Land Laws' as a Prelude to Internment," *Boston College Third World Law Journal* 19 (December 1998): 56.

2. *SFE*, October10, 1915, 26–27.

3. For an excellent study of the eugenics movement and its influence on immigration legislation, see Daniel Okrent, *The Guarded Gate* (New York: Scribner, 2018), 220.

4. The eugenics movement spawned forced sterilization laws in a number of states, which resulted in *Buck v. Bell*, and Oliver Wendell Holmes's pronouncement about generations of imbeciles.

5. 39 Statutes at Large 874.

6. *NYT*, January 17, 1917, 10.

7. 39 Statutes at Large 876.

8. *NYT*, February 6, 1917, 12.

9. *SFE*, February 6, 1917, 1.

10. *People v. Harada, et al.*, Riverside County Superior Court Case 7751.

11. *Documental History of Law Cases Affecting Japanese in the United States, 1916–1924*, Compiled by the Consulate General of San Francisco 2, 733.

12. Bruce Castleman, "California's Alien Land Laws," *Western Legal History* 7 (Winter/Spring 1994): 36.

13. *People v Harada.*

14. *Sacramento Star*, December 29, 1916, 1.

15. *Los Angeles Times*, April 5, 1917, Part 2, 1.

16. *Documental History*, 738.

Chapter 11. The Golden West

1. *SFE*, April 3, 1919, 2.

2. *Sacramento Bee*, April 1, 1919, 1, 9. Hostility to the Japanese was not in a vacuum, of course. Other nonwhite races, nationalities, or ethnic groups—Filipinos and Mexicans, for example—were also targeted both officially and unofficially. Still, the Japanese were certainly much the target of choice.

3. Roger Daniels, *The Politics of Prejudice: The Anti-Japanese Movement in California and the Struggle for Japanese Exclusion* (Berkeley: University of California Press, 1977), 85.

4. *NYT*, July 11, 1884, 3.

5. Both groups still exist.

6. Peter T. Conmy, *The History of California's Japanese Problem and the Part Played by the Native Sons of the Golden West in Its Solution* (Privately printed, 1942), 2.

7. Daniels, *The Politics of Prejudice*, 85.

8. Daniels, 6.

9. *SFE*, September 6, 1919, 1.

10. *Sacramento Bee*, September 2, 1920, 1.

11. Daniels, *The Politics of Prejudice*, 85.
12. *SFE*, November 4, 1920, 1.
13. *SFE*, November 4, 1920, 1.

Chapter 12. The Heart of an American

1. *Oakland Tribune*, June 3, 1903, 8.
2. His only son would die while serving in the U.S. Army in World War II.
3. *Honolulu Star Bulletin* (*HSB*), October 16, 1914, 4.
4. *HSB*, January 30, 1915, 1.
5. He would file a second, twenty-page typewritten brief in September 1915, the content of which was largely the same. The following extracts are from one or the other, but do not change the thrust of his argument.
6. *HSB*, June 9, 1915, 3.
7. Quoted in Ian Haney-Lopez, *White by Law: The Legal Construction of Race* (New York: New York University Press, 206), 56–57.
8. *HSB*, June 9, 1915, 3.
9. *HSB*, June 10, 1915, 2.
10. *Honolulu Advertiser*, August 1, 1915, 14.
11. *HSB*, January 3, 1916, 1.
12. *HSB*, March 24, 1916, 3.
13. *HSB*, March 25, 1916, 1, 8.
14. On the same day, Clemons ruled that two Filipino merchant seaman were eligible for citizenship because the Philippines was a protectorate of the United States.
15. *HSB*, March 30, 1916, 2.
16. *Honolulu Advertiser*, August 7, 1916, 1.
17. *HSB*, December 19, 1917, 7.
18. *HSB*, February 8, 1918, 2.
19. *HSB*, March 27, 1919, 1.
20. *Buffalo (NY) Times*, August 9, 1922, 2.
21. A companion case was also argued, *Yamashita v. Hinkle*, in which two Japanese immigrants who had been naturalized in Washington State prior to the 1906 law were denied the right to incorporate a real estate holding company, because the naturalizations were illegal, this upholding Washington's alien land law. California's alien land law had also contained an incorporation provision, which by extension was also upheld.
22. 260 U.S. 178 (1922).
23. 179 Fed. 1002 (1910).
24. The Court ruled against Yamashita also, thus voiding all previous naturalizations of the Japanese.
25. *SFE*, November 14, 1922, 1.
26. *Sacramento Star*, November 13, 1922, 10.
27. *HSB*, November 15, 1922, 6.

Chapter 13. What Meets the Eye

1. Some have speculated that immigrants from the Indian subcontinent were principal targets of the Asian Barred Zone, but more likely is that Congress had taken a broad brush to the issue and included a broad swath of nonwhite peoples.

2. Records and Briefs of the United States Supreme Court 484, 1072.

3. Records.

4. Records.

5. Records.

6. Records.

7. 261 U.S. 204 (1923).

8. Doug Coulson, "British Imperialism, the Indian Independence Movement, and the Racial Eligibility Provisions of the Naturalization Act: *United States v. Thind* Revisited," *Georgetown Journal of Law and Modern Critical Race Perspectives* 7 (2015): 37.

9. The *Thind* decision also had implications for Japanese war veterans. Responding to recruiting drives, 838 Japanese noncitizens from Hawaii had enlisted in the United States in the hopes of becoming citizens after they were discharged. They were placed in a separate company but were used only as replacements for white soldiers sent to France and did not see action themselves. Although 400 members of the company were naturalized in 1919, their citizenship was rescinded in 1922. One of the veterans, Hidemitsu Toyota, sued to regain his citizenship, but, with *Thind* on the books, lost in the Supreme Court in 1925. See https://java.wildapricot.org/resources/Documents/JAVA%20Fall%202015_FINAL%2025Nov15.pdf.

Chapter 14. Turning the Soil

1. After the Court's decision in *Yick Wo v. Hopkins*, which voided a discriminatory San Francisco ordinance aimed at Chinese laundry operators, anti-Asian state and local legislators became a bit more cautious in the language of draft legislation.

2. Theodore Roodner, "Washington's Alien Land Law—Its Constitutionality," *Washington Law Review* 39 (Spring 1964): 118.

3. *Terrace v. Thompson*, 274 F. 841, 843.

4. *United States Reports: Cases Adjudged in the Supreme Court* 24, 200.

5. *Reports*, 207.

6. Justices McReynolds and Brandeis thought there were no legitimate constitutional issues present and the case should have been summarily dismissed, and Justice Sutherland did not take part because arguments predated his appointment.

7. 263 U.S. 197 (1923). The plaintiff's contention that the commercial treaty between the United States and Japan included the right of individual

Japanese to enter into contracts to purchase land was dismissed, Sutherland asserting that the treaty was created to "establishing the rules to govern commercial intercourse between the countries."

8. *Strauder v. West Virginia,*100 U.S. 303 (1880). *Virginia v. Rives,* 100 U.S. 313 (1880). The "facially neutral" approach has been used extensively to sneak discrimination in through a legal back door, while numerous justices, including by Chief Justice Roberts in *Trump v. Hawaii,* have raised no objection.

9. 263 U.S. 313 (1923).

10. 263 U.S. 236 (1923).

11. *SFE,* November 13, 1923, 4.

12. Powell was one of the most influential legal scholars of the day. He would later teach at Harvard for twenty-five years and be elected president of the American Political Science Association.

13. Thomas Reed Powell, "Alien Land Cases in United States Supreme Court," *California*

Law Review 12 (1923–1924): 272.

14. Powell, "Alien Land Cases in United States Supreme Court," 274.

15. Ronald Takaki, *Strangers from a Distant Shore* (New York: Little Brown, 1989), 206.

Chapter 15. Slamming the Door

1. Marouf A. Hasian Jr., "Conserving the Nation's Germplasm: Nativist Discourse and the Passage of the 1924 Immigration Restriction Act," *Legal Studies Forum* 24 (2000): 163.

2. Hasian, "Conserving the Nation's Germplasm," 163.

3. "Outstanding Features of the Immigration Act of 1924," *Columbia Law Review,* 25, no. 1 (1925): 91.

4. "Outstanding Features," 90.

5. See, e.g., *San Bernardino Daily Sun,* March 31, 1924, 2.

6. Densho Encyclopedia, http://encyclopedia.densho.org/Immigration%20Act%20of%201924#cite_ref-ftnt_ref2_2–0.

7. *Sacramento Bee,* March 11, 1924, 1.

8. *Sacramento Bee,* March 11, 1924, 6.

9. *NYT,* April 15, 1924, 1.

10. *NYT,* April 28, 1924, 1.

11. *NYT,* May 9, 1924, 1.

12. *NYT,* May 9, 1924, 1.

Chapter 16. Banzai and Baseball

1. Historical Statistics of the United States, Series B304–330, https://www2.census.gov/prod2/statcomp/documents/HistoricalStatisticsoftheUnitedStates1789–1945.pdf.

2. It would decline by more than 10,000 in the next decade.

3. Library of Congress, https://www.loc.gov/classroom-materials/immigration/japanese/the-us-mainland-growth-and-resistance/.

4. Roxana Johnson, "Be Good Americans: The Message of the *Japanese American Courier*, https://depts.washington.edu/depress/japanese_american_courier_americanism.shtml.

5. Masato Shizume, "The Japanese Economy during the Interwar Period: Instability in the Financial System and the Impact of the World Depression," Institute for Monetary and Economic Studies, 2009, https://www.boj.or.jp/en/research/wps_rev/rev_2009/data/rev09e02.pdf.

6. Peace Preservation Law, https://msu.edu/~londo/FAU/4933_web/Peace_pres_law.htm.

7. Showa Restoration, http://motherearthtravel.com/history/japan/history-9.htm.

8. Josh Axelrod, "A Century Later: The Treaty of Versailles and Its Rejection of Racial Equality," https://www.npr.org/sections/codeswitch/2019/08/11/742293305/a-century-later-the-treaty-of-versailles-and-its-rejection-of-racial-equality.

9. United States Department of State Archive, https://2001-2009.state.gov/r/pa/ho/time/id/88313.htm.

10. The Kellogg–Briand Pact was an unenforceable multinational agreement to eliminate war as an instrument of national policy. Not an official treaty, it had little effect on territorial ambitions in Europe and Asia, but eventually many of the principles in Kellogg–Briand were incorporated into the United Nations charter.

11. Department of State, Office of the Historian, https://history.state.gov/milestones/1921-1936/mukden-incident. Also *SFE*, September 19–22, 1931.

12. *NYT*, September 19, 1931, 1.

13. Bill Savage, "Out of the Ballpark," http://thecore.uchicago.edu/Summer2016/departments/out-ballpark.shtml.

14. Vernona Gomez and Lawrence Goldstone, *Lefty: An American Odyssey* (New York: Ballantine, 2012), 185.

15. Many American newspapers incorrectly credited Ruth with the home run. Connie Mack, who was managing the American team, immediately offered Sawamura a contract, but Sawamura, still in high school, did not want to leave home. He died almost to the day ten years later, when his ship was torpedoed in December 1944. The Japanese equivalent of the Cy Young award is named for him.

16. Gomez and Goldstone, *Lefty*, 189.

17. John Gripentrog, "The Transnational Pastime: Baseball and American Perceptions of Japan in the 1930s," *Diplomatic History* 34 (April 2010): 251–252.

18. *SFE*, July 21, 1937, 2.

19. *NYT*, December 18, 1937, 1,10.

20. *SFE*, December 13, 1937, 1.

21. David Gompert et al., *Blinders, Blunders, and Wars: What America and China Can Learn* (Rand Corporation, 2014), 95.

22. Pedro A. Loureiro, "Japanese Espionage and American Countermeasures in Pre-Pearl Harbor California," *Journal of American-East Asian Relations* 3 (Fall 1994): 199.

Chapter 17. Loyalty

1. Pedro A. Loureiro, "Japanese Espionage and American Countermeasures in Pre-Pearl Harbor California," *Journal of American-East Asian Relations* 3 (Fall 1994): 200.
2. Loureiro, "Japanese Espionage and American Countermeasures," 197.
3. In later reports, Henry was updated to "Harry," although the reason for the change was never specified.
4. *Hanford Morning Journal*, March 5, 1936, 5.
5. *Santa Rosa Republican*, March 12, 1936, 5.
6. *Hanford Morning Journal*, March 5, 1936, 5.
7. Loureiro, "Japanese Espionage and American Countermeasures," 202.

Chapter 18. Fear and Fiction

1. Densho Encyclopedia, https://encyclopedia.densho.org/history/.
2. Densho Encyclopedia.
3. United States Commission on Wartime Relocation and Internment of Civilians, and United States, Congress, House Committee on Interior and Insular Affairs, *Personal Justice Denied: Report of the Commission On Wartime Relocation And Internment of Civilians: Report for the Committee On Interior And Insular Affairs* (Washington, DC: U.S. G.P.O., 1992), 61.
4. Commission on Wartime Relocation, 55.
5. Densho Encyclopedia, http://encyclopedia.densho.org/Saburo%20Kido#cite_ref-ftnt_ref4_4-0.
6. Commission on Wartime Relocation, 52.
7. Commission, 53.
8. Densho Encyclopedia, http://encyclopedia.densho.org/Munson%20Report.
9. Kenneth Ringle report, https://www.history.navy.mil/research/library/online-reading-room/title-list-alphabetically/r/ringle-report-on-japanese-internment.html.
10. Richard Reeves, *Infamy: The Shocking Story of the Japanese American Internment in World War II* (New York: Holt, 2015), 17.
11. *SFE*, December 24, 1941, 1.
12. *SFE*, December 8, 1941, 12.
13. Eric Muller, *American Inquisition: The Hunt for Japanese American Disloyalty in World War II* (Chapel Hill: University of North Carolina Pres, 2007), 3.
14. *Tulare Advance-Register*, December 9, 1941, 1.
15. *Santa Rosa Press Democrat*, December 10, 1941, 1.

16. G. Edward White, "The Unacknowledged Lesson: Earl Warren and the Japanese Relocation Controversy," *Virginia Quarterly Review* 55, no. 4 (1979): 613–629, https://www.vqronline.org/essay/unacknowledged-lesson-earl-warren-and-japanese-relocation-controversy.

17. White, "Unacknowledged Lesson."

18. White.

19. White.

20. Sumi Cho, "Redeeming Whiteness in the Shadow of Internment: Earl Warren, Brown, and a Theory of Racial Redemption," *Boston College Third World Law Journal* 19 (December 1998): 89.

21. White, "Unacknowledged Lesson."

22. White.

23. *Fresno Bee*, December 18, 1941, 10.

24. *San Bernardino Sun*, December 20, 1941, 2.

25. *Sacramento Bee*, January 6, 1942, 17.

Chapter 19. An Illusion of Disloyalty

1. Roberts Commission Report, http://www.ibiblio.org/pha/pha/roberts/roberts.html.

2. Roberts Commission Report.

3. Sumi Cho, "Redeeming Whiteness in the Shadow of Internment: Earl Warren, Brown, and a Theory of Racial Redemption," *Boston College Third World Law Journal* 19 (December 1998): 91.

4. Warren Olney, "Law Enforcement and Judicial Administration in the Earl Warren Era: Oral History Transcript," 228, https://archive.org/details/enforcementjudiooolnerich/pagc/228/modc/2up.

5. *Fresno Bee*, January 23, 1942, 6.

6. Olney, "Law Enforcement and Judicial Administration," 228.

7. *Oakland Tribune*, January 27, 1942, 15.

8. *SFE*, January 28, 1942, 1.

9. *Petaluma Argus-Courier*, January 30, 1942, 1.

10. Cho, "Redeeming Whiteness in the Shadow of Internment," 92.

11. *San Bernardino County Sun*, February 3, 1942, 1.

12. Olney, "Law enforcement and judicial administration," 230

13. Olney, 228–229.

14. Cho, "Redeeming Whiteness in the Shadow of Internment," 93.

15. Olney, "Law Enforcement and Judicial Administration," 229.

16. Olney, 229.

17. Cho, "Redeeming Whiteness in the Shadow of Internment," 94.

18. Cho, 96.

19. National Archives & Records Administration, https://www.ourdocuments.gov/doc.php?flash=false&doc=74.

20. Richard Reeves, *Infamy: The Shocking Story of the Japanese American Internment in World War II* (New York: Holt, 2015), 44.

21. Stetson Conn et al., *Guarding the United States and Its Outposts* (Washington, DC: U.S. Government Printing Office, 1964), https://history.army.mil/books/wwii/Guard-U.S./ch5.htm#b11.

22. Stetson Conn, *Guarding the United States and Its Outposts.*

23. Densho Encyclopedia, "Karl Bendetsen," https://encyclopedia.densho.org/Karl%20Bendetsen.

24. Densho Encyclopedia, "Bendetsen."

25. Hearings before the Select Committee Investigating National Defense Migration, House of Representatives, Seventy-seventh Congress, 10973–10974, https://archive.org/details/nationaldefensem29unit/page/10972/mode/2up.

26. Hearings before the Select Committee Investigating National Defense Migration, 10974, 11009, 11012.

27. Abigail G. H. Manzella, *Migrating Fictions: Gender, Race, and Citizenship in U.S. Internal Displacements* (Columbus: Ohio State University Press, 2018), 116.

Chapter 20. No Island Paradise

1. Richard B. Frank, "How Hawaii's Japanese Population Was Spared Internment during World War II," *Time,* March 13, 2020, https://time.com/5802127/hawaii-internment-order/.

2. Jane L. Scheiber, "Internal Security, the Japanese Problem, and the Kibei in World War II Hawaii," *University of Hawai'i Law Review* 35 (Spring 2013): 416.

3. Harry N. Scheiber et al., "Hawai'i's Kibei under Martial Law: A Hidden Chapter in the History of World War II Internments," *Western Legal History: The Journal of the Ninth Judicial Circuit Historical Society* 22 (2009): 11.

4. Scheiber, "Hawai'i's Kibei under Martial Law," 2.

5. Scheiber, 15.

6. Scheiber, 17.

7. *Honolulu Advertiser,* December 22, 1941, 1, 6.

8. Duncan Ryūken Williams, "The Forgotten Internment of Japanese Americans in Hawaii," *Lit Hub,* February 25, 2019, https://lithub.com/the-forgotten-internment-of-japanese-americans-in-hawaii/.

9. Williams, "The Forgotten Internment."

10. Frank, "How Hawaii's Japanese Population."

Chapter 21. Infamy

1. Richard B. Frank, "How Hawaii's Japanese Population Was Spared Internment during World War II," https://time.com/5802127/hawaii-internment-order/.

2. Later in the war, Gullion, even more of a bigot than DeWitt, would be investigated for involvement in an extreme right-wing group that was openly racist and anti-Semitic. He retired soon afterward because of ill health.

3. Richard Reeves, *Infamy: The Shocking Story of the Japanese American Internment in World War II* (New York: Holt, 2015), 45.

4. Reeves, *Infamy*, 41.

5. *SFE*, March 1, 1942, 7.

6. 55 *Statutes at Large* 173.

7. Digital Public Library of America, https://dp.la/exhibitions/japanese-internment/home-family

8. Library of Congress, https://www.loc.gov/classroom-materials/immigration/japanese/behind-the-wire/.

9. Densho Encyclopedia, http://encyclopedia.densho.org/Manzanar.

10. Densho Encyclopedia, http://encyclopedia.densho.org/442nd%20Regimental%20Combat%20Team.

Chapter 22. Four Who Refused

1. Peter Irons, *Justice at War: The Story of the Japanese American Internment Cases* (New York: Oxford University Press, 1983), 82.

2. John Tateishi, *And Justice for All: An Oral History of the Japanese American Detention Camps* (New York: Random House, 1984), 66.

3. Irons, *Justice at War*, 83.

4. Irons, 83.

5. Tateishi, *And Justice for All*, 68.

6. Tateishi, 68.

7. Tateishi, 71.

8. Peter Irons, *The Courage of Their Convictions* (New York: Free Press, 1988), 64.

9. Irons, *Courage of Their Convictions*, 65.

10. Irons, 67.

11. Tateishi, *And Justice for All*, 61.

12. Irons, *Justice at War*, 101.

13. Irons, 101

14. Irons, 102.

15. Densho Encyclopedia, https://encyclopedia.densho.org/Korematsu_v._United_States/.

16. Tateishi, *And Justice for All*, 76.

17. Tateishi, 72.

18. *SFE*, July 14, 1942, 4.

19. Irons, *Justice at War*, 257.

20. Warren did not disappoint, winning 60 percent of the vote and all but one county in the state.

21. *San Bernardino Sun*, September 9, 1942, 4.

22. Irons, *Justice at War*, 154.

23. *Los Angeles Times*, December 11, 1942, 23.

Chapter 23. A Caricature of Justice

1. On the same day, Ulysses Webb, as private citizen, appealed a ruling from district court that refused to bar the voter registration of American citizens of Japanese descent because they diluted the voting power of Caucasians. Webb claimed *Wong Kim Ark* was in error because the Constitution intended to establish a government "by and for white people." Webb was more or less laughed out of court.

2. 320 U.S. 81 (1943).

3. The First Amendment Encyclopedia, https://www.mtsu.edu/first-amendment/article/5/carolene-products-footnote-four.

4. 304 U.S. 144 (1938).

5. 304 U.S. 144 (1938).

6. 323 U.S. 214 (1944).

7. Tateishi, *And Justice for All*, 83.

Chapter 24. The Courage to Do What's Right

1. Irons, *Justice at War*, 273–274.

2. 323 U.S. 214 (1944).

3. 323 U.S. 283 (1944).

Chapter 25. Shame

1. Densho Encyclopedia, http://encyclopedia.densho.org/Minoru%20Yasui.

2. Densho Encyclopedia.

3. Ed Cray, *Chief Justice: A Biography of Earl Warren* (New York: Simon & Schuster, 1997), 240.

Selected Bibliography

Online Resources

Chinese Historical Society of America
Densho Encyclopedia
Digital History
Digital Public Library of America
Google Arts and Culture
Japanese American Veterans Association
Library of Congress Classroom Materials
Newspapers.com
San Francisco State University Collections

Reference Material

Annals of the Congress of the United States
Congressional Globe
Congressional Record
Records and Briefs of the United States Supreme Court
Statutes at Large
United States Reports

Books and Articles

Allerfeldt, Kristofer. "Race and Restriction: Anti-Asian Immigration Pressures in the Pacific North-west of America during the Progressive Era, 1885–1924." *History* 88, no. 1 (2003): 53–73.

Aoki, Keith. "No Right to Own? The Early Twentieth Century 'Alien Land Laws' as a Prelude to Internment." *Boston College Third World Law Journal* 19, no. 1 (1998): 37–72.

Bailey, Thomas. "California, Japan, and the Alien Land Legislation of 1913." *Pacific Historical Review* 1, no. 1 (1932): 36–59.

Berger, Bethany R. "Birthright Citizenship on Trial: *Elk v. Wilkins* and *United States v. Wong Kim Ark*." *Cardozo Law Review* 37, no. 4 (2016): 1185–1258.

Bowen, Francis, "Latest Form of the Development Theory." *Memoirs of the American Academy of Arts and Sciences*, n.s., 8, no. 1 (1861): 97–122.

Brudnoy, David. "Race and the San Francisco School Board Incident: Contemporary Evaluations." *California Historical Quarterly* 50, no. 3 (1971): 295–312.

Buell, Raymond L. "The Development of the Anti-Japanese Agitation in the United States." *Political Science Quarterly* 37, no. 4 (1922): 605–638; 38, no. 1 (1923): 57–81.

———. "Some Legal Aspects of the Japanese Question." *American Journal of International Law* 17, no. 1 (1923): 29–49.

"The California Alien Land Law." *Lawyer and Banker and Bench and Bar Review* 6, no. 3 (1913): 126–128.

Carbado, Devon. "Yellow by Law." *California Law Review* 97 (June 2009): 633–692.

Carr, Clare. "Battle for Chinatown: The Adaptive Resilience of San Francisco's Chinese American Community in the 1906 San Francisco Earthquake and Fire." *Rhodes Historical Review* 19 (Spring 2017): 80–105.

Castleman, Bruce. "California's Alien Land Laws." *Western Legal History* 7 (Winter/Spring 1994): 25–68.

Chambers, John S. "The Japanese Invasion." *Annals of the American Academy of Political and Social Science* 93 (January 1921): 23–29.

Chin, Gabriel, and Daniel K. Tu. "Comprehensive Immigration Reform in the Jim Crow Era: Chinese Exclusion and the McCreary Act of 1893." *Asian American Law Journal* 23, no. 1 (2016): 39–67.

Cho, Sumi. "Redeeming Whiteness in the Shadow of Internment: Earl Warren, Brown, and a Theory of Racial Redemption." *Boston College Third World Law Journal* 19 (December 1998): 73–170.

Collins, Charles Wallace. "Will the California Alien Land Law Stand the Test of the Fourteenth Amendment." *Yale Law Journal* 23 (1913–1914): 330–338.

Conmy, Peter T. "The History of California's Japanese Problem and the Part Played by the Native Sons of the Golden West in Its Solution." Privately printed, 1942.

Conn, Stetson et al. *Guarding the United States and Its Outposts.* Washington, DC: U.S. Government Printing Office, 1964.

Coulson, Doug. "British Imperialism, the Indian Independence Movement, and the Racial Eligibility Provisions of the Naturalization Act: *United States v. Thind* Revisited." *Georgetown Journal of Law & Modern Critical Race Perspectives* 7 (2015): 1–42.

Cray, Ed. *Chief Justice: A Biography of Earl Warren.* New York: Simon & Schuster, 1997.

Daniels, Roger. *The Politics of Prejudice: The Anti-Japanese Movement in California and the Struggle for Japanese Exclusion.* Berkeley: University of California Press, 1977.

Documental History of Law Cases Affecting Japanese in the United States. Privately printed. 1925.

Eom, Sujin. "The Specter of Modernity: Open Ports and the Making of Chinatowns in Japan and South Korea." *Traditional Dwellings and Settlements Review* 24 (2013): 39–50.

Everest-Phillips, Max. "The Pre-War Fear of Japanese Espionage: Its Impact and Legacy." *Journal of Contemporary History* 42, no. 2 (2007): 243–265.

Ferguson, Edwin E. "The California Alien Land Law and the Fourteenth Amendment." *California Law Review* 35, no. 1 (1947): 61–90.

Finkelman, Paul. "Coping with a New 'Yellow Peril': Japanese Immigration, the Gentleman's Agreement, and the Coming of World War II." *West Virginia Law Review* 117, no. 3 (2015): 1409–1459.

Fox, Stephen C. "General John DeWitt and the Proposed Internment of German and Italian Aliens during World War II." *Pacific Historical Review* 57, no. 4 (1988): 407–438.

Frank, Richard B. "How Hawaii's Japanese Population Was Spared Internment during World War II." *Time,* March 13, 2020. https://time.com/5802127/hawaii-internment-order/.

Gomez, Vernona, and Lawrence Goldstone. *Lefty: An American Odyssey.* New York: Ballantine, 2012.

Gompert, David C., Hans Binnendijk, and Bonny Lin. "Japan's Attack on Pearl Harbor, 1941." In *Blinders, Blunders, and Wars: What America and China Can Learn,* 93–106. RAND Corporation, 2014.

Gonzales, Richard. "Rebuilding Chinatown after the 1906 Quake." NPR, April 12, 2006. https://www.npr.org/2006/04/12/5337215/rebuilding-chinatown-after-the-1906-quake.

Gotō, Baron Shimpei. "The Anti-Japanese Question in California." *Annals of the American Academy of Political and Social Science* 93 (January 1921): 104–110.

Gripentrog, John. "The Transnational Pastime: Baseball and American Perceptions of Japan in the 1930s." *Diplomatic History* 34, no. 2 (2010): 247–273.

Hajimu, Masuda. "Rumors of War: Immigration Disputes and the Social Construction of American-Japanese Relations, 1905–1913." *Diplomatic History* 33, no. 1 (2009): 1–37.

Haney-Lopez, Ian. *White by Law: The Legal Construction of Race.* New York: New York University Press, 1996.

Hansen, Lawrence Douglas Taylor. "The Chinese Six Companies of San Francisco and the Smuggling of Chinese Immigrants across the U.S.-Mexico Border, 1882–1930." *Journal of the Southwest* 48 (Spring 2006): 37–61.

Hasian, Marouf A., Jr. "Conserving the Nation's Germplasm: Nativist Discourse and the Passage of the 1924 Immigration Restriction Act." *Legal Studies Forum* 24, no. 1 (2000): 157–174.

Hennings, Robert E. "James D. Phelan and the Woodrow Wilson Anti-Oriental Statement of May 3, 1912." *California Historical Society Quarterly* 42, no. 4 (1963): 291–300.

Hichborn, Franklin. *Story of the Session of the California Legislature of 1913.* San Francisco: Press of the James H. Barry Company, 1913.

Hofstadter, Richard. *Social Darwinism in American Thought.* New York: George Braziller, 1959.

Honjo, Eijiro. "From the Tokugawa Period to the Meiji Restoration." *Kyoto University Economic Review* 7, no. 1 (1932): 32–51.

Horie, Hideichi. "Revolution and Reform in Meiji Restoration." *Kyoto University Economic Review* 22, no. 1 (1952): 23–34.

Ichioka, Yuji. "Amerika Nadeshiko: Japanese Immigrant Women in the United States, 1900–1924." *Pacific Historical Review* 49, no. 2 (1980): 339–357.

———. "Japanese Immigrant Response to the 1920 California Alien Land Law." *Agricultural History* 58, no. 2 (1984): 157–178.

Ike, Nobutaka. "Western Influences on the Meiji Restoration." *Pacific Historical Review* 17, no. 1 (1948): 1–10.

Inui, Kiyo Sue. "California's Japanese Situation." *Annals of the American Academy of Political and Social Science* 93 (January 1921): 97–104.

———. "The Gentlemen's Agreement: How It Has Functioned." *Annals of the American Academy of Political and Social Science* 122 (November 1925): 188–198.

Irons, Peter. *The Courage of Their Convictions.* New York: Free Press, 1988.

———. *Justice at War: The Story of the Japanese American Internment Cases.* New York: Oxford University Press, 1983.

Iwata, Masakazu. "The Japanese Immigrants in California Agriculture." *Agricultural History* 36 (January 1962): 25–37.

Johnson, Roxana. "Be Good Americans: The Message of the *Japanese American Courier.* https://depts.washington.edu/depress/japanese_american_courier_americanism.shtml.

Kalhan, Anil. "*Trump v. Hawaii* and Chief Justice Roberts's '*Korematsu* Overruled' Parlor Trick." *American Constitution Society,* June 29, 2018. https://www.acslaw.org/expertforum/trump-v-hawaii-and-chief-justice-robertss-korematsu-overruled-parlor-trick/.

Kanzaki, Kiichi. "Is the Japanese Menace in America a Reality?" *Annals of the American Academy of Political and Social Science* 93 (January 1921): 88–97.

Karthikeyan, Hrishi, Gabriel Chin. "Preserving Racial Identity: Population Patterns and the Application of Anti-Miscegenation Statutes to Asian Americans, 1910–1950." *Asian Law Journal* 9, no. 1 (2002): 1–40.

Keith, Jeffrey A. "Civilization, Race, and the Japan Expedition's Cultural Diplomacy, 1853–1854." *Diplomatic History* 35, no. 2 (2011): 179–202.

Kennan, George. "The Fight for Reform in San Francisco." *McClure's Magazine,* September 1907, 547–560.

Kens, Paul. *Justice Stephen Field: Shaping Liberty from the Gold Rush to the Gilded Age.* Lawrence: University Press of Kansas, 1997.

Lee, Erika. *At America's Gates: Chinese Immigration during the Exclusion Era, 1882–1943.* Chapel Hill: University of North Carolina Press, 2003.

Le Pore, Herbert P. "Prelude to Prejudice: Hiram Johnson, Woodrow Wilson, and the California Alien Land Law Controversy of 1913." *Southern California Quarterly* 61, no. 1 (1979): 99–110.

Lew-Williams, Beth. *The Chinese Must Go: Violence, Exclusion, and the Making of the Alien in America.* Cambridge, MA: Harvard University Press, 2018.

Loureiro, Pedro A. "Japanese Espionage and American Countermeasures in Pre–Pearl Harbor California." *Journal of American-East Asian Relations* 3 (Fall 1994): 197–210.

M., Jenn. "A Tale of Two Nations: Victorian America and The Japan Craze."

NMSC Archeology & Museum Blog, March 18, 2014. https://nmscarcheologylab.wordpress.com/2014/03/18/a-tale-of-two-nations-victorian-america-and-the-japan-craze/.

Maclay, William, Kenneth R. Bowling, and Helen E. Veit, eds. *The Journal of William Maclay*. Baltimore: Johns Hopkins University Press, 1988.

Manzella, Abigail G. H. *Migrating Fictions: Gender, Race, and Citizenship in U.S. Internal Displacements*. Columbus: Ohio State University Press, 2018.

McClain, Charles J. "Tortuous Path, Elusive Goal: The Asian Quest for American Citizenship." *Asian Law Journal* 2 (1995): 33–60.

Menand, Louis. "Morton, Agassiz, and the Origins of Scientific Racism in the United States." *Journal of Blacks in Higher Education* (Winter 2001–2002): 110–113.

Miller, H. D. "The Great Sushi Craze of 1905, Part 1." *An Eccentric Culinary History*. https://eccentricculinary.com/the-great-sushi-craze-of-1905-part-1/.

Muller, Eric. *American Inquisition: The Hunt for Japanese American Disloyalty in World War II*. Chapel Hill: University of North Carolina Pres, 2007.

Nackenoff, Carol, and Julie Novkov. *American by Birth: Wong Kim Ark and the Battle for Citizenship*. Lawrence: University Press of Kansas, 2021.

Ngai, Mae M. *Impossible Subjects: Illegal Aliens and the Making of Modern America*. Princeton, NJ: Princeton University Press, 2004.

Okrent, Daniel. *The Guarded Gate*. New York: Scribner, 2018.

Older, Mrs. Fremont. *San Francisco: The Magic City*. New York: Longmans, Green, 1961.

Olney, Warren. "Law Enforcement and Judicial Administration in the Earl Warren Era: Oral History Transcript." https://archive.org/details/enforcementjudiooolnerich/page/228/mode/2up.

"Outstanding Features of the Immigration Act of 1924." *Columbia Law Review* 25, no. 1 (1925): 90–95.

Page, Thomas Walker. "The San Francisco Labor Movement in 1901." *Political Science Quarterly* 17, no. 4 (1902): 664–688.

Parr, Patrick. "American President Ulysses S. Grant Talks Peace in Meiji Era Japan." https://japantoday.com/category/features/lifestyle/american-president-ulysses-s-grant-talks-peace-in-meiji-era-japan.

Peffer, George Anthony. "Forbidden Families: Emigration Experiences of Chinese Women under the Page Law, 1875–1882." *Journal of American Ethnic History* 6 (Fall 1986): 28–46.

Phelan, James D. "Why California Objects to the Japanese Invasion." *Annals of the American Academy of Political and Social Science* 93 (January 1921): 16–17.

Powell, Thomas Reed. "Alien Land Cases in United States Supreme Court." *California Law Review* 12, no. 4 (1923–1924): 259–282.

Rast, Raymond W. "The Cultural Politics of Tourism in San Francisco's Chinatown, 1882–1917." *Pacific Historical Review* 76, no. 1 (2007): 29–60.

Reeves, Richard. *Infamy: The Shocking Story of the Japanese American Internment in World War II*. New York: Holt, 2015.

Roodner, Theodore. "Washington's Alien Land Law—Its Constitutionality." *Washington Law Review* 39 (Spring 1964): 115–134.

Salyer, Lucy. *Laws as Harsh as Tigers: Chinese Immigrants and the Shaping of Modern Immigration Law.* Chapel Hill: University of North Carolina Press, 1995.

Scheiber, Harry N., Jane L. Scheiber, and Benjamin Jones. "Hawai'i's Kibei under Martial Law: A Hidden Chapter in the History of World War II Internments." *Western Legal History* 22 (2009): 1–102.

Scheiber, Jane L. "Internal Security, the Japanese Problem, and the Kibei in World War II Hawaii." *University of Hawai'i Law Review* 35 (Spring 2013): 415–440.

Shizume, Masato. "The Japanese Economy during the Interwar Period: Instability in the Financial System and the Impact of the World Depression." Institute for Monetary and Economic Studies, 2009.

Sohoni, Deenesh. "Unsuitable Suitors: Anti-Miscegenation Laws, Naturalization Laws, and the Construction of Asian Identities." *Law & Society Review* 41, no. 3 (2007): 587–618.

Spencer, Herbert. *Essays on Education and Kindred Subjects.* Dutton 1861, 1911.

———. "Progress: Its Law and Causes." *The Westminster Review* 67 (April 1857): 445–465.

Startt, James D. *Woodrow Wilson and the Press: Prelude to the Presidency.* New York: Palgrave Macmillan, 2004.

Sullivan, Casey C. "13 Worst Supreme Court Decisions of All Time." *FindLaw,* October 14, 2015. https://www.findlaw.com/legalblogs/supreme-court/13-worst-supreme-court-decisions-of-all-time/.

Suzuki, Maseo. "Important or Impotent? Taking Another Look at the 1920 California Alien Land Law." *Journal of Economic History* 64, no. 1 (2004): 125–143.

Takaki, Ronald. *Strangers from a Distant Shore.* New York: Little Brown, 1989.

Tateishi, John. *And Justice for All: An Oral History of the Japanese American Detention Camps.* New York: Random House, 1984.

Tygiel, Jules. " . . . Where Unionism Holds Undisputed Sway: A Reappraisal of San Francisco's Union Labor Party." *California History* 62 (Fall 1983): 196–215.

White, G. Edward, "The Unacknowledged Lesson: Earl Warren and the Japanese Relocation Controversy," *Virginia Quarterly Review* 55, no. 4 (1979): 613–629.

Williams, C. C. *Congressional Career of the Hon. H. F. Page, Representative of the Second District of California and Renominated for a Fifth Term.* San Francisco: Francis, Valentine & Co., printers, 1880.

Williams, Duncan Ryūken. "The Forgotten Internment of Japanese Americans in Hawaii: A Dark Chapter in the History of Religious Persecution." *Literary Hub,* February 25, 2019. https://lithub.com/the-forgotten-internment-of-japanese-americans-in-hawaii/.

Wilson, Woodrow. *A History of the American People.* Vol. 5. New York: Harper and Brothers, 1903.

Woodworth, Marshall B. "Who Are Citizens of the United States? *Wong Kim Ark* Case—Interpretation of Citizenship Clause of Fourteenth Amendment." *American Law Review* 32, no. 4 (1898): 554–561.

Yang, Joshua S. "The Anti-Chinese Cubic Air Ordinance." *American Journal of Public Health,* March 2009. https://www.ncbi.nlm.nih.gov/pmc/articles/PMC2661442/.

Index